Frederick Betz

Stability in International Finance

Applications of Price Disequilibrium Theory

Springer

Frederick Betz
Department of Engineering and Technology Management
Portland State University
Portland, OR, USA

Department of Technology and Society
SUNY Korea, Incheon, Korea

ISSN 2191-5504 ISSN 2191-5512 (electronic)
SpringerBriefs in Economics
ISBN 978-3-319-26758-6 ISBN 978-3-319-26760-9 (eBook)
DOI 10.1007/978-3-319-26760-9

Library of Congress Control Number: 2015961053

Springer Cham Heidelberg New York Dordrecht London

Printed on acid-free paper

Springer International Publishing AG Switzerland is part of Springer Science+Business Media (www.springer.com)

For my dearest wife, Nancy, for her great help in the editing of the manuscript and assistance in trying to make the models of financial systems understandable.

Preface

Why are international financial systems unstable? To understand this, one must use a proper model for a financial market—a model which is not just normative but empirically valid. The traditional market model of price-equilibrium, while valid for commodity markets, is not empirically valid for financial markets. Instead, financial markets must be understood in a price-disequilibrium model. A price-disequilibrium model traces back to the studies of Irving Fisher, John Maynard Keynes, and Hyman Minsky.

We present here a three-dimensional supply-demand model which can depict how, over time, a financial market can move from a price-equilibrium toward price-disequilibrium, due to speculation—a financial bubble.

Financial bubbles occurred in the Asian Financial crisis in 1989, the Global Financial crisis in 2007–2008, and the Euro crisis of 2010–2015; and these bubbles have depressed national economies. They recur, despite the sophisticated information-communications technology of the modern Internet. Why?

And if we understand why financial bubbles occur and disrupt economies, what kind of regulation would be necessary to prevent bubbles? It would be a "public good" to anticipate and contain bubbles—instead of just "bailing out" banks, after fiscal crises freeze international finance and bring down economies.

Methodologically, we use cases in economic history to test the validity of economic theory and models. In using history as a technique, we will quote observers of the time, such as reports from news articles and from analyses by financial reporters and by economic theorists. In historical methodology, sources and quotes from sources provide direct evidence. Contemporary case studies often derive historical information from investigative reporters from interpretation by contemporary economists. Case methodology provides an important empirical technique upon which to construct and test societal theory and models.

Enumclaw, WA
September 2015

Frederick Betz

Acknowledgments

To my good friend and colleague, Elias Carayannis, who helped to guide me through the maze of the Greek Euro crisis.

Acknowledgements

Contents

Chapter 1
Price Disequilibrium Theory

Introduction

Even in the modern 'knowledge economy' in a global world, financial systems still continue to be central to global commerce. Technological advances in computer and communications have changed both knowledge and the economy and also the financial system. Globalization and technology have made international finance more powerful and important to the world; but they have increased volatility, instability, and fraud in international finance. For example, Martin Wolf wrote: "It is possible to identify … two huge shifts (in the economy). One is 'liberalization', the reliance on market forces across much of the world economy, including and notably, in finance. A second is 'technological change', in particular the information and communications technology revolution, which turbocharged the integration of economies, again, quite particularly, financial markets …. These great shifts of our time have permitted or created significant further changes. Among the most important have been: the emergence of a globalized world economy; soaring inequality in most economies; the entry of gigantic emerging economies (e.g., China and India) …, In brief, we have a world that is in the midst of historic shifts towards a more market-oriented, financially driven and globalized world economy …. It is a world that has seen downward shocks to the rate of inflation. It is also, it turns out, a world that is hugely crisis prone." (Wolf 2014)

Before the First World War of the twentieth century, Europe had the financial experience of three centuries of stable currencies: Dutch money in the 1600s and British money in the 1700s and 1800s. These were times of the so-called 'liberal hegemony' of the Dutch first and secondly the British Empire. But in the twentieth century after that First War, a stable international financial system (over the long term) did not exist. International financial systems became periodically unstable, triggering financial crises and resultant economic depressions in different nations.

Yet the global economy cannot develop properly without a stable international system—which should distribute wealth to economically productive activities. Does

F. Betz, *Stability in International Finance*, SpringerBriefs in Economics,
DOI 10.1007/978-3-319-26760-9_1

the current financial system distribute wealth to productivity in the world, or does it mostly facilitate 'casino banking'? How can a productive and stable modern international-financial-system be constructed?

During the nineteenth century, Britain provided the leadership of financial hegemony for the international world of commerce. But European financial leadership collapsed in 1914–1918, and particularly after the war when the French and British insisted on huge reparations from Germany. The German economy went through a horrendous inflation, as the German government printed money to pay their reparations. Then a new Reichsbank director fixed the Germany monetary system, and US investment flowed to Germany. But in the fall of 1929, the U.S. Wall Street stock-market crash triggered 3 years of bank runs, resulting in the rest of the decade in the 'Great Depression' of the U.S. In 1930–1931, this depression spread to Europe. The Reichsbank director resigned and went to work arranging financing for the Nazis. Then the Nazi government re-armed Germany and began the Second World War and the holocaust in Europe.

After the Second World War, the Allies of the USA, Britain, USSR, and France endeavored to construct a stable international financial system in the Bretton Woods Conference, by establishing the International Monetary Fund (IMF) and the International Bank for Construction and Development which became the World Bank. However, the IMF and World Bank failed to stabilize international finance, often instead only deepening economic corruption and depressions in financially-troubled nations.

For a few decades after the Second World War, the U.S. financial system temporarily contributed to international stability, with the dollar providing an international currency (earlier the British pound had been the international currency). Yet in 1971, the US dollar ended its exchange for gold (went off the 'gold standard'). Also financial systems changed under the impact of computer technology and by deregulation of bank practices. In the US, this culminated in a financial crisis in 2007, which froze the Wall Street banking system and brought international banking to a halt—a global financial crisis. Next in 2009, the looming defaults of several nations' sovereign bonds in European countries sent the European Monetary Union into financial crisis.

Although this traditional economic theory of 'perfect' markets was used in national fiscal policy, all markets (including financial markets) were considered in only a 'price-equilibrium-model'. This led government policy to operate mostly in a 'post-facto' mode rather than 'pre-emptive' mode—fixing economic recessions after they occur, rather than preventing them. For example, this was especially true of the 2009 U.S. recession, which was triggered by the 2008 global bank panic. About this, Binyamin Appelbaum wrote: "The Fed (Federal Reserve System) began 2007 still deeply immersed in complacent disregard for problems in the housing market. Fed officials knew that people were losing their homes. They knew that subprime lenders were blinking out of business with every passing week. But they did not understand the implications for the broader economy… August 2007 was the month that the Fed began its long transformation from somnolence to activism." (Appelbaum 2013) The Fed started the biggest bank 'bail-out' in U.S. economic history.

What was the soporific which, at the time, had put the Fed to sleep? It had been the then 'mainstream economic theory' of perfect markets. This soporific occurred not only in U.S. regulatory policy but also in British policy. Sir Mervyn King (Governor of the Bank of England in 2007) later said: "With the benefit of hindsight, we (Bank of England) should have shouted from the rooftops that a system had been built in which banks were too important to fail, that banks had grown too quickly and borrowed too much, and that so-called 'light-touch' regulation hadn't prevented any of this." (Wolf 2008) The big banks had gained such large capital assets, when if at risk, bank failures would bring down a whole economy.

As we noted, the 'mainstream economic theory' had paid little attention to the role of 'financial-bubbles-and-bank-panics' as precursors to recessions. For example in 2009, Paul Krugman wrote: "It's hard to believe now, but not long ago economists were congratulating themselves over the success of their field. Those successes—or so they believed—were both theoretical and practical, leading to a golden era for the profession .... Few economists saw our current crisis coming, but this predictive failure was the least of the field's problems. More important was the profession's blindness to the very possibility of catastrophic failures in a market economy .... There was nothing in the prevailing models suggesting the possibility of the kind of collapse that happened last year in 2008 ... Macroeconomists (remain) divided in their views. The main division was between those who insisted that free-market economies never go astray and those who believed that economies may stray now and then (but that any major deviations from the path of prosperity could and would be corrected by the all-powerful Fed). Neither side was prepared to cope with an economy that went off the rails despite the Fed's best efforts .... And in the wake of the crisis, the fault lines in the economics profession have yawned wider than ever." (Krugman 2013)

In the economic history of the United States, for example, there had been many events of financial crises, bank panics, and recessions—from the early 1800s to 2008 (Kindelberger and Aliber 2011).

- Panic of 1857—This was triggered by a excessive railroad investments, leading up to a stock market collapse, which triggered a bank panic and created an economic recession.
- Panic of 1873—Again, excessive investment created a stock bubble, whose collapse triggered a bank panic and subsequent economic recession.
- Panic of 1893—Again excessive investments in railroads, resulted in temporary overbuilding, triggering again a bank panic and recession—financial excess, market crash, bank panic, recession.
- Panic of 1896—Monetary policy about US currency began to be based both upon silver and gold, which, as monetary policy, created an economic depression when silver reserves declined.
- Panic of 1907—This was again a stock market failure, which began to trigger bank runs; but this was halted by JP Morgan bank. Stopping the bank panics prevented a recession. This event stimulated, 6 years later, the establishment of the U.S. central bank system (Federal Reserve System).

- Panic of 1929—A New York stock market bubble triggered 3 years of bank panics, resulting in the U.S. Great Depression, which lasted a decade.
- Panic of 2008—A U.S. real estate bubble was followed by the crash of a Wall Street financial derivatives market, and a global bank panic, creating a recession in the U.S.

Panics have also been international. For example in Asia in 1997, there was an Asian fiscal crisis, triggered first by real estate and stock bubbles in Thailand, and then by a sharp decline in exchange-rate and out-flow of foreign capital (Blustein 2003). In Europe in 2011, there were bank panics in Euro countries, due to excessive sovereign debts, which triggered bank panics, and resulting depressions, particularly in Southern Europe, in Greece, Portugal, and Spain.

The lesson from all this is that for fiscal policy, it is important to use an accurate macro-economic model. Financial markets should be modeled as price-disequilibrium objects. Using the right model for policy is important to the proper regulation of financial markets, which is critical in economic stability. Unstable financial markets result in 'deflation'—always due to 'overly-leveraged investments'. For example in 1933, Irving Fisher wrote: "(In deflation)… two dominant factors (are)… over-indebtedness to start with and deflation following soon after… the big bad actors are debt disturbances and price level." (Fisher 1933)

Deflation is the economic process which lowers the values of all capital assets. It typically occurs after a financial bubble, after banks have lent too much money to leveraged speculators (who had acted upon their cognitive reflexivity). When a financial bubble bursts, banks are left with worthless collateral, the collateral upon which they had lent to money to speculators. As bank collateral, the capital assets have deflated. Banks go toward insolvency, and bank runs occur. Credit is frozen; and the economy plunges into a recession/depression.

In the world of global trade, an unstable international financial system has been characteristic of twentieth century and continues into the twenty-first century. The mark of 'instability' in a financial system is a financial bubble. The pattern of financial instability begins with a financial bubble, which triggers bank panics, which stops commerce and plunges an economy into recession. Yet in the discipline of economics, there has been disagreement as to whether the pattern is 'accidental' or 'inherent' in financial markets. Economic theory divided into two schools, Exogenous and Endogenous, which respectively held that (1) financial systems were inherently stable as 'perfect markets' or (2) inherently unstable as 'disequilibrium markets'. The traditional Exogenous economic school held that instability in financial systems is 'outside' a perfect financial market; while the other Endogenous economic school held that instability is 'inside' (inherent to) financial markets, which can be periodically imperfect.

The historical evidence favors the Endogenous school. Instability has repeatedly occurred empirically in financial markets. We examine historical cases of stability and instability to construct a theoretical model for the requirements of stability in a global financial system. Can an international financial system be made 'stable' for the public good of a global world?

The basic theoretical model of the traditional exogenous school is the 'price-equilibrium model' of a commodity market. But empirically this may only apply to commodity-markets and not to financial-markets. This is the heart of the disagreement between the Exogenous and Endogenous Schools. Commodity markets can be 'perfect' with prices occurring at an equilibrium point of supply-meeting-demand; but in contrast, financial markets are frequently 'imperfect' with bubble pricing of capital assets, prices going off into the disequilibrium of a financial-bubble. The Endogenous school thinks that economic theory which is appropriate to the reality of financial markets is Hyman Minsky's 'disequilibrium theory'. We will explore this kind of approach, using disequilibrium theory to construct the requirements for a stable international financial system.

Methodology

To test the validity of economic theory, we will use contemporary case studies of economic crises. In the style of case studies, extensive direct quotes will be used in this book to provide references to sources of historical evidence. Contemporary cases are a blend of the case approach and historical methodology. In historical methodology, sources and direct quotes provide evidence of historical information and interpretation. Contemporary case studies derive historical information from investigative reporters on economic and financial events and on the interpretation of these events by contemporary economists and economic commentators. The direct quotes used in this book point to sources of historical evidence on the crisis events. Case studies in economics can be used to provide a basic empirical technique in institutional and micro-economic analyses of the validity of economic theory and models.

In scientific method, to be valid as a general theory, any social science theory must be examined either as an 'empirical law' or as a 'normative law'. Empirical laws are 'value-neutral', while normative laws are 'value-loaded'. In the social sciences, empirical laws explain what 'happened'; while normative laws explain what 'should-have-happened'. Empirical laws occur in reality; and while normative laws should occur in reality (but empirically, they may or may not).

The commodity market theory of 'price-equilibrium' is a normative law but not always an empirical law. The Exogenous School's price-equilibrium model of a 'perfect market' is an ideal (a norm) which economic markets should attain. But it is not generally true (always true) as an empirical law. This is because any particular commodity market may or may not be operating perfectly in a price-equilibrium point (at which price is set by market demand exactly matching supply). Empirically, a commodity market can be in price-equilibrium, but only when the actual conditions of the market enable such equilibrium. Any commodity market depends upon the actual conditions of the market, its market context. Even a commodity market is not empirically in price-equilibrium, except in a proper context, such as: the supply capacity being insufficient to meet demand, no monopolies over supply, safe and legal products in supply, etc.

Exogenous economists have termed the lack of proper conditions as 'market imperfections'. But empirically there are no 'imperfections' in a market! There is only a 'reality' in any market. Methodologically, 'imperfections' occur not in 'reality' but only in a 'theory'. A theory is 'imperfect' when it is not 'valid' in reality.

Still, the occurrence of a real condition of price-equilibrium in a commodity market (when supply equals demand) is a desirable condition. Price-equilibrium is a desirable characteristic of an economic system—a normative law. It can be applied to commodity markets for guiding policy. But it should never be applied to financial markets.

Regulatory policy based upon invalid theory has facilitated some economic disasters. For example, in U.S. financial policy in 2000, the misapplication of the theory of 'perfect' financial markets was used to argue against proper regulation of derivatives markets. But only 7 years later in 2007, the derivative market collapsed, triggering the bankruptcy (or near bankruptcy) of several Wall Street 'banks-too-big-too-fail'. US government policy of 'deregulation' had left the derivatives market unregulated. All this had been justified by Allen Greenspan, then Chair of the US Federal Reserve Systems. In 2000, he had argued to the U.S. Congress that all financial markets were 'perfect' and no regulation was needed for derivatives. Seven years later, U.S. mortgage derivative market crashed Wall Street. There are many studies of this crisis, which identify how economic theory was used to justify economic policy, which in turn allowed the disruptive conditions for the crisis, see for example, (Morgenson and Rosner 2011). Price disequilibrium theory describes how financial markets of capital assets can evolve over time.

Price Equilibrium Theory for Commodity Markets

Commodity markets exchange 'commodities'; and financial markets exchange 'capital assets'. The difference lies in economic value. Commodities have only one economic value: present-consumption. Capital assets have two economic values: present-rent and future-liquidity. This difference in economic values makes a difference in how economic agents behave in the two markets. In commodity markets, economic behavior aims toward a condition of supply-meeting-demand, a 'price equilibrium'. In financial markets, economic behavior aims for higher financial leverages, progressing toward a financial bubble, a 'price disequilibrium'.

First we review price-equilibrium theory for commodity markets. Commodities are produced goods which are consumed, such as: food, clothing, automobiles, etc. In commodity markets, the traditional economic model is a price-equilibrium model, Fig. 1.1. The theoretical principle expressed in this model is that in the supply and demand curves of the market, when supply equals demand a 'price equilibrium' will be reached.

In science, there is a difference between a model and a theory. A model is an accurate abstraction of reality of a natural object and can be directly validated (or

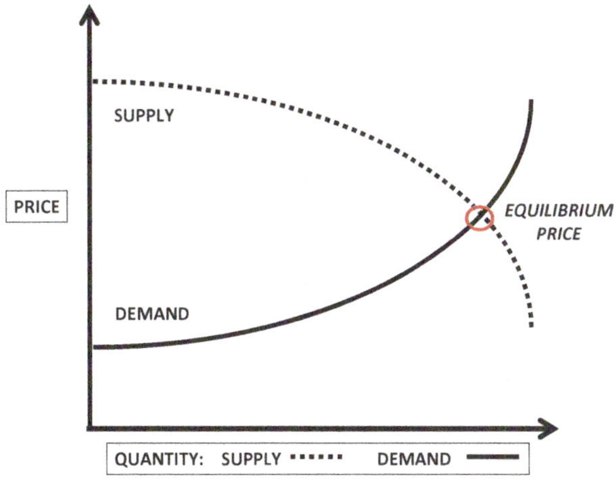

Fig. 1.1 Economic equilibrium pricing of a commodity when supply equals demand

invalidated) by comparison to experience (or experiment or history). A theory is a semantic language of principles in which valid models can be constructed. In the economics model, an equilibrium-price point is desired, as then the market is in balance between supply and demand. This is model expresses a theoretical normative principle. The equilibrium price establishes a stable condition of supply–demand equality, and then the market is efficient as to matching supply and demand. Such a market is in principle 'perfect'; this principle has been called the 'invisible hand of the market place'. Such a market needs no regulative interference to control supply or demand. This is a desirable economic state, a normative theory.

Modeling a Financial Market in the Neo-Keynesian School

But is this equilibrium principle empirically true of all markets, including financial markets? Hard experience with repeated financial crisis points to the fact that while commodity markets can be empirically perfect, financial markets are not necessarily perfect over time. As just noted, this 'perfect' model was actually used in 1999 in the United States to justify congressional de-regulation policy—by classically-oriented economists such as Robert Rubin, Lawrence Summers, and Alan Greenspan. They justified the deregulation of U.S, banking in the passage of the 1999 Gramm–Leach–Bliley Act. This act repealed that part of the 1924 U.S. Glass-Steagle Act, which had separated investment and commercial banking. And 'deregulation' allowed the creation of integrated banks—which proved to be 'too-big-to-fail' and needed 'bail-out' by the US Government in 2008. The 'too-large-to-fail-banks' created major economic risk in the whole financial system, due to their unregulated and fraudulent derivative trades.

The question is whether the equilibrium-price market model is ever accurate for modeling financial markets? Early in economic theory, Irving Fisher (Fisher 1933) and later John Maynard Keynes (Keynes 1936) had identified that instability occurs repeatedly in financial markets leading to a debt deflation. Later, this was elaborated by Hyman Minsky (1975). Martin Wolf wrote about Minsky: "Hyman Minsky (1919–1996), fascinatingly, a post-Keynesian product of the Chicago School, developed one of the most comprehensive critiques of pre-crisis … His crucial points were three: first, he believed that instability is an inherent feature of a dynamic capitalist economy, not just of the financial system; second, he doubted whether any regulatory rules could contain this instability durably; and, finally, he believed that the combination of 'Big Government' with the 'Big Bank' (the central bank) was the only way to contain the consequences of severe instability." (Wolf 2014)

The Neo-Keynesians argued that the Neo-Classical economists were too narrowly focused on viewing an economy only as a production system (commodity markets). Ben Bernanke wrote: "Economists have not always fully appreciated the importance of a healthy financial system for economic growth or the role of financial conditions in short-term economic dynamics …." (Bernanke 2007) Bernanke was pointing out the school of classical economists had assumed that 'instability' of financial markets had little or no effect upon an economy. About this, Hyman Minsky commented: "As Ben Bernanke points out the dominant microeconomic paradigm is an equilibrium construct … that determines relative prices …. (The assumption is that) money and financial interrelations are not relevant to the determination of these equilibrium variables …. But if the basic microeconomic model is opened to include 'yesterdays, todays, and tomorrows' … (then finance can influence price equilibrium)." (Minsky 1993) Minsky was emphasizing that the temporal dynamics (time-dimension) of financial markets did have an effect upon the stability of an economy.

Minsky had argued that a 'dimension-of-time' needs to be introduced into economic models. Drawing upon John Maynard Keynes work, Minsky wrote: "In the *General Theory*, Keynes sought to create a model of the economy in which money is never neutral (to pricing). He did this by creating a model … in which the price level of financial … assets is determined in (financial) markets …. Each capital and financial asset yields an income stream, (which) has carrying costs and possessing some degree of liquidity …. The price level of assets is determined by the relative value … (of) income … and liquidity …." (Minsky 1982)

In Keynes' model of a financial system, a 'time-dependence' is implicit in the concept of a 'capital asset' having both a 'present-income' and a 'future-liquidity' (Keynes 1936). A capital-asset is an investment which creates income and can later be sold. It produces an income stream (present-income) and also can be sold in the future (future-liquidity). The time dimension is from ($\mathbf{T_1}$) of a present-income to ($\mathbf{T_2}$) of future-liquidity. This present-to-future ($\mathbf{T_1}$ to $\mathbf{T_2}$) temporal process occurs in a financial system as a transaction of 'credit-debt'. Minsky wrote: "Every capitalist economy is characterized by a system of borrowing and lending …. The fundamental borrowing and lending act … is an exchange of 'money-now' for 'money-in-the-future'. This exchange takes place … in a negotiation in which the borrower

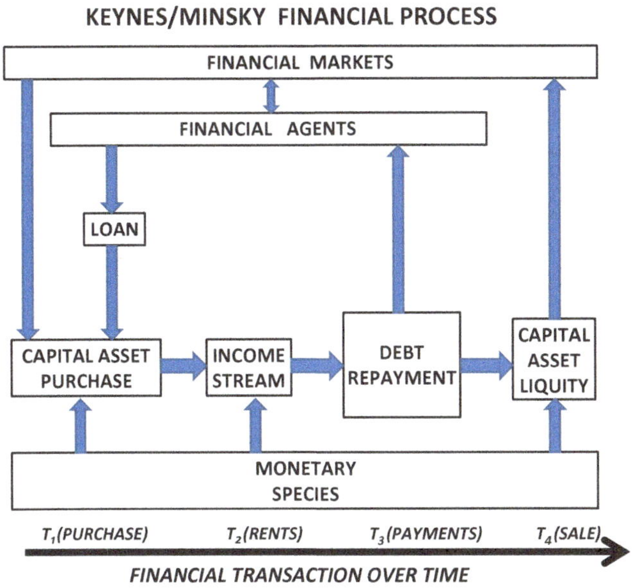

Fig. 1.2 Transactions of capital assets in the Keynes/Minsky depiction of financial markets

demonstrates to the satisfaction of the lender—that the money of the future part of the contract will be forthcoming….The money in the future is to cover both the interest and the repayment of the principle of the contract." (Minsky 1975)

A financial market makes the credit-debt contracts sellable over time, as a future-liquidity. Thus in a financial sub-system, three things are essential: (1) credit-debt transactions as a fundamental financial process, and (2) a capital-asset market for liquidity of the asset, and (3) money as a medium of value-exchange. Using Minsky's emphasis on a time dimension to model a financial market, the author diagramed such a temporal financial process, as in Fig. 1.2 (Betz 2014).

A financial capital-asset transaction occurs over time, beginning with a loan for an asset purchase, followed by rents (income stream) from the productivity of the capital asset, which are used for payments of the loan until the sale of the asset. Financial agents provide a purchase loan to the purchaser of the asset, receiving in turn from the purchaser loan payments on the debt over time from T_1 through T_3. Financial markets price the capital asset for purchase at time T_1 and later for sale at time T_4.

Debt makes a financial process operate. Yet one aspect of debt can destabilize the process; and this is 'leverage'. To increase profit, a financial system uses debt to finance the purchase of capital assets. Profits can be increased through financial leverage; and this is the financial rational of 'leverage' (more 'present-debt' toward greater 'future-wealth'). However, when present-debt is too large (too highly leveraged), it might not create future-wealth but, instead, bankruptcy. *Excessive 'leverage' increases the likelihood of bankruptcy and not future-wealth.* This was earlier pointed out by Irving Fisher, who called a financial state of excessive-leverage as 'debt deflation.' (Fisher 1933). Later Hyman Minsky called a state of excessive financial leverage as 'Ponzi finance' (Minsky 1982).

'Leverage' is the borrowing of a large percentage of the purchase price of a capital asset. Leverage increases profit when a capital asset is sold, but also increases risk of loss if the asset is not sold. Paul McCulley has also emphasized the importance of the economic role of 'leverage' in finance. McCulley wrote: "At its core, capitalism is all about risk taking. One form of risk taking is leverage. Indeed, without leverage, capitalism could not prosper…. And it is grand, while the ever-larger application of leverage puts upward pressure on asset prices. There is nothing like a bull market to make geniuses out of levered dunces….(Speculation) begets ever riskier debt arrangements, until they have produced a bubble in asset prices. Then the bubble bursts…." (McCulley 2009)

Thus leveraged 'present-debt' can increase 'future-wealth'; but 'excessive leverage' can lead to 'bankruptcy'. In Fig. 1.3, we graph this impact of leverage on a price equilibrium model—by modifying the 2-dimentional 'price-equilibrium chart'—with the addition of a third-dimension of time. This graph shows a supply–demand curve at two different times, T_1 and later T_2. In the time-dimension, one can see how a 'price-disequilibrium' situation can arise over time, as a 'financial bubble'.

It is 'excessive leverage' in the financing of a financial market which allows a financial bubble to occur. If no speculation occurs in an asset market (financial market)

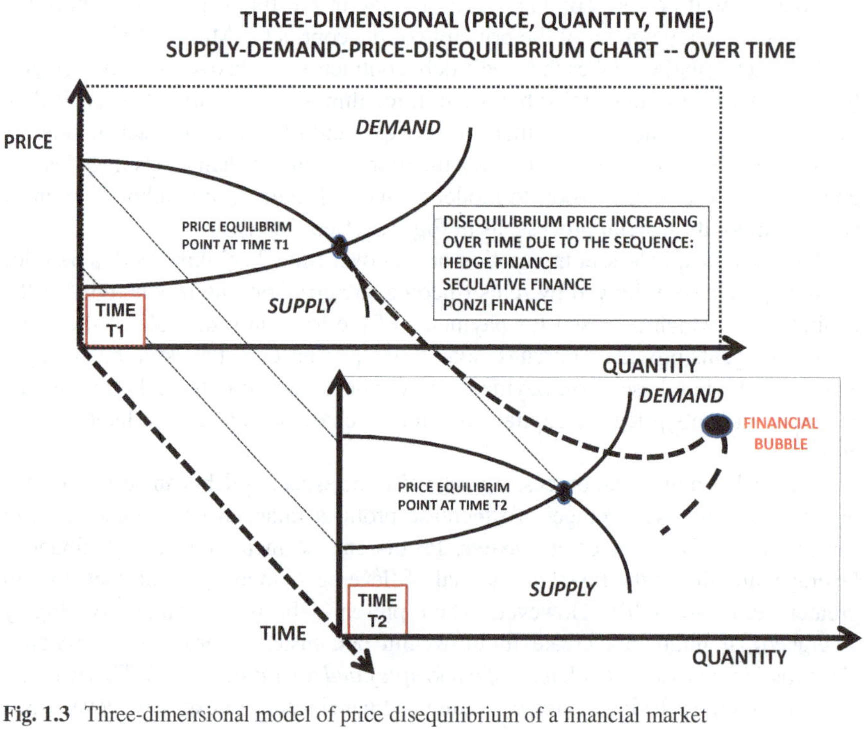

Fig. 1.3 Three-dimensional model of price disequilibrium of a financial market

then the equilibrium prices at T_1 and T_2 could be the same. But when speculation in the future-price at time T_2 occurs in a financial market, a price bubble can begin. *Fueled by 'leveraged speculation' in the future price of an asset, a 'disequilibrium pricing' of the asset grows—increases and increases until the financial bubble bursts.* Then the banks which funded the 'leveraged speculation' hold assets greatly decreased in value (from the bursting of the bubble); and this places these banks at risk of 'insolvency'. When depositors perceive a bank has put itself at risk, through funding too much speculation, depositors run to take their money out of the bank—a bank panic. Bank panics close down risky banks and freeze available credit. When too much credit is frozen in an economy, businesses have no access to operating funds and are forced to lay off workers or close doors.

History: U.S. Dot.com Financial Bubble

Financial bubbles have led to bank panics, which created credit freezes, which have led to business failures and unemployment—triggering an economic recession/depression. Financial bubbles can be seen in stock markets. Figure 1.4 shows the NASDAQ stock market index in the United States for the time period from 1970 to 2010.

Here one can see the 'dot.com' stock bubble from 1995 to 2000. Investor enthusiasm for businesses in the new Internet financed the start-up of hundreds of dot-com new ventures from 1998 to 2000. And the price index of the NASDAQ market rose from the stock index of '2000' in the year 1998 to '6000' in the year

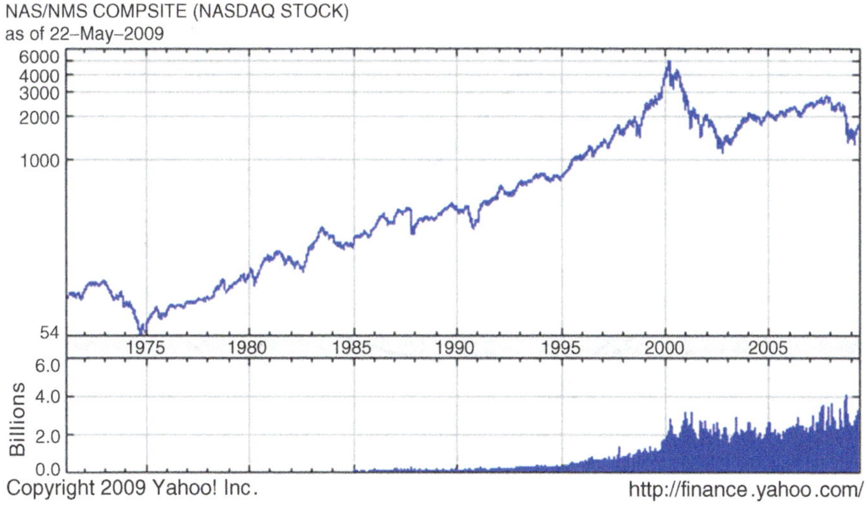

Fig. 1.4 U.S. NASDAQ stock market index 1970–2010

2000—a threefold growth in 2 years, a stock market bubble. The financial bubble burst in the year 2000, declining back to the index level of '2000'—a threefold drop—wiping out the earlier stock market increase. Billions of dollars were lost by venture capitalist funds in this sudden collapse, due to their investments in new Internet companies—hence called the 'dot.com' stock bubble.

Joseph Nocera and Tim Carvell summarized that time: "The Internet decade has seen the unscrupulous rewarded, the dimwitted suckered, the ill-qualified enriched at a pace greater than at any other time in history. The Internet has been a gift to charlatans, hypemeisters, and merchants of vapor….And despite all that, it still changes everything." (Nocera and Carvell 2000) In the year 2000, the U.S. NASDAQ stock market peaked at a then historic high of 6000

Upon a price-disequilibrium curve, one can fit a chart of a stock-market index over time onto the 'Price-Time' plane of the three-dimensional price-disequilibrium graph, as in Fig. 1.5.

This shows that a boom in a stock-market index charts is actually a 'price-disequilibrium graph' of the stock-price-index over time. The advantage of looking at it this way is to allow one to apply Minsky's categories of financial status to the stock-market graphs. When the average 'price-to-earnings' (P/E) of a stock market is in the 10–15 range, then the financial state of the stock market is in a 'Conservative-financial' range. When the average 'price-to-earnings' (P/E) of a stock market is in the 16–25 range, then the financial state of the stock market is

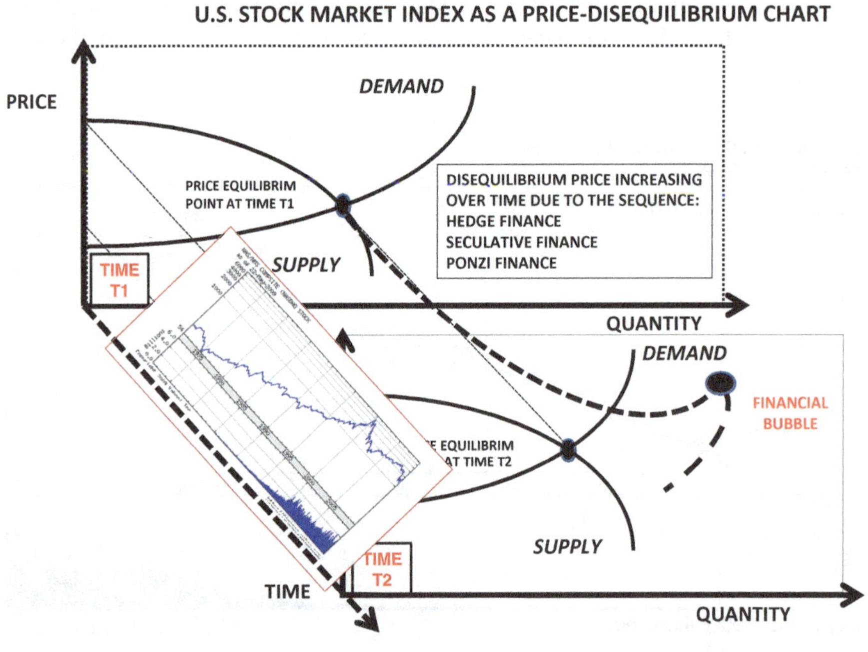

Fig. 1.5 Stock market index as a chart on the price-time plane of a price-disequilibrium model

in a 'Speculative-financial' range. When the average 'price-to-earnings' (P/E) of a stock market is above 25, then the financial state of the stock market is in a 'Ponzi-financial' state. And Minsky emphasized that when any financial market is in a 'Ponzi-financial' state, a financial bubble exists, just ready for bursting.

Because of the phenomena of financial bubbles, economic instability was seen by Neo-Keynesians as *inherent* to economic financial models. For this reason, the Neo-Keynesian School was called the '*endogenous*' school of economics, meaning instability is *indigenous* (inside) to an economy—through the disequilibrium pricing of asset markets in a financial bubble. The Neo-Classical Synthesis School was called an '*exogenous*' school of economics because they believed instability was *external* to the economic system, of perfect markets.

> *As a precursor—when financial markets track away from an equilibrium pricing point (demand increasing dramatically over time with excessive leverage and without supply increasing)—then a financial bubble can be anticipated.*
>
> *Regulatory intervention should occur before the critical time of Ponzi financing, as this time indicates a forthcoming devaluation—a bursting of the bubble.*

Reflexivity in Financial Markets

In financial markets, the behavior of financial agents is a critical factor. Why does Ponzi finance occur in speculator thinking? This creates the financial bubbles. To explain this, one must examine at the 'thinking' of speculators—the cognition of economic agents. George Soros had called this 'cognition' in financial markets as a kind of 'reflexivity' in thinking: "What makes reflexivity interesting is that a prevailing bias (in a market) has ways, via market prices, to affect the so-called fundamentals that market prices are supposed to reflect…. It does not happen all the time, but when it does it gives rise to the boom/bust sequences and other far-from-equilibrium conditions that are so typical of financial markets." (Soros 1988) Soros was pointing to the economic phenomena that prices in a financial market do not always depend upon the 'fundamentals' of current business (such as profits and revenue) but may rise to higher prices due to the bias of traders in the market, such as anticipating economic growth.

Soros defined 'reflexivity' as a 'cognition-action' interaction by participants in a society. The interaction is between: (1) what people think about a possible future and their actions based upon such thinking and (2) how a particular future may occur influenced by the action. He called this a "cognition-participation" interaction in influencing future outcomes of events in society. People think about the future, having 'expectations' of the future. People can then act in the present to make future expectations come true. All human actions occur in the present, aimed at an envisioned future outcome.

This reflexivity (between present-thinking-and-present-action as impacting upon future outcomes) is essential to how a financial market can move from a price-equilibrium to a price-disequilibrium. As an example of a stock market bubble,

Soros explained the dot.com bubble of 1995–2000 (shown earlier in Fig. 1.5). George Soros wrote: “In the Internet and telecom boom, inflated stock prices accelerated the introduction of new technologies. There was a misconception involved.... In the technology boom, the error was (that)... stocks were valued at a *multiple-of-revenue* (not valued about earnings) and growth was financed by selling stock (not by following sound business plans). Expectations were inflated, until they became unsustainable.... Eventually a turning point was reached.” (Soros 1988) The reflexivity was the interaction between investors’ ‘expectations’ and the ‘inflated stock prices’. That reflexivity resulted in a rapid rise of prices in the stock market to a financial bubble. This burst when investor ‘thinking’ saw the bubble as unsustainable (too high prices of stocks) and sold out (bust). All stock market bubbles are driven by a ‘reflexivity’ between a present ‘expectations & purchases’ and a ‘future’ unsustainable-situation’. Increasing leverage used in speculation creates a financial bubble, as prices rise away from a market price equilibrium toward a disequilibrium in capital-asset prices.

The technology of the Internet was real and would continue to create business opportunities. A decade later, the largest stock offerings were in Internet companies, such as Google, Facebook, Twitter, etc. In any stock market ‘reflexivity’, Soros emphasized that there were two kinds of factors—an underlying trend in the market (such as technology) and the expectations of investors about the future. *It is the interaction between underlying-trends and investor-expectations which provide the reflexivity that moves financial markets from equilibrium to disequilibrium pricing.*

In society, ‘cognition’ which choses an ‘action-in-the-present’ can help bring about an ‘anticipated-future’. Sociologists have called such a consciousness of the consequences-of-action-in-society as occurring either as expected or unexpected—‘foreseen consequences’ or ‘unforeseen consequences’.

A financial bubble is an ‘unforeseen’ economic consequence of financial markets, driven by the increasing of leverage in trading by speculators. George Soros commented: “If there is any place where the theory of perfect competition ought to be translated into practice, it is in the stock market. Yet there is little empirical evidence of an equilibrium, or even a tendency for prices to move toward an equilibrium.... Existing theories about the behavior of stock prices are remarkably inadequate.... The market price of a stock is supposed to tend toward its fundamental value over a period of time so that an analysis of fundamental values (e.g., earnings-per-share) provides a useful guide to investment decisions.... I take a totally opposite point of view. I do not accept the proposition that stock prices are a passive reflection of underlying values.... I contend that the market evaluations are always distorted and... the distortions can affect the underlying values. Stock prices are not merely passive reflections; they are active ingredients in a process in which both stock prices and the fortunes of the companies whose stocks are traded are determined.” (Soros 1988)

Because of (1) the time dimension of financial markets and (2) the cognitive reflexivity of economic agents in a financial market (speculators), financial markets are never empirically a ‘perfect market’. It is the reflexivity in economic agents which creates the disequilibrium pricing process of financial markets—the process toward financial instability.

Case: U.S. Stock Market Conglomeration Bubble

For example, a context dependency occurred in the reflexivity in U.S. stock market in the 1960s. George Soros analyzed the U.S. stock market boom in the 1960s, fueled by corporate conglomeration: "The first time I used the model systematically was in the conglomerate boom of the late 1960s. It enabled me to make money both on the way up and on the way down. The key to the conglomerate boom was a prevailing misconception among investors. Investors had come to value growth in per-share-earnings and failed to discriminate about the way the earnings growth was accomplished. A few companies learned to produce earnings growth through acquisitions. Once the market started to reward them for their performance, their task became easier because they could offer their own highly priced stock in acquiring other companies." (Soros 1988)

The trick for speculation in corporate conglomeration lay in the financial 'magic' number of Price-to Earnings (P/E). For companies having a record of little or no earnings growth, stocks might be purchased at a ratio of P/E = 10. This means that earning of that level over 10 years would return the capital invested of the stock purchase. The problem was this. At what rate would a company grow in earnings? Therefore at what multiple of present earnings should a stock be purchased, to reflect expected earnings growth in the future? About this, George Soros wrote: "In theory, the process works as follows. Let us assume that all of the companies involved have the same intrinsic growth in earnings but the stock of the acquiring company sells at twice the earnings multiple of the acquired ones; if the acquiring company manages to double its size, its earnings-per-share jump by 50 %, and its growth rate increases accordingly.... Several of the path-breakers were high-technology companies with a strong defense component, whose management recognized that their historic growth rate could not be sustained indefinitely.... They started to acquire more mundane companies, but, as their per-share earnings growth accelerated the multiple expanded instead of contracting. Their success attracted imitators and later on even the most humdrum companies could attain a high multiple by going on an acquisition spree." (Soros 1988)

'Reflexivity' was in the participants' 'expectation' that share price would increase as earnings-per-share grew. This expectation of the future price was reflexively made real in the future by purchasing shares at a higher price. This reflexivity created the 'boom' in stock market growth. This growth by acquisitions could not last forever. It was a temporary corporate growth strategy that had a time limit. The boom became a bubble when stock investors realized that there was indeed a time limit to the strategy. An expectation-by-investors of growth-without-limit was unsustainable. George Soros calls such expectations by investors in a given market at a given time as a market 'bias'. Soros wrote: "Markets are always biased in one direction or another. Markets can influence the events that they anticipate." (Soros 1988)

One can see the impact of the investor bias in the 1960s for corporate conglomeration in the share-price chart of Teledyne, then one of the conglomerates, Fig. 1.6.

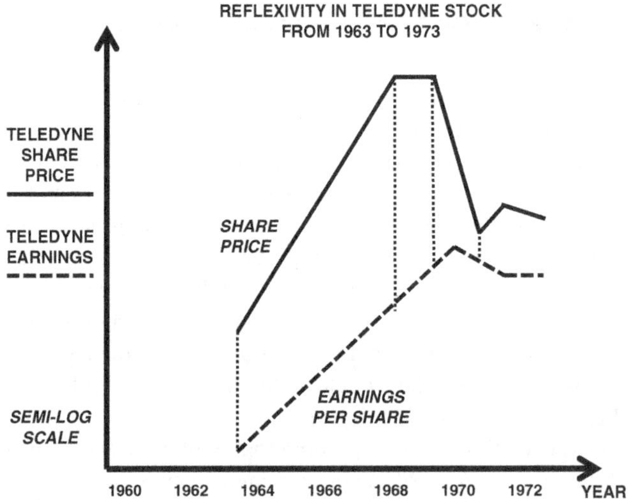

Fig. 1.6 Market reflexivity occurring in Teledyne stock prices

> Teledyne's share-price climbed before the earnings-per-share grew, as investors anticipated continued corporate growth through business acquisitions—through corporate conglomeration. This growth occurred from 1963 to 1968, as earning-per-share grew. But from 1968 through 1969, some investors began to perceive that continuing earnings growth from business acquisitions was not eternally sustainable, and stopped buying shares at higher prices. Share price leveled off from 1968 to 1969. As this expectation became widely shared, the prevailing investor bias about the company changed, and investors sold shares, precipitating a dramatic share-price fall, from 1969 through 1970. This is an example of Soros' concept of 'reflexivity' in financial markets, as present-decisions-by-investors are based upon expectations-of-the-investors-about-the-future. *'Reflexivity' in societal events is that societal participants can affect the future due to actions-in-the-present based upon thinking-about-the-future.*
>
> As a footnote—in 2014, Teledyne Technologies still existed as a U.S. industrial conglomerate, with global operations. In 1960, Henry Singleton and George Kozmetsky had founded the company as Teledyne. In 1996, was acquired by Allegheny Ludlum Corporations and became part of Allegheny Teledyne. In 1999, that conglomerate broke into three companies, Teledyne Technologies, Allegheny Technologies, and Water Pik Technologies. (http://en.wikipedia.org/Teledyne_Technologies, 2014)

As seen in this example, a kind of 'model' was implicit in the investor process of 'reflexivity', which contains an investor bias in a market at a time. Soros argued that financial markets are never a 'perfect' economic market because investors are never completely rational, 'unbiased'. But all financial markets operate within some investor bias at the time. The 'investor bias' is a shared expectation of the future of the market.

Economic behavior, such as 'reflexivity' in market traders' cognition, is why the connections between economic models are not merely information transfers (as assumed in the economic theory of a perfect market). Connections are themselves economic activities. As activities, the 'connections' are themselves 'processes'. But such processes cannot be modeled context-free (without any context).

Each connection is context dependent upon the market and the time of the market. In the example of Teledyne, the context-dependent economic process was 'corporate conglomeration'. But this context did not last forever in the U.S. stock market. It lasted through the decade of the 1960s and ended in the decade of the 1970s—during which the OPEC oil cartel totally changed the economic and financial pictures of the world. In the case of the dot.com stock bubble of 1995–2000, it grew and ended upon overly-zealous expectations of rapid profitability in the Internet.

Summary

We have reviewed the price-disequilibrium model of financial markets, in contrast to the price-equilibrium model of commodity markets. The price-disequilibrium model derives from financial transaction theory in which capital-assets traded in a financial market have two economic values in time, a current rent and a future liquidity. Also since capital assets purchases (and trading) use credit (debt loans), leverage in the loans varies when a market gets 'hot'. Excess leverage for high prices can then crash the market. Thus instability is inherent in the dynamics of financial markets, allowing for periodic financial bubbles.

Financial systems instabilities usually begin with a 'financial bubble' and, they often are followed by bank panics and economic recessions. Thus one needs to track a financial bubble, as a likely precursor to bank panics and recessions. We have reviewed (1) how to model the Minsky-Keynes model of financial transactions, and (2) how to extend the 'equilibrium-price' model to a 'disequilibrium-price' model, through adding a third dimension of time.

Theory is a semantic language of 'principles' in which models of 'reality' (models of real objects) can be constructed. In economics, theory consists of 'normative principles' about how economic systems should operate—markets should be 'self-price-regulating' in proper contexts. Thus a price equilibrium model can be accurate for a market of 'commodities' (in the proper context) but not for a financial market of 'capital assets'. For a financial market, a price-disequilibrium model is accurate to depict real financial markets. Thus in empirical reality, some regulation is necessary for both kinds of markets to display the economic ideal (theory) of market self-regulation. We will explore what kind of regulation is needed for international financial markets to approach the economic ideal of 'self-regulation' and 'stability'.

References

Appelbaum, B. (2013, January 18). Days before 2007 crisis, fed officials doubted need to act. *New York Times*.

Bernanke, B. S. (2007). *Global imbalances: Recent developments and prospects*. Berlin, Germany: Budesbank Lecture. Retrieved September 11, 2008 from http://www.federalreserve.gov/newsevents/speechbernanke20070911a.htm

Betz, F. (2014). Disequilibrium pricing theory. *Theoretical Economics Letters, 4*(1). Retrieved February, from http://www.scirp.org/journal/tel

Blustein, P. (2003). *The chastening: Inside the crisis that rocked the global financial system and humbled the IMF*. New York: Public Affairs Books.

Fisher, I. (1933, October). The debt-deflation theory of the great depression. *Econometrica*.

Keynes, J. M. (1936). *The general theory of employment, interest, and money*. New York: Harcourt Brace.

Kindelberger, C. P., & Aliber, R. Z. (2011). *Manias, panics, and crashes: A history of financial crises* (6th ed.). New York: Palgrave Macmillan.

Krugman, P. (2013). How the case for austerity has crumbled. *The New York Review of Books*. Retrieved June 6, 2013 Issue, from http://www.nybooks.com/articles/archives/2013/jun/06/how-case-austerity-has-crumbled/

McCulley, P. (2009, February). *Saving capitalistic banking from itself*. Newport Beach, CA: PIMCO.

Minsky, H. (1975). *John Maynard Keynes*. New York: Columbia University Press (reprinted in 2008 by McGraw Hill).

Minsky, H. P. (1982). *Can 'it' happen again? Essays on instability and finance*. Armonk, NY: M.E. Sharpe.

Minsky, H. (1993). Comment on Ben Bernanke, 'credit in the macro-economy'. Hyman P. Minsky Archive, Paper 361. Retrieved from http://digitalcommons.bard.edu/hmarchive/361

Morgenson, G., & Rosner, J. (2011). *Reckless endangerment: How outsized ambition, greed, and corruption led to economic Armageddon*. New York: Henry Holt and Company.

Nocera, J., & Carvell, T. (2000, October 30). 50 Lessons. *Fortune* (pp. 136–137).

Soros, G. (1988). *The alchemy of finance*. New York: Simon & Schuster. ISBN 0-671-66338-4 (paperback: Wiley, 2003; ISBN 0-471-44549-5).

Wolf, M. (2008, April 8). Why Greenspan does not bear most of the blame. *Financial Times*.

Wolf, M. (2014). *The Shifts and the Shocks: What we've learned-and have still to learn-from the financial crisis*. London: Penguin Press.

Chapter 2
International Grid of Capital Flows: Innovation, Crisis, and Off-shore Banking

Introduction

Disequilibrium financial markets are now embedded in international financial networks, which direct the flow of capital around the world. These international cash flows are involved in the process of international banking; and the modern technologies of information and communications (IC) have increased the speed, volume, and complexity of international flows. But at the end of the twentieth century, the global world began to experience destabilizing international flows—particularly in the Asian financial crisis of 1997, Global financial crisis of 2007, and Euro crisis of 2010. In using the IC technologies, how has international banking increased the frequency and intensity of international financial crises?

Did the IC technology somehow encourage the failure of international financial institutions in performing with basic financial 'integrity', 'honesty', and 'prudence'? To answer these issues, one must observe the financial system within an IC network, a kind of financial 'grid'. We use the concept of a 'financial grid' and model the grid as a network of institutional intermediaries, matching financial supply-to-demand. To construct this topological model, we review the recent history of investment banking and of the organization of off-shore banking into an unregulated but centralized international financial grid.

Most of the literature on international capital flows have focused upon the issue of—whether capital should be allowed to flow freely into and out of the country or should the country try to control the flow? Barry Eichengreen wrote: "The implications of capital mobility for growth and stability is one of the most contentious and least understood issues of our day. The controversy is long standing; one only need recall Nurkse's emphasis on destabilizing capital flows in the 1920s or Keynes's and Whites' effort to construct an international regime with limits on capital mobility following World War II. But the depth of disagreement in both academic and policy circles was pointed up by the Asian crisis (in 1998). This event which followed on the heels of widespread capital liberalization in the first half of the 1990s, convinced

F. Betz, *Stability in International Finance*, SpringerBriefs in Economics,
DOI 10.1007/978-3-319-26760-9_2

many observers that early opening to international capital markets is a recipe for disaster. But it also led others to the opposite conclusion." (Eichengreen 2004)

Underlying this disagreement on capital liberalization (about its liability or benefit to economic growth) has, however, been a common assumption—that the 'structure' of the banking institutions controlling capital flow has remained unchanged over the twentieth century. And this empirically was not true. The introduction of information and communications (IC) technologies (e.g. computers and electronic networks) into the financial sector has changed financial transactions (process and products). In the course of the last years of that century and into the first years of the twenty-first century, IC technologies have electronically developed banking networks into a kind of financial grid.

The investigative financial reporter Suzanne McGee used the term 'financial grid' to describe the U.S. Wall Street institutional infrastructure as an 'abstraction'. A 2009 meeting of a U.S. Senate Banking Committee was trying to understand the financial collapse of Wall Street in 2008. One senator asked the question: "Does Wall Street owe the American people an apology?" The question was asked of the then Chair of the Federal Reserve System, Ben Bernanke. Susan McGee reported his response: "He tried to describe to the committee the concept of 'Wall Street'. After a lot of hemming and hawing, Ben Bernanke finally replied that… 'Wall Street' is a… is a… is an abstraction.'" (McGee 2010)

The abstraction to which Bernanke was referring is that of a 'system'—not a place nor buildings nor a business but a process of functional transactions—a financial system. The abstraction is about how institutions in the financial system provide services. But Wall Street is a private system, and to understand why the public needed to 'bail-out' a private system, Suzanne McGee used the analogy of an electrical power system to a financial system. McGee wrote: "Wall Street, in its totality, involves more than what happens on the floor of the New York Stock Exchange or within the walls of any single investment banking institution. It has become a labyrinth of many different groups and institutions, all of which have one thing in common: they make the whole money grid work more smoothly and more efficiently." (McGee 2010)

An electrical power grid needs to be regulated for the public good, to ensure power generation and distribution companies perform their job of continuously delivering 'power'. In McGee's view, so too must the grid of financial systems be regulated to ensure they perform their job of continuously delivering 'money'. Yet in the last half of the twentieth century, there were political moves to deregulate banking in America and Europe. Why was there such an effort to deregulate international banking, even as destabilizations occurred? How had the international banking become 'casino banking'—banks gambling depositors' monies on massive trading and on producing unsound products of high risk and little public good?

One of the unsound products innovated by Wall Street's new 'casino banking' mentality in the beginning of this century was called 'securitization'. It brought down Wall Street in 2008; and in 2009, the U.S. Congress established an inquiry to investigate the crisis. Phil Angelides was appointed Chairman of the U.S. Congress Financial Crisis Inquiry Commission: "I came into my position as chairman of the commission with what I thought was a reasonable understanding of the American financial system, and I had this quaint notion that it was a system designed to allocate capital to the economy for the purposes of creating jobs in enterprise and long-term sustained wealth for our society. I must tell you that over the course of the last year and half, I, along with my fellow commissioners, undertook a journey of revelation. As we did our investigation, we were surprised, we were shocked, we were fascinated and often appalled at what we found. I often felt as if I had entered my local community bank, had opened a door that I wasn't supposed open, and when I opened it, I saw a casino floor as big as New York, New York. And, I may add, that unlike Claude Raines in Casablanca, I was truly shocked at the level of gambling that was going on in Wall Street." (Angelides 2011)

Wall Street was part of the new international financial grid, which reached down even to local community banks. What kind of international bank regulation is needed to ensure a stable international financial system which allocates capital to economic activity of job creation—instead of mostly 'gambling'?

Disequilibrium Systems Model of a Financial Grid

The traditional function of investment banking occurs in what has been called a 'financing life cycle' of business. Investment banking services involves finding investors to finance the start of a business, loaning money to the business to finance its growth, taking the business public by issuing stock, maintaining a trading market in the stock, and assisting the business to issue bonds for operations or acquisitions. Some investment banks (venture capital firms) specialize in financing the 'start-up' stage of a new business; while the traditional Wall Street investment banks specialize in the underwriting the public offering stage. In offering public stock, investment banks had to ensure the continuing market for stock by participating in a stock exchange (e.g. having a seat on the New York Stock Exchange). Traditional investment banks also sold corporate bond issues for further corporate financing.

In a network of banking, Irving Minsky viewed investment and commercial banks as a layered banking system. (Minsky 1975) Investment banks draw upon commercial banks for leveraged investment loans. The commercial bank takes in deposits of savings, and the investment banks produce financial products to sell to investors and commercial banks (demand for investments). An investment bank creates the financial intermediation process by formulating a financial product, which is based upon two economic values: (1) the estimated market value of the capital asset and (2) the interest rate (rent) of the financial product. This financial product is then available for sale in a financial market (e.g. corporate equity stocks in a stock market or derivatives in a derivative market or international currency exchanges in a currency exchange market). The economic value of the financial product is determined by its pricing in its financial market; and if a financial bubble occurs in the market (such as the housing bubble in 2005 in the mortgage derivative market), then the bubble can burst, dropping the market. Thus the financial product value depends upon: (1) its initial value when sold and (2) its later value when traded in a market.

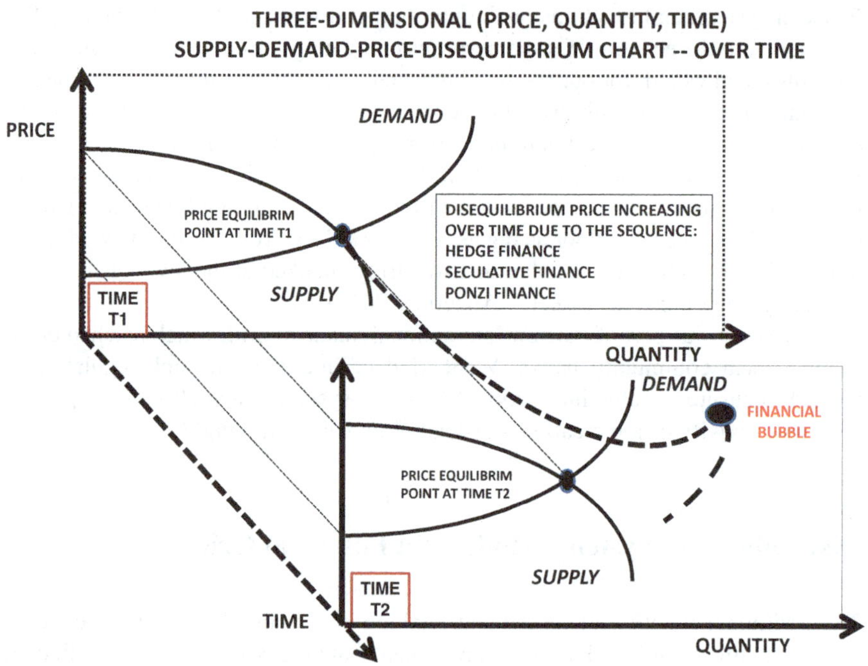

Fig. 2.1 Disequilibrium price model of a financial market over time

In the first chapter, we derived the he Keynes-Minsky price disequilibrium transaction in a financial market as a disequilibrium-price model; and we show this again in Fig. 2.1.

We recall that in a financial market, financial products of capital assets are traded, and a capital asset has two economic values—current rent and future liquidity. Over time from T_1 to T_2, trading in the market can move from a price-equilibrium point to price disequilibrium, when a market gets hot and traders borrow money to purchase the asset at higher and higher prices. This is possible using greater leverage in the loans the trader gets to trade in the market. Debt makes a financial process operate. Yet one aspect of debt can destabilize the process; and this is 'leverage'. To increase profit, a financial system uses debt to finance the purchase of capital assets. Profits can be increased through financial leverage; and this is the financial rational of 'leverage' (more 'present-debt' toward greater 'future-wealth'). However, when present-debt is too large (too highly leveraged), it might not create future-wealth but, instead, bankruptcy.

We can now use this disequilibrium model of a financial market as the central piece in modeling how the products of that market are produced and sold. This is the basic economic role of investment banking to create and sell financial products of capital assets.

As shown in Fig. 2.2, the investment bank process can be depicted in systems notation, with a 'disequilibrium financial market model' in the middle of the

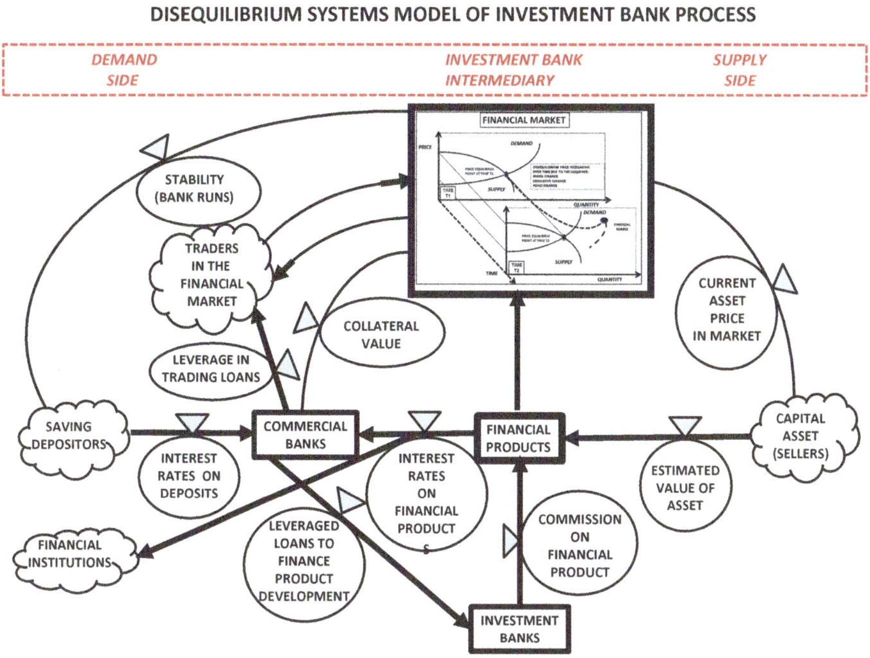

Fig. 2.2 Disequilibrium systems model of financial products produced for a financial market

system—with a demand side and a supply side. The financial market is composed of financial products created by investment banks—products which match capital supply (demand side) to capital need (supply side). The investment bank creating financial products for a financial market is the center of the systems model. To the right side (supply side) of the systems model are sellers of capital assets, and to the left side are buyers of capital assets (demand side). The investment banks are the banking intermediary which create the financial products which sell capital assets to buyers.

In systems notation, the 'cloud' symbols are 'sources' as origins of things entering the 'flow' of the system—things which flow along the 'arrow' lines of the system. The 'rectangle' symbols are stocks of things which receive, send, or hold the things flowing along the arrows. The 'circle-with-triangle' symbols are 'control valves' which control the 'rate-of-flow' of things along the arrows of the system. The 'system' model of an institutional process indicates a flow of things between sources and stocks in the system, controlled by valves along the flow lines.

In the case of a systems model of investment bank procedures, there are two sources: a source of savings (buyers) and a source of assets (sellers). The flow is 'capital' from a source of savers to a source of asset sellers, through the intermediary of the creation and trading of 'financial products'—products created by investment banks and traded in a financial market. The 'price-disequilibrium' aspect of the investment process model is in the financial market—which over time might go into a financial bubble (due to trader speculation in the market) and then a Minsky moment occurs when the financial bubble collapses.

As a financial intermediary, an investment bank brings together a financial *supply side* of capital assets to trade in a market with a financial *demand side* of buyers of the assets. For example, when an investment backs assists a private company in making a public offering of stock, the private company sells equity assets as stock and purchasers of the stock buy equity in the company.

The source in the *supply side* for the financial products are sellers of capital assets. The value of the financial product is controlled by a rate of the estimated-value-of-the-asset compared to the current-asset-price trading in the financial market. In financing the creation of a financial product, investment banks often get loans from commercial banks; and there is leverage in the product-development loans. (For example in a 2007 case of securitized mortgage bonds, an investment bank's hedge fund within Bear Sterns borrowed 100 % of the cost of the mortgage they purchased for securitization for 1 year from the commercial Bank of America—even when the mortgage wouldn't pay back principle for 30 years.)

To model the *demand side* of financial products, the source of savings are individuals who make deposits in commercial banks, and the commercial banks purchase financial products. Also other financial institutions (mutual funds, hedge funds, pension funds, insurance companies) purchase financial products. The interest rate on the financial product is the controlling rate for its purchase by commercial banks and financial institutions. Commercial banks also make leveraged loans to traders in the financial market; and the trader's purchase of financial products is then held as collateral by the banks. Commercial banks use interest from a financial product to pay interest to their savings depositors.

Thus the *stability* of the commercial banks can then depend (1) upon the quantity of financial product purchased by the bank and (2) upon the value of the collateral held on loans to traders. If the financial market collapses, then commercial banks are saddled with valueless financial products and the bad loans to the traders. The banks can become insolvent. (For example, in the New York stock market collapse of 1929, stocks held as collateral in banks which made loans to traders purchasing stocks-on-margin became valueless; and many of these banks went bust, through 1930, 1931, 1932. Later in the 2007 derivatives market crash, some large U.S. banks (holding mortgage bonds as collateral) collapsed; and others holding such collateral would have collapsed, except for the U.S. government bail-out.

Thus the disequilibrium model of a financial market is composed of the financial products which trade capital assets; and the financial market may move toward a price disequilibrium, if and when the market becomes hot, as traders bid the price of the financial product higher into a financial bubble. *As traders bid higher prices in the market, they need increasing larger leverage in the loans for purchase.* When the leverage in the loans gets too high, then the market grows into a financial bubble and can collapse. In a financial market collapse, the financial products which the commercial banks have held as collateral can become valueless (toxic assets). The banks can become insolvent and collapse (bank runs).

This models the 'abstraction of Wall Street' in terms of a price-disequilibrium systems model of a financial market—created in the process of connecting the supply side (sellers) to the demand side (buyers), with investment banks acting as financial intermediaries. Suzanne McGee wrote: "All of the players (on Wall Street) perform functions that link the 'buy side,' those who have capital and want to invest it profitably, and the 'sell side,' those entities in need of capital. 'At its heart, when it is doing what it does best, Wall Street is a superb gatekeeper, making matches between investors and businesses, governments, or anyone else who needs to finance something,' explains Mike Heffernan, a former Morgan Stanley banker." (McGee 2010)

The sellers and buyers of financial products have different interests, which the investment bank must bridge in creating a financial product. Suzanne McGee wrote: "The sell side wants to get as much capital on the most favorable terms possible from the buy side—investors who range in size and importance from individuals to mutual fund conglomerates such as Fidelity, and include hedge funds, private equity funds, foundations, college endowments, pension funds, venture capital partnerships, and ultra-wealthy individual investors such as Microsoft cofounder Paul Allen or financier George Soros. In a perfect world, the sell side would love free money—with no interest payable, no specific term for repayment, and no promises about increasing the value of the investment. It is the myriad institutions that collectively make up Wall Street that (in exchange for a fee) bring together the two parties and negotiate a compromise: the terms on which the buy side is willing to invest some of its capital and the sell side is willing to agree to in order to get its hands on that capital. Banks have been fulfilling that kind of function in more limited ways for centuries.... Wall Street exists to help investors and those in need of capital find their way through the financing maze. Investment bankers still not only link the two sides but also help them sort out what terms are fair for the kind of capital being sought." (McGee 2010)

In the twenty-first century, how did it happen that 'Wall Street' investment banking in the U.S. moved away from this traditional economic role toward 'casino banking'? Casino banking gambles high-risk financial products of questionable quality, little public good, and prone to market bubbles. Why did Wall Street take this path?

History: Wall Street 'Mayday'

Historically, Wall Street investment banks had collected fixed fees for buying or selling of stock by investors on the stock exchange. While corporate start-ups, IPOs, and bonds were occasional events, earning commissions for the investment banks, the continuous trading of stocks provided a steady stream of income for the investment banks. But a large stream of steady profits from stock trading came to a sudden end for Wall Street investment banks. Suzanne McGee wrote: "May 1, 1975, has gone down in the history of the Street as "Mayday," the date the Securities and Exchange Commission had dictated would mark the end of fixed trading commissions in the stock market. Overnight, Wall Street's comfortable existence was shaken; its long-standing business model was turned upside down." (McGee 2012)

Trading stock on the New York Stock Exchange cost a fixed fee (dependent upon the dollar value of the trade). This generated a steady and large income stream for the investment banks. McGee quoted Fred Joseph, former CEO of Drexel Burnham: "I was a big producer, because I'd do one trade in connection with a deal. I could make a $500,000 fee without discussing it with the client. This was due to the fee being fixed and institutional investors making large and frequent trades." (McGee 2012)

Fixed commissions on executing stock trades provided a secure and continuous base of revenue for U.S. investment banks. The commissions produced large profits which financed overhead activities such as 'investment research' by the Wall Street banks. When the fixed commission structure was deconstructed, investment banks had to turn to intermittent and non-recurrent business activities to generate large commissions. Suzanne McGee quoted Wilbur Ross about the change: "Wall Street's Mayday changed the whole nature of Wall Street; what we did and who we were. Research suddenly had no value in its own right and wasn't being subsidized. So the clever people on the Street said, 'Okay, we'll use these smart and well-paid people to bring in investment banking business.'" (McGee 2010)

With this change in revenue flow, Wall Street could not afford to protect the investor with financial research or even financial due diligence. This was the beginning of the evolution of Wall Street investment banks from acting as proper financial intermediaries to casino banking—trading, pumping, and dumping. Suzanne McGee wrote: "The ugly end to the U.S. dot-com boom in early 2000 drove that message home to Wall Street decision makers like nothing else had done. They had spent the waning years of the twentieth century chasing the kind of fees that had been the bread and butter of Wall Street: taking start-up technology companies public, raising both debt and equity for the likes of WorldCom and AT& T Wireless, and pocketing merger advisory fees by helping companies such as Cisco and JDS Uniphase snap up innovative young companies.... But that happiness could endure only as long as the market bubble kept inflating.... The fact was that Wall Street firms no longer needed to rely purely on the fees they earned for overseeing processes such as underwriting, sales and trading, or advising on mergers. These intermediary functions were profitable only when they could be done in tremendous volumes, as had happened at the height of the dot-com boom. The longer the slump that began in 2000 lasted, the more Wall Street needed to find an alternative source of revenue, preferably one with a higher profit margin." (McGee 2010)

Institutional Change in Wall Street

After 1973, the history of Wall Street can then be recounted as a series of disequilibrium bubbles: (1) in the 1970s, there was the Eurobond market, (2) in the 1980s, there were the leveraged buyouts and junk bond financing, (3) in the 1990s, there was the Dot.com bubble and off-book company transactions, (4) in the 2000s, there was securitization and secrecy jurisdictions.

An economic system is implemented as processes operated by institutional procedures. The procedures standardize the economic processes, so that at a given time in a society the system can be described in a steady-state—economic transactions occurring within standardized procedures of an institutional structure. When an event in an economic system alters the institutions and their procedures, then the processes change from a prior steady-stage (stasis) to a different stasis. In societal dynamics theory, one can depict societal change as a sequence of stasis (steady-state) processes, altered by events which change institutional structure in a society. (Betz 2011) As shown in Fig. 2.3, the 'Mayday' event of 1973 when the US Security Exchange Commission (SEC) ordered that stock trading commissions be negotiated; and afterwards, Wall Street financial institutions sought more revenue from 'financial products' rather than trading commissions.

Wall Street Goes to London: Eurodollar Market

After 'Mayday', a second 'change' event for Wall Street occurred, when branch offices were opened in London, for avoiding the U.S. bank regulations about international financing operations. Suzanne McGee wrote: "Wall Street's fee income from its traditional businesses—buying and selling stock on behalf of its clients and underwriting their debt and equity businesses—was threatened. The solution? New products that would address new concerns…Globalization also created new market opportunities. In 1971, the United States abandoned the Bretton Woods system of fixed exchange rates, creating a thriving market for options and futures contracts on foreign currencies, such as the British pound, Japanese yen, and Swiss franc. The Eurobond market was another attractive new opportunity. Born in London's financial markets in the 1960s, it involved issuing dollar-denominated debt outside the United States, meaning that the issues didn't need to be registered with the SEC and that the companies selling debt didn't need to abide by U.S. accounting rules." (McGee 2010)

The bonds were issued in dollar currency by international companies and sold by bank offices in the City of London. Investors found the bonds acceptable in an international currency, paying good interest and avoiding regulations (banking or taxes) by particular nations. Susanne McGee wrote: "The Eurobond market was one of the

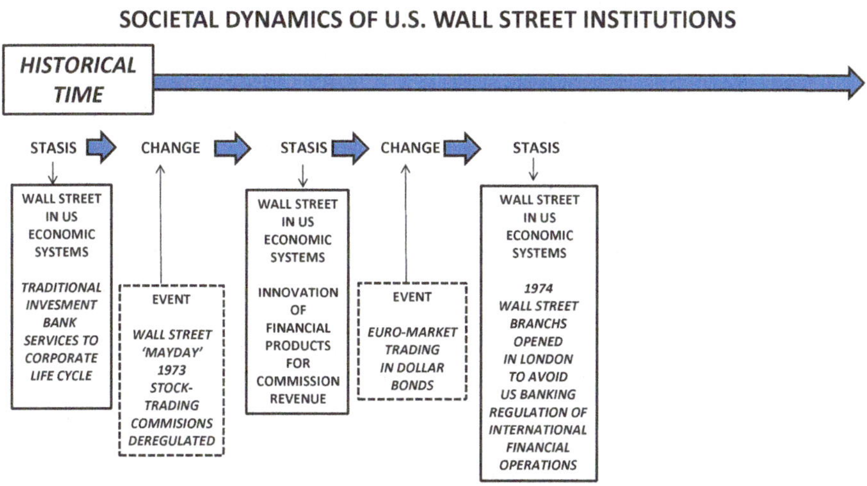

Fig. 2.3 Change events in evolution of Wall Street investment banking

fastest-growing capital markets around—and, like options, it was a lucrative alternative to plain-vanilla bond deals, rewarding underwriters with higher fees. But trying to build a Eurobond business drove home, yet again, the need for a large and stable base of capital. Not only did trying to grab market share in Eurobonds mean establishing a presence in London, but players such as Morgan Stanley and Goldman Sachs (among the early arrivals) would need to compete with giant commercial banks such as Deutsche Bank and Credit Suisse, institutions that, unlike their U.S. counterparts, faced no domestic rules against using their giant commercial banking balance sheets to help them muscle in and grab investment banking business." (McGee 2010)

Thus Wall Street's first financial innovation after the Wall Street 'Mayday' was to create and sell Eurobond in the international financial market. This required Wall Street to establish British branches in London, to avoid the U.S. regulatory restrictions on international financial operations by US investment banks.

How did establishing a London branch of a Wall Street investment bank enable the Wall Street bank to escape regulation, national or international? This occurred after the Second World War when the Bank of England decided not to regulate the British banks much (a regulatory 'light touch'). Nicholas Shaxson wrote: "Nobody quite agrees when this new strain of offshore activity first emerged, but it was probably first spotted by a financial regulatory authority in June 1955 when staffers at the Bank of England, the UK's central bank, noticed some odd trades going on at Midland Bank (now part of the globetrotting HSBC). Exchange rates in those days were mostly fixed against the dollar. Banks in London were not supposed to trade in foreign currencies unless it was for financing specific trades for their clients, and they were not allowed to lend against deposits in foreign currencies. Midland Bank was apparently contravening UK exchange controls by taking U.S. dollar deposits that were not related to a specific commercial transaction. And it was also offering interest rates on these dollar deposits that were substantially higher than those permitted by U.S. regulations." (Shaxson 2011)

The Bank of England had 'looked the other way' (as regulators) in allowing Midland Bank to violate regulations. This opened the lucrative investment bank business in the City of London to take dollar deposits with higher interest rates than offered in the U.S. Dollar deposits followed into the Midland Bank and to other British banks (which also had noticed the implicit 'deregulation'); and the Eurodollar market was born. In Fig. 2.4, we add an international plane to a national plane of the disequilibrium systems model of a commercial-investment bank financial grid.

The commercial or investment banks located in a nation could avoid their nation's bank regulations by opening a bank branch in London. Shaxson wrote: "A Bank of England official called in Midland's chief foreign manager for a chat, to ask why the bank was contravening official controls. Afterward he noted down that the Midland official 'appreciates that a warning light has been shown'. Luckily for Midland, though, Britain was struggling to shore up its shaky foreign exchange reserves, and the Bank was reluctant to snuff out a new area of international business. 'We would be wise, I believe, not to press the Midland any further,' the Central Bank concluded." (Shaxson 2011)

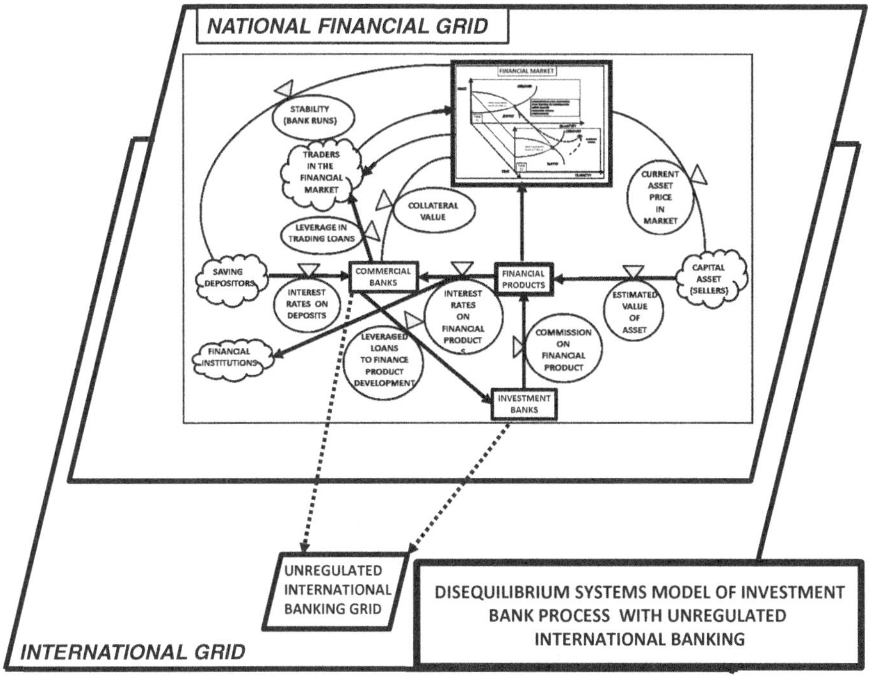

Fig. 2.4 Investment bank process with unregulated international banking

This British practice of 'light regulation' (e.g. only a warning light without any regulatory restriction) by the Bank of England effectively created an unregulated international banking network (financial grid) centered in the City of London. Thus the first step in the evolution of Wall Street banking was to 'go abroad' to London.

Wall Street Junk Bonds

After the Wall Street 'Mayday' and the opening of London branches, the financial products of Wall Street could expand, periodically innovating new financial products which could be sold at home and abroad. The first financial innovation after 'Mayday' was a new concept of the 'junk bond'. Junk bonds were corporate bonds issued without collateral. There was no capital-asset-value backing the bond (as a loan). The junk bonds were highly risky in that: if the bond issuer failed, there was no underlying asset to seize. Why were they issued and sold? The issuer could use money the bonds raised to buy companies which did have assets; and these purchases were called 'leveraged buy-outs'. The junk bond innovation of Wall Street financed the leveraged buy-outs of ongoing businesses—but loaded the businesses with debt, reducing the productivity and competitiveness of a 'captive' business—and thereby the competitiveness of the U.S. economy. As indicated in Fig. 2.5, Wall Street went from assisting economic growth in the U.S. economy to stifling growth—trading not in corporate 'productivity' but in corporate 'control'.

Suzanne McGee wrote about the 'junk bond' financial innovation: "At a lavish dinner celebrating the fortieth anniversary of Institutional Investor magazine in 2007, Henry Kravis, a cofounder of the giant buyout firm KKR, was one of the evening's honorees—the forty 'Legends of Wall Street.' (That group also included John Gutfreund of Salomon Brothers.) In his speech, Kravis chose to laud Michael Milken, the investment banker who had popularized the "junk bond" during the 1980s. Without Milken, Kravis told the audience, KKR couldn't have done the gargantuan deals that made it famous, and the entire buyout business (which had generated $357 billion in deals in the United States alone the previous year, each of which produced massive fees for Wall Street investment banks) would have been stillborn." (McGee 2010)

In 1970, Drexel Firestone was an investment bank focused upon selling bonds and providing stock trading services. Michael Milken began working as a bond salesperson. In 1973, I.W. Burnham purchased the firm and changed its name to Drexel Burnham Lambert. Burnham gave Milken $2 million to trade in bonds and Milken doubled it in 1 year. Burnham increased the capital available to Milken to trade and gave him a 35 % commission on trading profits. Connie Bruck wrote: "The world that Milken created for his faithful… would transform the face of corporate America. It would introduce terror and mayhem into countless corporate boardrooms. It would cause frightened managements to focus on short-term gains and elaborate takeover defenses…. It would cause the loss of jobs, as companies were taken over and broken up… In doing all these things, the good and the bad, Milken's machine would stir hatreds and prejudices…. Experts would debate whether the value that Milken's onslaught had added to American business outweighed the damage…." (Bruck 1988)

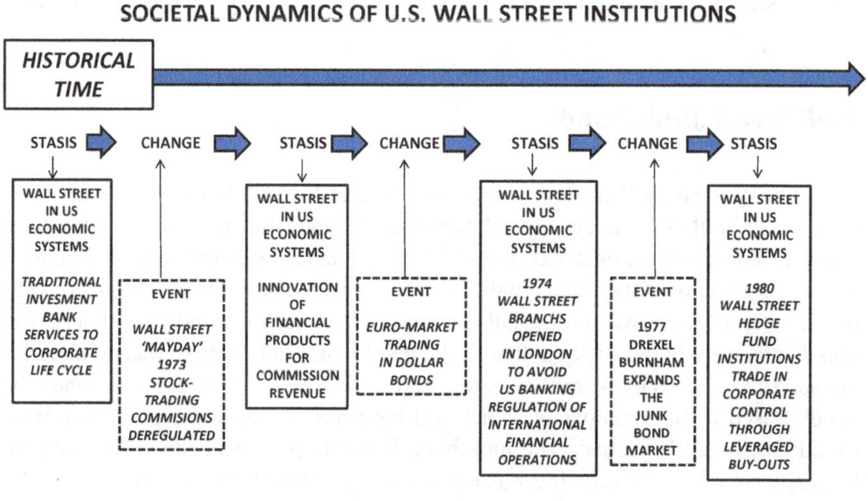

Fig. 2.5 Change events in the evolution of Wall Street

Milken focused on selling and trading bonds without underlying assets, 'junk bonds'. Junk bonds had existed for a long time, as bonds without adequate evidence that the corporation which issued the bond could fulfill its financial contract. What Michael Milken did was to realize that there could be a new market for a new kind of junk bond—a bond without past-value but perhaps future-value. The junk bonds were issued to buy-out existing companies. And for this junk bond market there were new sellers (buy-out artists and hedge-funds) and new buyers (savings & loan banks, insurance companies, and pension funds). This scheme is modeled in Fig. 2.6.

In this disequilibrium model of Drexel's junk bond market, the investment bank of Drexel Burnham led in formulating junk bond offerings for corporate raiders. The Savings & Loan Bank industry (recently deregulated) eagerly bought the junk bonds because of their high interest rates. Other financial institutions, such as insurance companies, also bought the junk bonds. When the junk bond market collapsed, many of the S&L banks went bankrupt, as their junk bonds became worthless.

As Milken at Drexel began to stir the junk bond market, more sellers went to Milken to create junk bonds. They were the 'corporate raiders', people who bought corporate control by buying a corporation's stock, using junk bond financing. With 'junk bond' funding in the 1980s, over a quarter of American corporations were so 'traded'—taken over.

Connie Bruck has listed some of the well-known corporate raiders in the 1980s, who included: Carl Icahn, Victor Posner, Nelson Peltz, Robert M. Bass, T. Boone

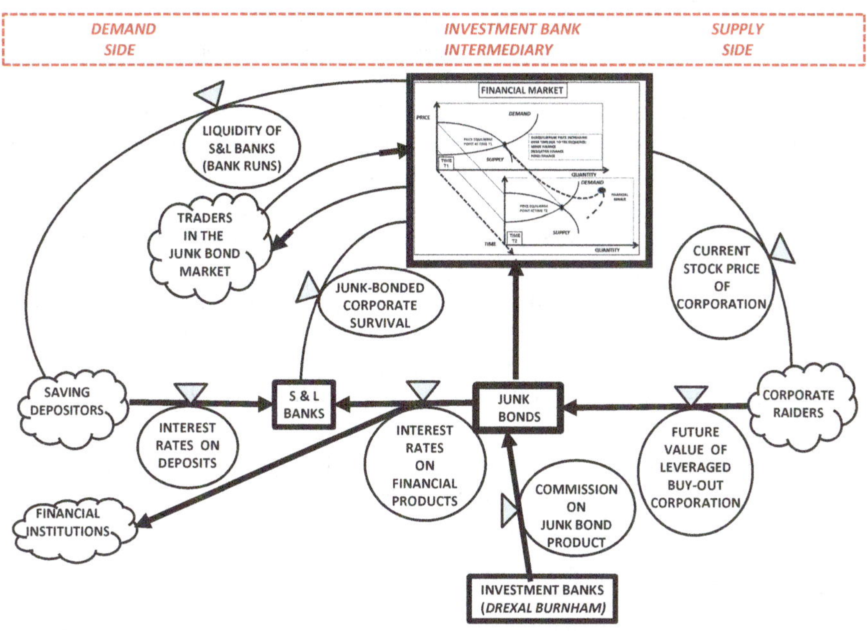

Fig. 2.6 Disequilibrium systems model of corporate leveraged buy-outs

Pickens, Harold Clark Simmons, Kirk Kerkorian, Sir James Goldsmith, Saul Steinberg and Asher Edelman. Connie Bruck wrote that: "Michael Milken raised pools of capital for the raiders through Drexel's junk bond offerings. For example, in 1984, Milken sold a $750 million blind pool of junk to enable Ronald Perelman to take over Revlon, a leading cosmetics maker. Perelman sold off four of Revlon's divisions to reduce debt and later in 1966, Perelman sold his stock in Revlon through a public offering which made Revlon again a public company." (Bruck 1988) A captured corporation (such as Revlon), between being 'private' and then flipped again as 'public', had been greatly burdened to handle the enormous junk debt.

The profitability in the trade derived from transferring the debt liability from the 'trader' to the 'traded corporation'. The 'take-over raider' which issued 'junk bonds' as the raider's liability; but the liability was next transferred by the raider onto the captive corporation. The raider could do this by taking the company private in the 'buy-out'. Then as a private company, the raider could transfer his bond-liability onto the company books, since the company was the raider's private property. In this way, a 'taken-over' captive company' was loaded with the additional debt to pay for its own 'take-over'. This was a private good for the take-over artist but not necessarily a private good for the corporation. The corporate raider 'investor' then had no further liability for the junk bonds previously issued, a nice financial trick.

Kohlberg Kravis, Roberts & Co (KKR) was a private equity company which pioneered the trading of American corporations through 'leveraged buy-out' financing. It was founded in 1976 by Jerome Kohlberg, Henry Kravis and George Roberts. They had worked together at Bear Sterns, where they started some leveraged buy-outs. Then they left to form their own firm; and proceeded to buy out over 160 companies worth $400 billion in private equity transactions.

An example of the heavy burden of debt KKK could put upon a company was its 'captured' First Data Corp. Henny Sender wrote: "Sometime soon (in 2014), KKR hopes to mark its investment in First Data back to 100 cents on the dollar, allowing the private equity group to start preparing a heavily indebted company it took private at the peak of the 2007 buyout boom for an initial public offering… It has been a long way back for a $30bn deal that was one of the largest buyouts ever. At the depths, KKR held the payments processor and information company on its books at 60–70 cents." (Sender 2014)

As a private company owned by KKK, First Data had been loaded with the junk debt (which KKK transferred from it to First Data). Then First Data was no longer 'profitable', as its revenues after 2007 went only to pay expenses to service interest on junk debt. Thus the value of First Data had declined to 60–70 % of it 'buy-out' price; and in 2014, KKK needed to invest some of its own capital into First Data to make it a competitive company—and to make it show profits, so that KKK could 'flip it' by taking it again public. In 2014, Greg Roumeliotis wrote: "First Data is one of many corporate cleanups quietly underway in the world of private equity, as the industry deals with a debt binge in the years before the 2008 financial crisis." (Roumeliotis 2014)

The captured corporation had to pay off the junk debt used to capture the corporation; and often could make no investments for the future (such as R&D and new products). Later (and hopefully) after the captured corporation paid off some of the debt and achieved profits again, the corporation could be taken public again, reaping enormous profits on the investment by the raiders—providing an infinite rate of profit to the raider-trader because they borrowed the money and never held liability for the debt. Some of the stock sales proceeds might be used to pay down some of the debt; but proceeds first went to enrich the corporate raider. Wall Street investment banking went from helping corporations to begin and grow to 'flipping' corporations—a private good with a questionable public good.

But junk bonds had also an impact upon buyers, creating 'bank runs' on the U.S. Savings & Loan banks (S&L) in the late 1980s. From 1986 to 1995, one third of the S&L banks went bankrupt. S&L banks were chartered to fund home mortgages in the United States, restricted to mortgages with homes as collateral. In 1980 and 1982, the U.S. Congress deregulated the S&L industry, allowing these banks to invest in anything and many invested in Milken's junk bonds. When Milken went to jail in and the junk bond imploded then, the S&Ls holding junk bonds went insolvent. The U.S. regulatory agencies then closed 1043 out of 3234 S&Ls.

Wall Street Securitization and Secrecy Jurisdictions

After 2000, Wall Street next moved into 'securitization' for financial products. But Wall Street's financial invention of the 'securitized mortgage' was really a fraudulent financial asset because (1) the rent had been stripped from the mortgage bonds and sold separately as a derivative and (2) the investment bank creators (e.g. Bear Sterns, Goldman Sachs, etc.) had not paid for the mortgages but only borrowed for them, with the long-term mortgages purchased by short-term loans. By creating a fraudulent capital asset (not really a capital asset) and also by borrowing-short-and lending-long to purchase the mortgages, the investment banks had not been selling financial products (derivatives) as a real capital asset product (with both rents and future liquidity). They had gone from a banking 'integrity' to 'casino banking'—gambling that the bonds underlying the derivatives might never have to be sold. The mortgage bonds the investment banks held (and had not paid for) then became the 'toxic assets' to the investment banks—because the bonds could not be again sold (having no interest income). Then the government would have to buy from them in the bail-out.

We earlier noted that Irving Minsky specified for financial markets to trade real capital assets, the assets would have to have both rents and future liability. (Minsky 1975) Had the then chair of the U.S. central bank appreciated Minsky's insights about the nature of a financial market, he should not have allowed Wall Street investment banks to sell the so-called 'securitized' mortgage-based-derivatives. Yet, instead in 2000, the Chair of the U. S. Federal Reserve Bank had argued to the U.S. Congress that the derivative market need not and should not be regulated. (Wolf 2008)

The financial innovation event of 'securitization' is shown in Fig. 2.7, along with a second event of 'secrecy jurisdictions'.

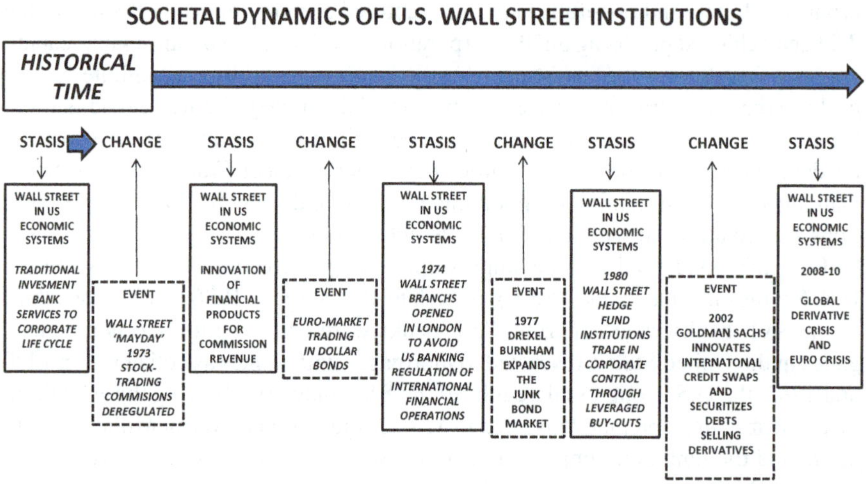

Fig. 2.7 Change events in the evolution of Wall Street

In addition to the financial innovation of 'securitization', Wall Street also innovated ways to keep debt off of government books. This was a process which Nicholas Shaxson called 'secrecy jurisdictions'—making debt secret. (Shaxson 2011) Wall Street created this product as a so-called 'credit swap'. Wall Street sold loans (disguised as currency credit-swaps) to municipalities in the US and in Europe, advertising low-interest rates in the short-term. The 'catch' was that the interest rates were tied to a currency exchange rate; and if the currency exchange rate changed the interest could jump higher.

For example, variable-interest-rate loans were sold to French cities, with the euro exchange rate coupled to the Swiss franc. Some of the financial results of 'credit-swaps' can be seen in the case of a small town in France, Châtcauncuf-Les-Martigues. Noemie Bisserbe wrote: "The mayor of this sleepy town near the Mediterranean coast gathered a crowd in the community hall on a recent day to discuss complex instruments that most of them had never heard of: financial swaps. Over 3 h, he described how a loan pegged to the Swiss franc that municipal officials took out years ago had become so burdensome that the southern French town could no longer afford to build the school it needed. Like several hundred cities across France, Chateauneur-les-Martigues took out a variable-interest-rate loan in the mid-2000s to restructure debt and reduce interest payments. The loans offered very low interest rates for the first few years, before the rate would start to vary according to the value of the Swiss franc." (Bisserbe 2015)

The loans were made to cities with an initial low interest rate but coupled to the exchange rate of the Euro to the Swiss franc. These loans carried large commissions for the investment banks. Buyers bought them, assuming the risk was low based upon the integrity of municipalities. But in 2015, with the Euro crisis continuing in Greece, the value of the Euro dropped and that of the Swiss franc rose. Then the variable interest rates of the loans climbed. Noemie Bisserbe wrote: "Now, with the euro having sunk... scores of municipalities across France have come to rue the day they accepted the offers. Interest rates on some loans started to increase during the financial crisis. That has accelerated in the 6 months since the Swiss National Bank abandoned a cap on the franc's value versus the euro.... The loan mess is turning into a municipal crisis for the French government... A handful of mayors have filed complaints against Dexia, claiming they weren't informed about the risks involved and seeking to cancel the loans.... Chateauneur-les-Martigues says that, even if the government paid 60 % of the fees to terminate its loan, the town still would need to pay 13 million euros in capital, interest and fees to get out of the 6.6 million euro loan it took out 8 years ago." (Bisserbe 2015)

This innovation by Wall Street investment banks to lure municipalities into variable-rate loans was obviously not in the long-term 'public good' of the cities. But after the Wall Street 'Mayday', investment banks around Wall Street no longer looked out for the public good interest of their clients—neither sellers nor buyers. Their goal was focused upon commissions on products, for which neither the seller nor buyer might really benefit.

Also suffering during this same period was Greece; and about Greece, Robert Reich wrote: "The Greek debt crisis offers another illustration of Wall Street's powers of persuasion and predation, although the Street is missing from most accounts. The crisis was exacerbated years ago by a deal with Goldman Sachs, engineered by Goldman's current CEO, Lloyd Blankfein. Blankfein and his Goldman team helped Greece hide the true extent of its debt, and in the process almost doubled it.... In 2001, Greece was looking for ways to disguise its mounting financial troubles. The Maastricht Treaty required all eurozone member states to show improvement in their public finances, but Greece was heading in the wrong direction. Then Goldman Sachs came to the rescue, arranging a secret loan of 2.8 billion euros for Greece, disguised as an off-the-books "cross-currency swap"—a complicated transaction in which Greece's foreign-currency debt was converted into a domestic-currency obligation using a fictitious market exchange rate." (Reich 2015) At the time, Blankfein was head of the department selling cross-currency swaps, and later he was promoted to the CEO of Goldman Sachs.

The 'cross-currency swap' was really a loan to Greece disguised as an exchange into Euros of other currencies. Robert Reich wrote: "As a result, about 2 % of Greece's debt magically disappeared from its national accounts.... For its services, Goldman received a whopping 600 million euros ($793 million). That came to about 12 % of Goldman's revenue from its giant trading and principal-investments unit in 2001—which posted record sales that year. The unit was run by Blankfein." (Reich 2015)

It was in 2006 when Lloyd Blankfein became CEO of Goldman Sachs, after the previous head of Goldman Sachs, Henry Paulson, was nominated for U.S. Secretary of Treasury. (As Treasury Secretary, Paulson proposed to Congress the Emergency Economic Stabilization Act of 2008, which authorized him to spend up to $700 billion to buy the 'toxic assets' of Wall Street. These 'toxic assets were the mortgage-based (securitized) derivatives, which Wall Street investment banks had sold world-wide and which triggered the Global Financial crisis of 2008.) While derivatives were being manufactured by Goldman Sachs and others, Blankfein in 2006 received $54.4 million dollars as salary and bonus from Goldman Sachs. In 2007, Blankfein earned again $54 million dollars. But in 2014, he received only $24 million, since profits in Goldman Sachs had declined after the 2008 Wall Street debacle.

In 2010, U.S. Senate investigations about the 2008 Wall Street financial crisis, Lloyd Blankfein was called to testify. James Quinn reported: "Lloyd Blankfein has admitted that he believes Goldman Sachs has no moral obligation to tell clients it is betting against a product it is asking them to buy. The stark admission—made by the bank's chairman at the end of a more than 9-hour marathon hearing before the US Senate—came in spite of his assertion that 'I think people trust us' as he tried to fend off accusations that Goldman inflated the US housing bubble. Senator Carl Levin told the veteran banker that he wouldn't trust Goldman. Levin repeatedly asked whether the bank would disclose its position: 'When they're buying something you solicit them to buy, and then you're taking a position against them?' Mr. Blankfein responded: 'I don't believe there is any obligation' to tell investors. I don't think we'd have to tell them, I don't think we'd even know ourselves.'" (Quinn 2010)

Traditionally an important aspect of banking is its 'public good' in ensuring that financial transactions are honest, sound, and transparent—banking integrity. But in 2010, the head of Goldman Sachs (then the most successful international investment bank in the world) did not believe in the integrity of his firm (and even doubted it could distinguish integrity, when he said: 'I don't think we'd even know ourselves.') This rejection of banking' integrity' for its clients astounded Senator Levin. James Quinn reported: "His (Blankfein's) responses are key in the light of the Securities and Exchange Commission's civil fraud charges against Goldman Sachs in connection with a $1bn mortgage-backed derivative which the regulator alleges was mis-sold to investors, allowing one investor to benefit over another." (Quinn 2010)

In addition to Goldman Sachs, other Wall Street institutions in the financial grid were eager to also engage in unethical financial operations in 'off-market' transactions both in the fraudulent 'derivatives' and in the 'credit swaps'. Robert Reich wrote: "Until 2008, European Union accounting rules allowed member nations to manage their debt with so-called off-market rates in swaps, pushed by Goldman and other Wall Street banks. In the late 1990s, JPMorgan enabled Italy to hide its debt by swapping currency at a favorable exchange rate, thereby committing Italy to future payments that didn't appear on its national accounts as future liabilities. But Greece was in the worst shape, and Goldman was the biggest enabler. Undoubtedly, Greece suffers from years of corruption and tax avoidance by its wealthy. But Goldman wasn't an innocent bystander: It padded its profits by leveraging Greece to the hilt—along with much of the rest of the global economy. Other Wall Street banks did the same. When the bubble burst, all that leveraging pulled the world economy to its knees." (Reich 2015)

An interesting term, this 'off market'! Economically, financial markets are supposed to be open and transparent in order for the optimal prices to be set in equilibrium of supply-and-demand. Why then would financial market makers, such as Goldman Sachs and JPMorgan want to distort the sovereign bond market by hiding bond-like transactions in 'off-market credit swaps'? Let us call these 'off-market credit swaps' a financial innovation of 'secrecy jurisdictions', whose purpose was to make secret and hide government debt profligacy from the international bond markets.

Goldman Sachs had a good thing going for their executives. Investment banks could innovate, such as (1) hide government debt in a 'secrecy jurisdiction' until the sovereign bond market bursts and (2) 'securitize' mortgage debt until the mortgage market bursts. In all cases of financial catastrophes, bankers appeared to believe that the governments of America and Europe would bail out 'banks-too-big-to-fail'. Since none of the investment bankers involved in the financial innovations of the decade of 2000s went to jail, the governments involved judged that all the innovations in the international financial grid of 'light regulation' were legal. The governments, by letting their banks bring down the financial system and then bailing them out, signaled that all was legal, only unfortunate.

But were they ethical? Robert Reich judged: "Goldman Sachs and the other giant Wall Street banks are masterful at selling complex deals by exaggerating their benefits and minimizing their costs and risks. That's how they earn giant fees. When a client gets into trouble—whether that client is an American homeowner, a US city, or Greece—Goldman ducks and hides behind legal formalities and shareholder interests. Borrowers that get into trouble are rarely blameless, of course. They spent too much and were gullible or stupid enough to buy Goldman's pitches. Greece brought on its own problems, as did many American homeowners and municipalities. But in all of these cases, Goldman knew very well what it was doing. It knew more about the real risks and costs of the deals it proposed than those who accepted them. 'It is an issue of morality,' said the shareholder at the Goldman meeting where Oakland came up. Exactly." (Reich 2015)

As intermediaries creating their financial products, investment banks in the twenty-first century were less interested in banking ethics and more interested in banking commissions.

History: Offshore Banking Grid

We have constructed a model of the international financial grid focused upon the production of financial products (for financial markets) by investment banks; and also we have reviewed some of the sellers of capital assets for such products (e.g. corporate raiders); but what about the buyer side. Who are the 'buyers' of the innovative financial products?

Who would buy a 'junk bond'? They are highly risky, depending upon the ability of the captured corporation to pay off its leveraged junk-bond debt. Who would want companies to be loaded with debt until they were uncompetitive?

Who would buy a 'securitized product'? A securitized product pays only the interest from a capital asset, without the risk-reducing collateral of the 'principle' of the asset. Accordingly if the interest failed to be paid, there is no collateral to back the loan.

Who would by a currency-exchange swap? Who would want to help countries and cities hide their debt? And who would believe in a 'credit default swap' as a real insurance contract?

The answer to these questions is probably: 'no one'. Certainly no bank (or financial institution) which was committed to exercising 'due diligence' (finding out whether or not the loan is a good risk). So why would some banks buy the products, not exercising due diligence? The answer is that some banks did buy the products, disregarding due diligence; and many of these were banks in the so-called 'off-shore' banking industry.

An investigative financial reporter, Joanne Ramos, pointed to offshore banks as critical elements of the modern international financial grid. Ramos, wrote: "In a globalized economy, money moves instantly and anonymously across borders. This can benefit terrorists, drug traffickers and rogue nations in need of cash. Keeping such customers out of the world's sprawling financial system is becoming ever harder. Financial regulators have another big concern. Footloose capital transmits not just tainted money but financial crises too. The huge growth in the use of esoteric derivatives and the rise of hedge funds have made it increasingly difficult to understand where financial risk lies, partly because much of it is hidden away on islands with variable supervision. Offshore holdings now run to $5 trillion-7 trillion, five times as much as two decades ago, and make up perhaps 6–8 % of worldwide wealth under management, according to Jeffrey Owens, head of fiscal affairs at the OECD. Cayman, a trio of islands in the Caribbean, is the world's fifth-largest banking centre, with $1.4 trillion in assets. The British Virgin Islands (BVI) are home to almost 700,000 offshore companies." (Ramos 2007)

The offshore banking industry has turned out to be a critical institutional sector of the international financial grid, having the volume to buy in large amounts the questionable financial innovations sold by the investment banking industry. Offshore banks buying these questionable investments were not performing 'due diligence' in financial trading. This was because off-shore banks had no means of investing the huge amounts of the international cash flow going into their deposits—except through international investment banks. As noted, from 6 to 8 % of the world's wealth flowed into the offshore banking industry.

Other investigative reporters have also examined the off-shore industry. Nicholas Shaxson also emphasized the importance of the institutional role of off-shore banks: "Towering inequalities in Europe and the United States, not to mention in underdeveloped countries, cannot be understood properly without exploring the role of secrecy jurisdictions. The systematic looting of the former Soviet Union, and the merging of the nuclear-armed country's intelligence apparatus with organized crime, is substantially a story that unfolds in London and its offshore satellites. The political strength of Saddam Hussein had important offshore underpinnings, as does the power of North Korea's Kim Jong-Il today. Prime Minister Silvio Berlusconi's strange hold over Italian politics is significantly an offshore story. The Elf affair, which helped powerful French elites float above and out of reach of French democracy, had secrecy jurisdictions at its heart.... The narcotics industry alone generates some $500 billion in annual sales worldwide. To put this into perspective, that is twice the value of Saudi Arabia's oil exports. The profits made by those at the top of the trade find their way into the banking system, the asset markets, and the political process through offshore facilities. You can only fit about $1 million cash into a briefcase. Without offshore, the illegal drugs trade would be more like a cottage industry." (Shaxson 2011)

The offshore banks (outside proper bank regulatory authority) make money by helping people and corporations to hide money from taxes and also to launder money gained from illegal or corrupt activities. The off-shore banking institutions include locally licensed banks and financial institutions. What happens to all these deposits (e.g. $1.4 trillion in the Cayman Islands), since the offshore banks and institutions have no financial investments in which to put all that savings? They invest (buy) products sold by the investment banks with branches in the City of London. Nicholas Shaxson wrote: "London's first claim to be a tax haven is.... its role as the creator and developer of the Euromarkets—Wall Street's giant escape route from the checks and balances of U.S. financial regulation. Here the subsidiaries and affiliates of U.S. commercial banks have long been allowed to engage in, among many other things, investment banking, "casino banking," as some have called it—something the Glass-Steagall Act of 1933 explicitly prohibited. Over the years, as this business became more integral to their global banking models, Wall Street could increasingly pressure the U.S. government to do away with the original restrictions to allow them to do at home what they already did offshore, and this was arguably the main factor that led to the repeal of Glass-Steagall in 1999." (Shaxson 2011)

Here is the connection between Wall Street's 'Mayday' (the end of regulated commissions) and Wall Street's search for deregulation. In the London-based Eurodollar market, Wall Street institutions went to London to engage in selling unregulated international financial products. The London branches of Wall Street investment banks have been central to the sale of the products which blew up Wall Street in 2008. Nicholas Shaxson wrote: "London provides endless loopholes for U.S. financial corporations, and many U.S. banking catastrophes can be traced substantially to those companies" London offices. The unit that blew up the insurance company American International Group (AIG), putting the U.S. taxpayer on the hook for $182.5 billion, was its four-hundred-strong AIG Financial Products unit, based in London. The court-appointed examiner looking into the collapse of Lehman Brothers in September 2008 found it had used a trick called Repo 105 to shift $50 billion in assets off its balance sheet, and that while no U.S. law firm would sign off on the transactions, a major law firm in London was delighted to oblige, without breaking the rules.... A little-noticed IMF paper in July 2010 estimated that by 2007 the seven largest players in the market—Lehman Brothers, Bear Stearns, Morgan Stanley, Goldman Sachs, Merrill/ BoA, Citigroup, and JPMorgan—had shifted $4.5 trillion off their balance sheets in this way. (Shaxson 2011)

To understand the 'buy-side' of the international financial grid, one must analyze the 'off-shore banking industry', as depicted in Fig. 2.8. One needs two topological planes: one to diagram the system of financial transactions in the grid and a second to diagram the institutional connections of off-shore banks to the centralized international investment banking system. These two planes are (1) the disequilibrium financial systems plane and (2) the institutions of the off-shore banking network which connect to an international financial center. The offshore banking network operates by: (a) collecting savings deposits from individuals & corporations seeking financial secrecy, (b) setting up an institutional account with an investment bank in the City of London financial center, and (c) purchasing financial products from the investment banks in London.

Two topological planes are necessary because there are two different networks in the financial grid: (1) investment bank network and (2) off-shore banking network. These two networks are connected through the City of London Financial Center. This model shows that the offshore-bank network is financially effective because it ties into a central location, the City of London Financial Center. The City of London does not regulate the international investment banks dealings with the offshore network—as sellers (investment banks) and buyers (offshore banks)—of financial innovations which may or may not have any public good. And the model emphasizes that some of the international buyers of the investment banks 'financial innovations' were the off-shore banks which needed high-interest income to pay interest

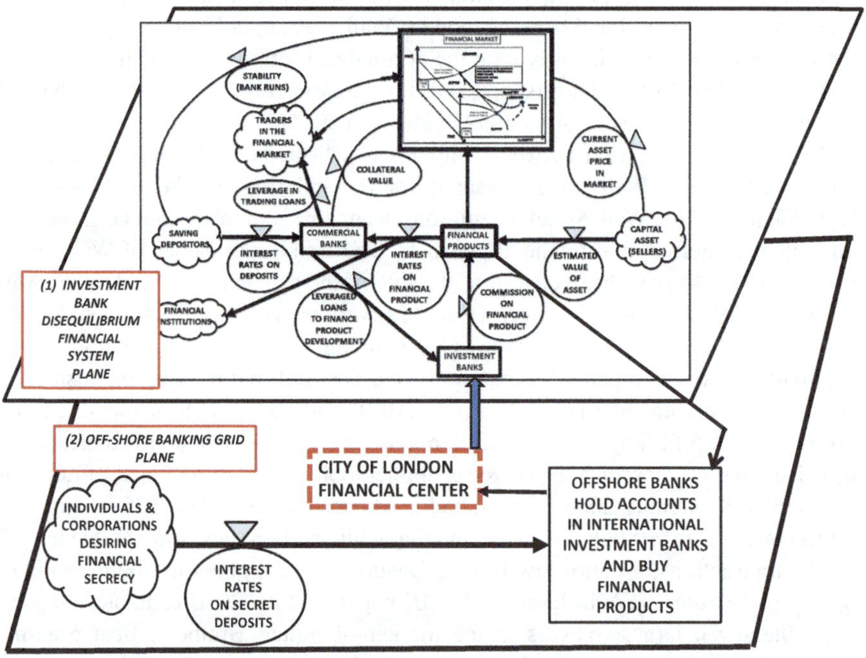

Fig. 2.8 Modern international financial grid with off-shore banking

to their secret clients—individuals and corporations depositing in the off-shore banks. These off-shore banks do not care about the soundness of the financial products', just as long as the investment banks assure them that they are low-risk and bear high interest.

How does the City of London act as a center for the off-shore banking network? Nicholas Shaxson wrote: "The next component of the City's offshore status is its role in running, protecting, and being fed by Britain's offshore spider web. This web of partly British tax havens around the world provides the City with three things. First, it captures passing foreign business and assets nearby and channels them, and the business of handling them, to London, just as a spider web catches insects. Second, it is a storage mechanism for assets. Third, it is a kind of money-laundering filter that lets the City get involved in foreign dirty business but at sufficient distance to minimize the stink." (Shaxson 2011)

The historical impact of the Bank of England allowing the Midland Bank to engage in foreign exchanges was to begin the deregulation of banks located in the City of London. Later in 1986, London financial deregulation was enacted formally by the Margaret Thatcher's government. The London Stock Market would no longer charge fixed trading commissions and investment banks could act for both buyers and sellers in the trading. Nigel Lawson wrote: The radical reform of the London Stock Exchange came to be known as 'Big Bang' … Without that reform, it is doubtful if London would have retained its place as Europe's pre-eminent financial centre, and certain that it would not have become the foremost truly international financial centre of the modern globalized economy that it is today, to the great benefit of the British economy as a whole … in 1979, the Office of Fair Trading decided to launch an investigation into the restrictive practices of the London Stock Exchange, in particular the system of fixed minimum commissions …. The problem, as I (Lawson) saw it, was not merely the restrictive practices themselves: in addition to fixed minimum commissions, these included the 'single capacity' rule, which enforced a separation between brokers acting as agents for their clients on commission and jobbers who made the markets and theoretically provided liquidity by holding lines of stocks and shares on their books; the requirement that both brokers and jobbers should be independent and not part of any wider financial group; and the exclusion of all foreigners from stock exchange membership." (Lawson 2003)

Thus a London 'Mayday' occurred in the 'Big Bang' in London, which then deregulated fixed commissions on stock trades in Britain, forcing British investment banks to financially 'innovate' (just like the U.S. Wall Street). Nicholas Shaxson wrote: "By the early 1980s the main elements of the modern offshore system were in place and growing explosively. An older cluster of European havens, nurtured by old European aristocracies and led by Switzerland, was now being outpaced by a new network of more flexible, aggressive havens in the former outposts of the British Empire, themselves linked intimately to the City of London. A state within the British state, the City had been transformed from an old gentleman's club operating the financial machinery of empire, steeped in elaborate rituals and governed by unspoken rules about what "isn't done," into a new, brasher, deregulated global financial center dominated by American banks and linked intimately to this new British spider web." (Shaxson 2011)

Public Good (or Bad) in the Financial Grid

As we previously noted, there is a long-standing and wide-spread debate in economics about the good or harm of international capital flows for national economic development. Barry Eichengreen wrote: "The normal presumption in economics is that markets know better than governments and that, left to their own devices, they allocate resources reasonably well. Yet the suspicion remains that there is something different about international financial markets. The founding fathers of the Bretton Woods System, Harry Dexter White and John Maynard Keynes, certainly thought so. The Bretton Woods Agreement negotiated under their guidance, although encouraging economic liberalization generally, authorized (indeed, encouraged) countries to retain restrictions on international financial transactions." (Eichengreen 2004)

A view of the 'public good' aspects believed to be about international capital flows (and shared by many) is that the flows direct capital into a developing country (in order to finance development). Eichengreen wrote: "International financial transactions transfer resources from high-saving to low-saving countries." (Eichengreen 2004)

This is how the contemporary financial grid should work, but does it? And this is why the empirical reality of institutional practices (micro-economics) should be investigated in particular historical contexts. Does general economic theory really work in a particular time and place of history? The empirical evidence is that in the present historical context of the early twenty-first century is that there is harm being done in the modern international financial grid.

The non-profit organization of Global Financial Integrity examined 'harm' by measuring the net flows of capital from and into developing countries. This net-flow is important because one economic need of poor countries is capital for development. If there is a net flow of capital out of a developing country, then wealth needed for economic development is being lost to the future of the country. The surprising findings of Global Financial Integrity is that the international financial grid has been sending capital not 'into' but 'out of' developing countries—a negative capital flow. Dev Kar and Joseph Spanjers wrote: "This report, the latest in a series of annual reports by Global Financial Integrity (GFI), provides estimates of the illicit flow of money out of the developing world—as a whole, by region, and by individual country—from 2003 to 2012, the most recent 10 years of data availability. The study finds that between 2003 and 2012, the developing world lost US$6.6 trillion in illicit outflows. In real terms, these flows increased at 9.4 % per annum. After a brief slowdown during the financial crisis, illicit outflows are once again on the rise, hitting a new peak of US$991.2 billion in 2012." (Kar and Spanjers 2014)

The negative flow is continuing and significant. Kar and Spanjers wrote: "To put this in perspective, the cumulative total of official development assistance (ODA) to the developing countries in this report from 2003 to 2012 was just US$809 billion. In 2012, the last year in this study, ODA to these countries stood at US$89.7 billion, according to OECD data sourced from the World Bank. That means that for every single one of those US$89.7 billion in development aid that entered these developing countries in 2012, over US$10 in illicit financial flows (IFFs) came out.... GFI measures illicit financial outflows using two sources: (1) outflows due to deliberate trade mis-invoicing (GER) and (2) outflows due to leakages in the balance of payments, also known as illicit hot money narrow outflows (HMN). The vast majority of illicit financial flows, 77.8 % in the 10-year period covered in this report, are due to trade mis-invoicing." (Kar and Spanjers. 2014)

'Mis-invoicing' is a deliberate attempt to make secret the real nature of the financial transaction. The reasons for 'mis-invoicing' (hiding the nature of the transaction) are to (1) avoid national exchange restrictions, (2) reduce taxes, and (3) hide government corruption. Kar and Spanjers wrote: "Potential drivers of trade mis-invoicing can be related to regulatory, fiscal, and governance issues although their relative importance can vary from one country to another.... In 2013, there were 113 countries that maintained exchange restrictions. Such practices give rise to differences in exchange rates between different exchange markets or among approved official transactions. There is a tendency for black markets in foreign exchange to develop as private economic agents seek to profit from the differences in exchange rates.... Fiscal issues can also drive trade mis-invoicing. While importers may initially pay more by over-invoicing imports, they will continue to do so as long as the reduction of corporate profits (due to larger import costs) outweighs the increased import duties payable, which allows the company to pay a lower corporate profits tax.... Finally, governance issues and corruption in particular tend to be a major driver of illicit flows. Le and Rishi find that there is a significant link between corruption and capital flight, based on the World Bank Residual method adjusted for trade mis-invoicing." (Kar and Spanjers 2014)

In Nicholas Shaxson's study of oil corruption in Angola, he was impressed with the scale of the corruption: "My personal belief, based on years of investigating Angola's economy ... is that official estimates (equivalent to just over 9 % of its $51 billion in oil and diamond exports during that time) simply have to be a gross underestimate of the losses. Many billions have disappeared offshore through opaque oil-backed loans channeled outside normal state budgets, many of them routed through two special trusts operating out of London." (Shaxson 2011)

The impact of the offshore banking sector of the financial grid has been particularly great for crime (money laundering), as well as for corruption (flows of petrodollars from 'less-developed countries' dictators). For example in 2004, Lucy Komisar wrote: "A detailed analysis of Saddam Hussein's secret money-laundering techniques shows here for the first time how he used the same offshore money launderers as Osama bin Laden. That covert money network, based in the tax havens of Switzerland, Liechtenstein, Panama and Nassau, helped bankroll the war machines of both Iraq and al-Qaida." (Komisar 2004)

The existence of a banking network (devoted to secrecy) networked into a banking network (devoted to transparency) provide the institutional framework for economic abuses of the financial grid—assisting tax-avoidance, criminal activity, governmental corruption, and financial fraud.

Macro-Economic Models and Micro-Economic Institutional Analysis

In mathematical framework of topology, we have constructed a price-disequilibrium model of a financial market embedded within a systems dynamics model of intermediary financial institutions (in order to connect financial product supply to demand). This provides a model of the transaction processes in international capital flows—a macro-economic model of an international financial grid. Moreover this methodological use of a systems dynamics *macro-economic* model provides a graphic structure in which to embed the empirical reality of the *micro-economic* institutional procedures of financial institutions—operating in a specific historical context. The macro-economic model can express general economic theory, while the micro-economic institutional context can express historical reality. How is the grid connected? How does a historical grid really work? What kinds of financial products and innovations flow through the grid? What public benefit do these products give (if any)?

What is particularly interesting in this model is that two kinds of networks are connected through a centralized feature. The networks of off-shore banks and international investment banks are interconnected by banking located in London—creating a grid wherein vast sums of capital can flow in an unregulated and surprising manner. Nicholas Shaxson described the importance of the connection between the two networks: "Financial deregulation and globalization? Offshore is the heart of the matter. The rise of private equity and hedge funds? Offshore. Enron? Parmalat? Long Term Capital Management? Lehman Brothers? AIG? Offshore. Multinational corporations could never have grown so vast and powerful without the tax havens. Goldman Sachs is very, very much a creature of offshore. And every significant financial crisis in the world since the 1970s, including the latest global economic crisis, is very much an offshore story. The decline of manufacturing industries in many advanced countries has many causes, but offshore is a big part of the story. Tax havens have been central to the growth of debt in our economies since the 1970s. The growth of complex monopolies in certain markets, or insider trading rings, or gigantic frauds, almost always involves secrecy jurisdictions as major or central elements. This is not to say that all of these problems don't have other explanations too. They always do. Tax havens are never the only story because offshore exists only in relation to elsewhere. That is why it is called offshore. Without understanding offshore, we will never properly understand the history of the modern world." (Shaxson 2011)

The unregulated off-shore banking sector operates not upon 'transparency' of financial transactions but upon 'secrecy'. Secret transactions connect buyers (wishing tax avoidance or money laundering) to deposits in off-shore banks which then connect to financial products of investment banks, through unregulated banking in the City of London financial center. The secrecy in the connected networks has created conditions of financial abuse.

An example of structure-to-function relations (and about the function of secrecy in the structure of the connected networks) can be seen in events related to government regulation. After the financial debacle of unregulated derivatives trading and of proprietary trading by integrated banks, Lucy Komisar wrote: "As I write this (in July 2010), the U.S. Senate is debating a major financial reform bill in which the credit default swap, a kind of (insurance for) derivatives, plays a significant part. An amendment to that bill, proposed by Senators Carl Levin (D-MI) and Jeff Merkley (D-OR), would ban banks from proprietary trading. There are a lot of high-rolling bankers who do not want that amendment to pass, because it will mess up their plans to repatriate foreign profits into the United States, untaxed, by trading in derivatives on their own accounts. The clearinghouse ICE Trust U.S. forms a central part of these plans. What is ICE Trust U.S., and who owns it? ICE US Holding Co., which was established in 2008 as the parent of ICE Trust U.S., is located in the Cayman Islands. Yet none of the owners of ICE US Holding Co. are based in the Caymans. Among the owners of the Cayman's company are Citigroup, Goldman Sachs, J.P. Morgan, Merrill Lynch and Morgan Stanley, which are headquartered in New York. Bank of America, which now owns Merrill Lynch, is based in Charlotte, North Carolina. (Komisar 2010)

Thus of the 700,000 companies in the British Virgin Islands and Cayman Islands, there was at least one 'blind' company for Wall Street banks—Citigroup, Goldman Sachs, J.P. Morgan, Merrill Lynch, Morgan Stanley, and Bank of America. Why were they hiding? Their business was to provide 'secrecy jurisdictions'; and to do secret business, you must be secret. The modern offshore system operations were making finances secret. Secret financial transactions turned out to provide a big market for international investment banks.

Nicholas Shaxson summarized the negative impact of a regulated financial grid coupled to an unregulated financial network: "The secrecy jurisdictions, by applying a sort of super-lubricant to the flow of capital around the world, dramatically widen these chasms inside capitalism. They are the supreme generators of remoteness and artificiality: creating secrecy barriers and generating unfathomable complexity as corporations garland their financial affairs around the world's tax havens to fox the world's tax authorities and regulators, and to shield particular investors against other nations' laws and regulations. As we have discovered since 2007, the system was wildly inefficient: consider the wealth destroyed and the costs heaped onto the shoulders of taxpayers. Capital no longer flows simply to where it gets the best return but to where it can secure the best tax subsidies, the deepest secrecy, and to where it can most effectively evade the laws, rules, and regulations it does not like. None of this has anything to do with allocating capital more efficiently. Keynes would have viewed the explosion in offshore finance since the 1970s—and the massive capital flight it fostered—with horror." (Shaxson 2011)

Now if this off-shore banking network (centralized in the City of London) remains unregulated and of questionable ethics, why would established banks use such a system? Joseph Stiglitz is a Nobel laureate for economics and former World Bank Chief Economist; and in 2010, he said to the reporter Lucy Komisar: "You ask why, if there's an important role for a regulated banking system, do you allow a non-regulated banking system to continue? It's in the interest of some of the moneyed interests to allow this to occur. It's not an accident; it could have been shut down at any time. If you said the US, the UK, the major G7 banks will not deal with offshore bank centers that don't comply with G7 banks regulations, these banks could not exist. They only exist because they engage in transactions with standard banks." (Komisar 2010) The secrecy of the financial grid is protected by banking interests who generate a lot of wealth for their own private good and who lobby government institutions not to regulate (or regulate with only a 'light touch') the processes in the financial grid.

Summary

Again, our modeling approach is to use mathematical 'topological' models' to show 'structure' (as in a macro-economic model) but connected into 'institutional processes' (as in a micro-economic model). Topological models (planes of connected graphs with processes) provide an effective methodology for a cross-disciplinary approach to structure-function explanations of societal phenomena. The topological model shows both the structure of macro-economic processes and the functional details of institutional processes which control flows in the structure. Applied to economic systems, structure-function modeling (in topological form) enables the description of how macro-economic structures really operate in the empirical reality of institutional economics.

For the empirical input of current institutional economics, we have used case studies of the international financial system written mostly by investigative financial reporters. This is a method which historians use to draw upon contemporary writings as sources for historical analysis. We also use extensive quotes from these original case materials to point to the historical documentation about a case. Economic historians also draw upon such sources, which contributes a cross-disciplinary perspective on the reality economic theory and models in historical situations.

A systems dynamics disequilibrium-pricing model of a financial grid provides the structural framework (macro-economic) for a functional analysis of actual institutional procedures (micro-economics). As shown in Fig. 2.9, one can add into the disequilibrium systems model of the international financial grid a third plane of networks (3) into which the planes of investment bank processes (1) and the planes of the off-shore bank processes (2) all connect. This emphasizes the importance of a network structure in the financial grid, as operated with information-communication technologies.

Plane 3 of the grid expands to the product processes in Plane 2 of investments and also to Plane 2 in the deposit processes of the offshore banks. This disequilibrium systems model of the networks in modern financial grid depicts four particular features.

1. The grid partitions into a legitimate regulated network (investment banks) and an illegitimate unregulated network (off-shore banking);
2. The illegitimate unregulated network of off-shore banking serves purposes of tax-avoidance, laundering of government financial corruption, and illegal criminal finances;

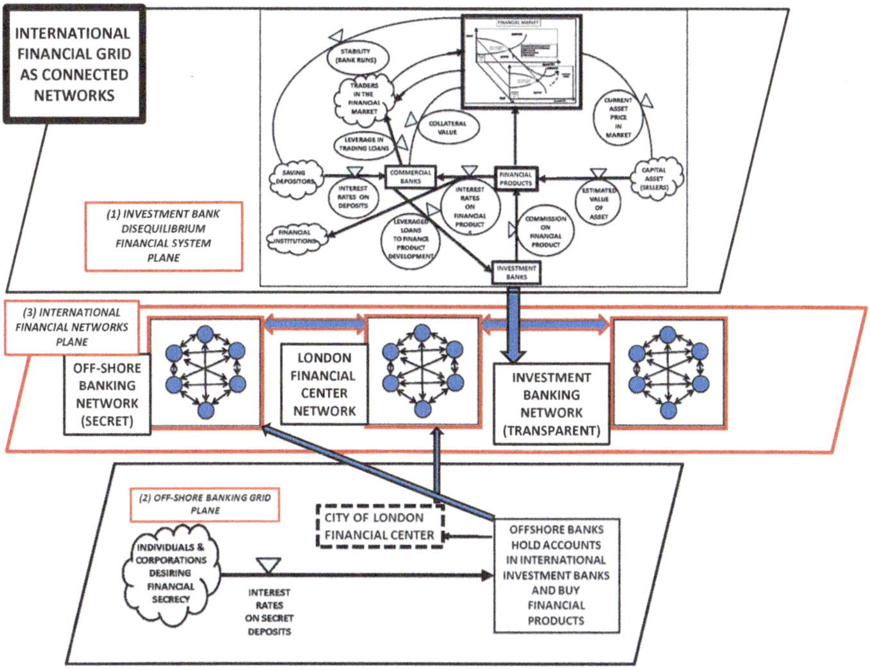

Fig. 2.9 Three networks connecting together as the international financial grid

3. The two networks (regulated and unregulated) connect through an 'unregulated international financial center' in the City of London—connecting the investment bank products between legitimate and/or illegitimate sellers and buyers;
4. Because of the lack of international regulation in the international grid, investment bank products may serve private good but may not always serve the public good; while the unregulated network economically serves private good but seldom public good;
5. The circulation in the whole network of private-good products can create instability through Minsky financial bubbles in the financial markets of the financial innovations by the international investment banks.
6. Without the (presently unregulated) cooperation between the investment banks (in national regulated domains) with commercial banks (in offshore unregulated domains), the abuse of capital flows could not occur at the recurrent events of quick and large-scale global financial crises. The off-shore banking sector provides the size of capital needed to purchase imprudent financial products in large volume.

Through modeling the processes of the international finance institutions as an international capital-flow grid, one can pinpoint where and how the practices of the institutions (micro-economics) affect the public good and the stability of international financial system (macro-economics). In this case of financial markets, it is important to use the methodology of disequilibrium systems modeling as a macro-economic format, into which can place the empirical micro-economics of actual institutional procedures. The 'empiricism' of the macro-model occurs as to how exactly 'real institutional procedures' control the 'real flows' of capital—for the private good of a financial system, and hopefully for the public good rather than harm.

The limits of this present model of the international financial grid is that it is primarily a structural framework; and for a fully developed model, one needs to add quantitative data about the flows in the system. It is presently difficult to get information on the quantity of flows in the model. Future research could focus (1) upon measurement of quantitative flows in the system arrows and (2) developing quantitative algorithms for the amount of control a valve has upon flow.

References

Angelides, P. (2011). Justice, reform, and rebuilding in the wake of the financial crisis. Levy Economics Institute of Bard College. 20th Annual Hyman P. Minsky Conference on the State of the US and World Economies. April 13–15, 2011, New York City.

Betz, F. (2011). *Societal dynamics*. New York: Springer. ISBN 978-1-4614-1278-6.

Bisserbe, N. (2015). Toxic loans wallop French towns. *Wall Street Journal*. Retrieved July 20, from http://www.wsj.com/articles/toxic-loans-wallop-french-towns-1437411450

Bruck, C. (1988). *The predators' ball*. New York: Simon and Schuster (Published with a new chapter by Penguin Books. 1989).

Eichengreen, B. (2004). *Capital flows and crises*. Cambridge, MA: MIT Press.

Kar, D., & Spanjers, J. (2014). *Illicit financial flows from developing countries: 2003–2012*. Global Financial Integrity. Retrieved December, from http://www.gfintegrity.org/wp-content/uploads/2014/12/Illicit-Financial-Flows-from-Developing-Countries-2003-2012.pdf

Komisar, L. (2004). Saddam's secret money laundering trail. *The Komisar Scoop*. United Press International (UPI). Retrieved June 2, 2004, from http://www.thekomisarscoop.com/2004/06/saddam%E2%80%99s-secret-money-laundering-trail/

Komisar, L. (2010). The Wall Street ICEcapade. *The Komisar Scoop*. May 18. *The American Interest*, July-Aug 2010 (online May 18, 2010). Retrieved from http://www.thekomisarscoop.com/tag/credit-default-swaps/

Lawson, N. (2006). *Big Bang 20 years on – New challenges facing the financial services sector*. (Collected Essays with a Foreword by Nigel Lawson). London: Centre For Policy Studies.

McGee, S. (2010). *Chasing Goldman Sachs: How the masters of the universe melted Wall Street down...And why they'll take us to the brink again*. New York: Crown.

Minsky, H. (1975). *John Maynard Keynes*. New York: Columbia University Press (reprinted in 2008 by Mc Graw Hill)

Quinn, J. (2010). Goldman boss Lloyd Blankfein denies moral obligation towards clients. *The Telegraph*. Retrieved April 28, from http://www.telegraph.co.uk/finance/newsbysector/banksandfinance/7642325/Goldman-boss-Lloyd-Blankfein-denies-moral-obligation-towards-clients.html

Ramos, J. (2007). Places in the sun: Offshore financial centres. *The Economist*. Retrieved February 22, from http://www.economist.com/node/8695139

Reich, R. B. (2015). How Goldman Sachs profited from the Greek debt crisis. *The Nation*. Retrieved August 3–10, from http://www.thenation.com/article/goldmans-greek-gambit/

Roumeliotis, G. (2014). KKR doubles down on First Data, leading $3.5 billion investment. *Reuters*. Retrieved June 19, from http://www.reuters.com/article/2014/06/19/firstdata-kkr-idUSL6N0P03AL20140619

Sender, H. (2014). KKR seeks to make the numbers work at First Data. *Financial Times*. Retrieved September 18, from http://www.ft.com/intl/cms/s/0/3adee562-3d30-11e4-a2ab-00144feabdc0.html?siteedition=intl#axzz3RXONojG6

Shaxson, N. (2011). *Treasure Islands: Uncovering the damage of offshore banking and tax havens*. New York: St. Martin's Press/Palgrave McMillan.

Wolf, M. (2008). Why Greenspan does not bear most of the blame. *Financial Times*, April 8.

Chapter 3
Dynamics of Government Fiscal Instability

Introduction

Not only can stock markets crash in financial bubbles, nations also can collapse in government fiscal bubbles. How did the financial grid assist in making a national fiscal crisis deeper? As previously noted, international investment banking assisted Greece in hiding the size of it national debt. How did the continuously increasing debt finally trigger a fiscal crisis in Greece, depressing its economy and destabilizing governments?

One needs to understand how government fiscal policies can create a national crisis and even an international financial crisis. One connection between national fiscal systems and the international financial system is that governments can use foreign investment in the form of sovereign bonds to fund budget deficits (when their tax base is insufficient to balance their annual budget). But when deficits continue to grow, year after year, until government debt exceeds the confidence of the international bond market, then governments can be placed in peril of default. The national currency exchange rate plunges, and banks become insolvent. Bank runs occur, and the credit freezes in the national economy. A depression follows. Governments fall. The society descends into economic chaos. We next examine the case of Greece's fall into economic chaos in 2009–2010.

Historical Case: Greek Euro Crisis 2009

We review the beginning in 2009 of the Greek fiscal crisis. Then bond raters began the downgrading of Greek sovereign bonds, as Bill Koenig reported: "Fitch Ratings said it downgraded Greece's long-term foreign currency and local currency issuer default ratings to A- from A. The outlook is negative." (Koenig 2009)

The financial market responded negatively to the ratings downgrade, as Helena Smith and Ashley Seager reported: "Financial markets around the world sold off,

F. Betz, *Stability in International Finance*, SpringerBriefs in Economics,
DOI 10.1007/978-3-319-26760-9_3

after Greece's credit rating was cut amid mounting concerns about its fiscal health. European stock markets tumbled, and the euro weakened sharply with investors becoming increasingly worried about debt problems worldwide. The fallout also followed a ratings downgrade for six companies in Dubai, reinforcing fears of a global debt crisis. The Fitch rating agency cut Greece's long-term debt to BBB+ from A minus. It marked the first time in 10 years that the country has seen its rating pushed below an A grade. The agency cited: 'The weak credibility of fiscal institutions and the policy framework… (is) exacerbated by uncertainty over the prospects for a balanced and sustained economic recovery.'" (Smith and Seager 2009)

Since Greece was a part of the Euro Dollar fiscal union, the potential of its default affecting the whole of the Euro union. Smith and Seager reported: "After the (rating) decision, the euro slipped against the dollar and other major currencies, highlighting anxiety over the possible repercussions it could have for the eurozone if Greece defaulted, on what has become the most expensive debt in the EU. European stock markets also took fright, with the pan-European FTSEurofirst index slipping 1.5 %, while in London the FTSE 100 shed 1.65 % to close at 5223.13, down 87.53 points on the day. The euro fell by 2 % against the yen and by 0.6 % against the dollar to $1.472." (Smith and Seager 2009) Greece's bonds went into 'price-disequilibrium', as the 'interest rate' on new issues of Greek bonds accelerated, Fig. 3.1.

The jump in interest rates on Greek Sovereign bonds in 2010 went from 3.47 % in January to 9.73 % in July. This is what Paul McCulley called a 'Minsky moment'—the time when market speculators realize a recent rapid price rise is a financial bubble and that market collapses. (McCulley 2007) Bond traders' confidence failed about the Greek government's capability to solve its fiscal problem. Bonds must return both interest on the loan and principle at maturity. Suddenly, the market feared a debt default. The market for new Greek bonds collapsed, as traders demanded higher and higher interest rates on new bonds.

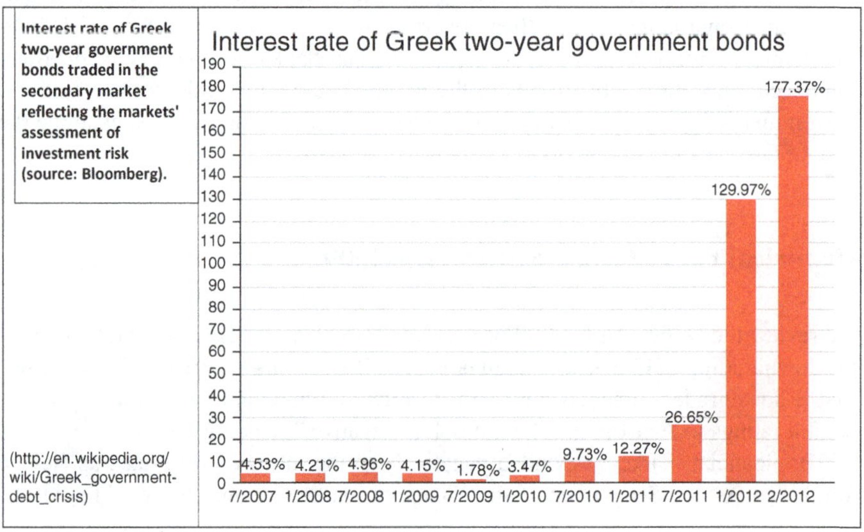

Fig. 3.1 Interest rate of Geek government bonds

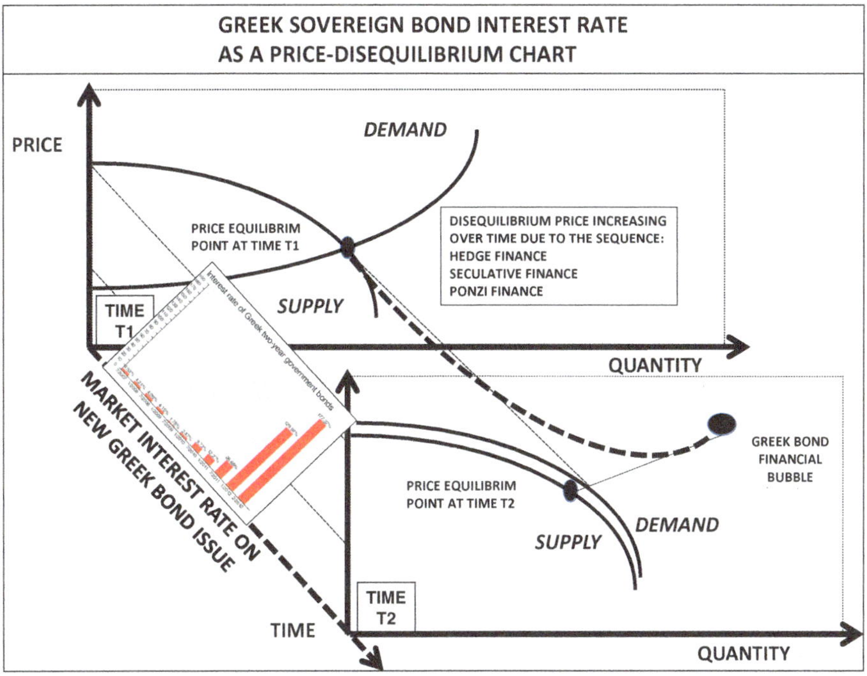

Fig. 3.2 Greek bonds interest rates on the price-time plane of the disequilibrium-price model

We recall this kind of anticipation is what George Soros has called 'reflexivity' in a financial market. (Soros 1988) Anticipating a possible government default, traders would not buy new Greek sovereign bonds, except at very high interest rates. The interest rate on Greek bonds jumped from 12.27 % in January 2011 to 26.65 % in August 2011. Then in January 2011, it leapt to 129.9 % and then 177.37 %. This was a 'price disequilibrium' in the Greek bond market—a market 'reflexivity' anticipating future government bond default. Figure 3.2 shows the Greek bond 'financial bubble' in the 'rapid rise of interest rates' on a price-disequilibrium model.

The time chart of Greek bond interest rates fits empirically upon the Price-Time-Plane, of a three-dimensional financial market disequilibrium model. The 'Minsky moment' (from speculative finance to 'Ponzi' finance) had occurred, not in bond-market speculation, but in the Greek government's fiscal policy.

Systems Dynamics Model of Greece's Sovereign Bonds

But while the price-disequilibrium model displays the outcome of 'instability' in a financial market (financial bubbles), it does not explain the societal process leading up to the Greek fiscal bubble. To explain the process, we next apply the modeling technique of systems dynamics, as depicting two sources of government finance: 'tax revenues' and 'sovereign bond issues'. As a system feed-back loop, we will

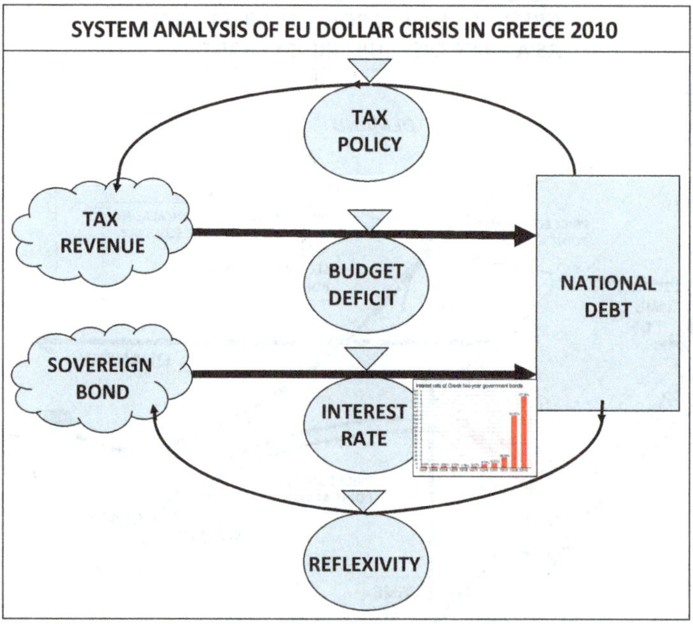

Fig. 3.3 Systems model of government fiscal policy

apply George Soros' concept of market 'reflexivity' between the bond-market and the government debt. The point of a systems analysis is to highlight the critical factors which led to the government fiscal crisis.

Earlier Michael J. Radzicki and Robert A. Taylor had sketched a systems dynamics model for the U.S. Government deficit and debt, using one source of revenue, taxes. (Radzicki and Taylor 1997) We now extend their model, with two sources of revenue, taxes and bonds and also add feed-back loops for tax policy and market reflexivity. This is shown in Fig. 3.3.

We recall that arrows depict flows of 'things' from sources to stocks of the things. Sources are denoted in a cloud symbol; and stocks of things building up from the flow is depicted in a rectangle symbol; and control of a flow is depicted as a symbol of a triangle-over-a-circle. National debt can be indicated as build-up (accumulation) of debt from the issuance of sovereign bonds. When tax revenue is insufficient to fund a government budget, then the 'stock' of national debt will accumulate. This occurs when a government finances budget deficits through issuing sovereign bonds. The interest rates on the sovereign bonds will vary in bond markets, considering the risk of investments in the government bonds. As shown in the figure, the Greek bond interest rates rose dramatically in and after 2009, when market confidence declined over the soundness of Greek government policy, about its fiscal responsibility. The level of 'interest rate' operated as a kind of 'control valve' on the 'flow' of sovereign bonds into the 'stock' of national debt.

Confidence in the future value of Greek bonds had been undermined by the size of the Greek debt to Greek tax revenue. Smith and Seager reported: "Greece has the

GREEK GOVERNMENT TAX REVENUE AND BUDGET EXPENDITURE FROM 2002 TO 2013

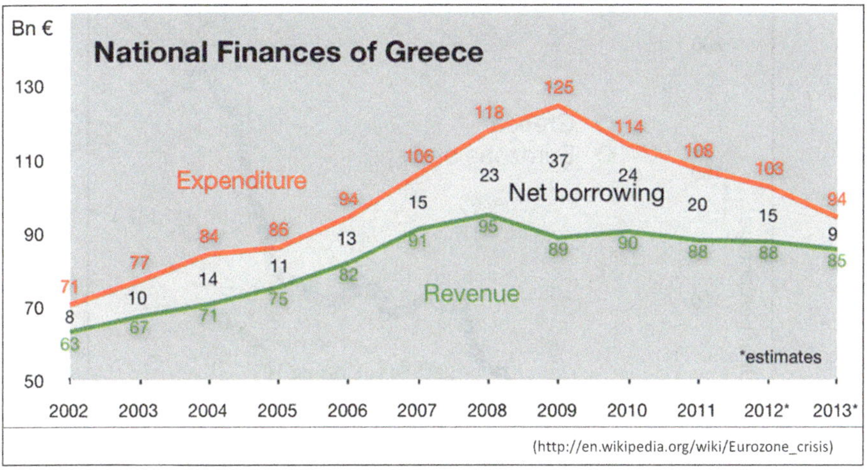

Fig. 3.4 Annual net borrowings by the Greek governments

highest debt ratio within the 16-member eurozone, with the finance minister, Giorgos Papaconstantinou admitting that 'the fiscal situation is dramatic'. Next year, it is forecasted to reach 124.9 % of gross domestic product." (Smith and Seager 2009) Figure 3.4 shows the tax revenues and government budget expenditures in Greece over the early part of the twenty-first century. Over this decade from 2002 through 2013, net borrowing from abroad was needed to cover the annual budget deficit of the Greek governments. When the fiscal crisis occurred in 2009, it was because the international financial market had lost confidence in Greece's government's ability to honor its debt.

Frequently governments try to act, but usually only after a fiscal crisis begins. At the onset of the fiscal crisis in 2009, the Greek government was urged to try to face the problem. Smith and Seager reported: "The head of the European Central Bank, Jean-Claude Trichet, appealed to the prime minister, George Papandreou, to enact 'courageous measures'. 'The situation in Greece is very difficult,' Trichet told the European parliament's economic committee. 'This calls for very difficult, very courageous but absolutely necessary measures.' Last week the country was formally put under EU supervision, (and it was) revealed … that the public deficit was 12.7 % of GDP—more than four times the EU's permitted level …. Appearing on CNN, Papandreou rejected the prospect of Greece going bankrupt, saying it was 'a responsible country' and would not default on its debt. The socialists have announced that they will curb the deficit by cutting tax evasion and trimming public expenditure." (Smith and Seager 2009)

Thus one of the system dynamic results of a continuing Greek government budget-deficit was to increase the national debt over time, as shown in Fig. 3.5.

This continuing budget deficit acted as a second kind 'valve' controlling the rate of accumulation of national debt, as shown in Fig. 3.6.

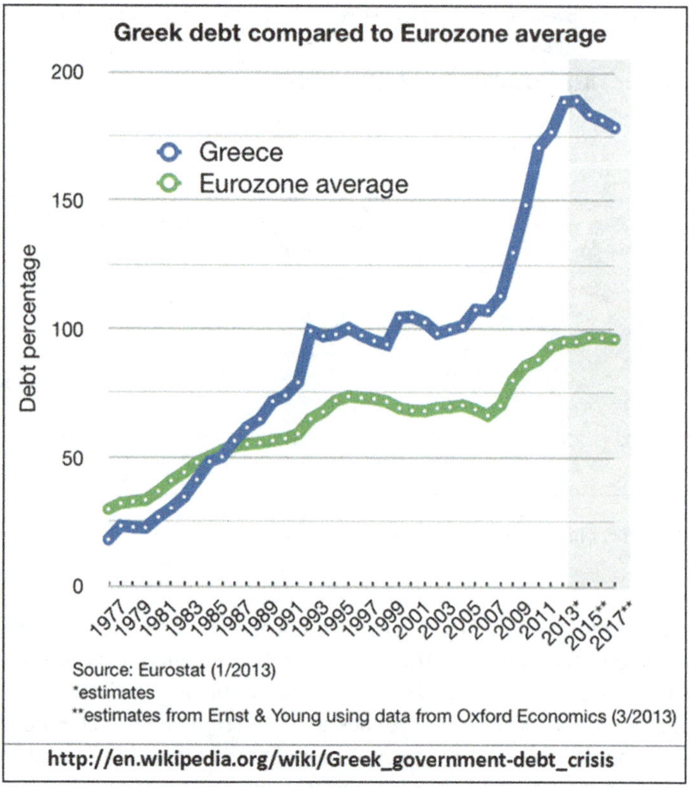

Fig. 3.5 Greek national debt as a percentage of gross domestic product

In systems dynamics terms, the national debt is a kind 'stock', which is increased or decreased by the 'flow' of annual deficits (or surpluses) from the annual government budget process. We can place this charted information about the budget deficit as a 'control valve' on the 'flow line' from the tax revenue 'source' to the 'stock' of national debt (national debt chart). These charts add more information to the systems dynamics model of the Greek financial system.

One sees how the system's 'control valve' of the 'Budget Deficit' kept, over time, increasing the nation's 'stock' of its 'National Debt'. In every economic fiscal crisis, a government promises to take 'courageous measures', such as cutting tax evasion and trimming public expenditure. Often it has been both a wide-spread-tax-evasion and a high-public-expenditure which has led to governmental fiscal crises. An earlier example was the Argentine fiscal crisis in 1999. (Betz 2013) This was the case in Greece, as we will next see.

In systems terms, how did this continuing situation, (of the Greek governments' fiscal condition) finally trigger the bond market reaction (a Minsky moment of Greek fiscal crisis)? As we noted, this was a 'reflexivity' in bond market perception; and we have indicated 'reflexivity' as a 'feed-back' loop from the perception of the

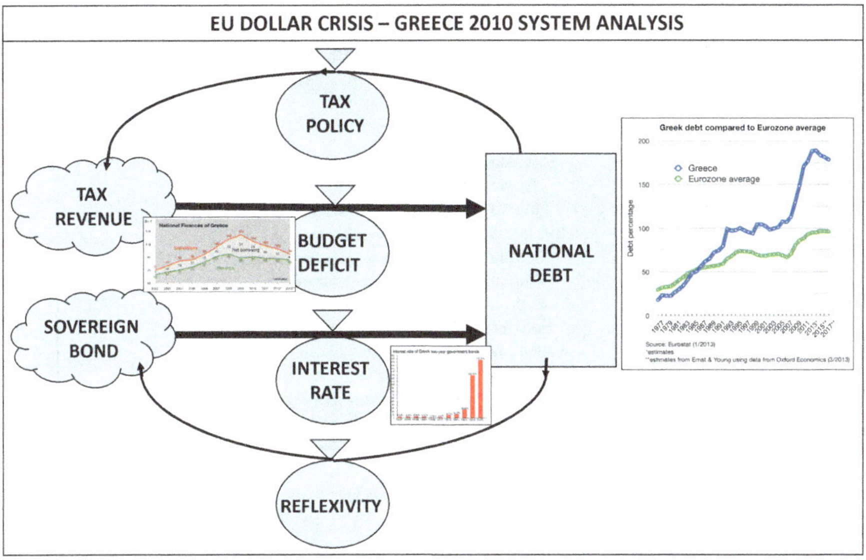

Fig. 3.6 Systems model of Greek fiscal policy with charts of relevant information

status of Greek national debt back onto the 'risk' in the Greek bond market. The 'reflexivity' of bond traders cognition was their expectation about whether or not the Greek government could continue to honor their bonds or default on payments due on their sovereign bonds.

But how does one measure (or chart) indications of reflexivity in sovereign bond markets? One indicator of the 'reflexive perception' is the so-called 'debt roll-over'. A government often needs to issue new sovereign bonds to finance the paying off of previous bonds whose maturity date is reached. Debt roll-over is the issuing of new debt to pay off maturing debt; and for Europe in 2010, this is shown in Fig. 3.7.

Internationally, Greece stood out as requiring 20 % of its debt to be refinanced each year—by paying off old bonds coming due through issuing new bonds (roll-over). And over 80 % of this bond refinancing would need international purchases of Greek bonds. This was a very difficult financial situation, and bond traders lost confidence in Greece being able to continue such annual 'roll-overs'—refinancing.

A second indicator of the 'reflexive perception' about Greek finance by bond traders is how much national debt is being accumulated as a percentage of annual economic output or Gross Domestic Product (GDP). This indicates how many years of annual production could a country need to pay off its debt. Of course, no country could ever devote all of its production in 1 year (100 % of debt to GDP) to pay off debt. People would starve in that year. But if a country could devote 10 % of its annual production (10 % of economic revenue devoted to taxes), then a country could pay off in 10 years. But even devoting 10 % of production to paying off debt is unlikely, for this would be over and above the annual budget needs for government service. Accordingly, when national debt approaches the same value of GDP,

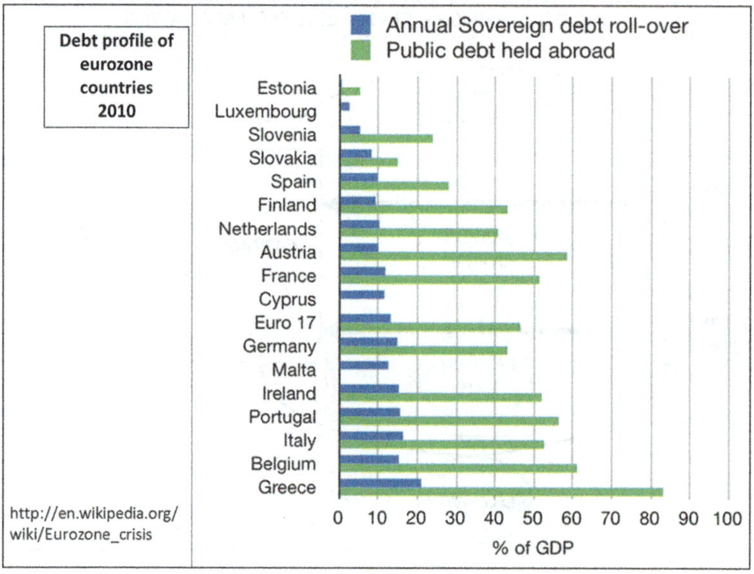

Fig. 3.7 Percentage of debt to GDP in 2012 requiring issuing of new bond issues (Debt Roll-Over)

bond traders get nervous about the ability of governments to continue to service their debt, to pay interest on their bonds, to refinance their debt—and not to default on debt. Figure 3.8 shows the Greek history of debt to GDP.

The important information on this chart is indicated by the red line. The red line is government debt as percentage of GDP. One sees that in 1995, total Greek government debt began to exceed (greater that 100 %) total GDP. And then in 2010, debt jumped up to 140 % of GDP, a sudden rise of 40 % over the long period of excessive debt for the past 15 years. This sudden rise contributed to the reflexive perception by the bond market that Greek government financing was unsustainable. It was in the fall of the preceding year (2009) that bond raters had begun rating down Greek sovereign bonds. When 2010 began, interest rates on new Greek bonds jumped higher.

Compared to other European countries, Greece's high debt and large deficit was exceptional, as shown in Fig. 3.9. This chart summarizes the 'reflexive perceptions' about the unsoundness of Greek government fiscal policy. In 2009, the bond market began to see that Greece was in situation of an unsustainable debt-to-GDP ratio.

As shown in Fig. 3.10, we can add all these charts about reflexivity to the systems diagram, on the system 'feed-back loop' between stock of national debt and the sovereign bond market. These charts add more information of what was happening in the Greek fiscal system.

This graphic form of system-dynamics model (adding charts of information upon a system dynamics model) enables one to 'sort out and relate' the relevant empirical information (which can often be found in the form of charts). Organizing

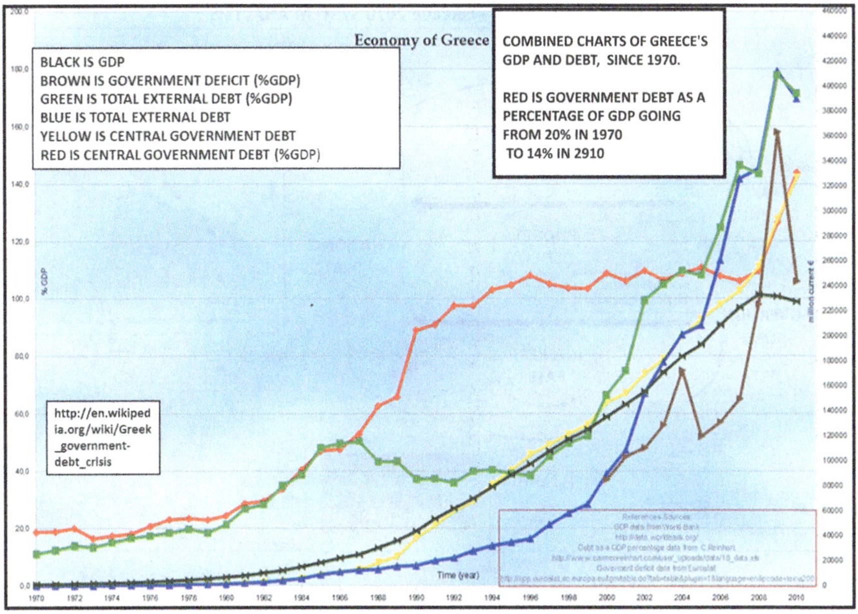

Fig. 3.8 Greece's percentage ratios to government debt to GDP

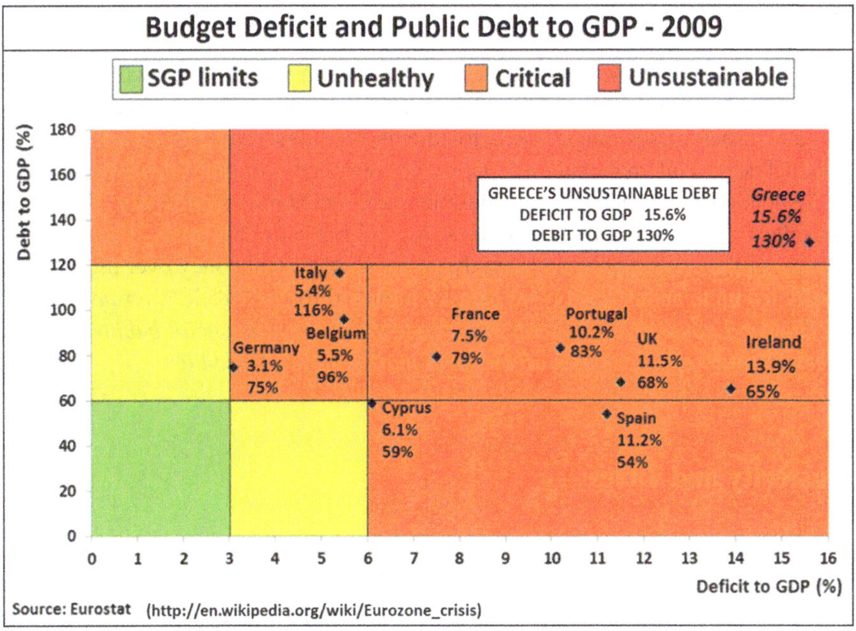

Fig. 3.9 In 2009, Greece's budget deficit and public debt as ratios to GDP

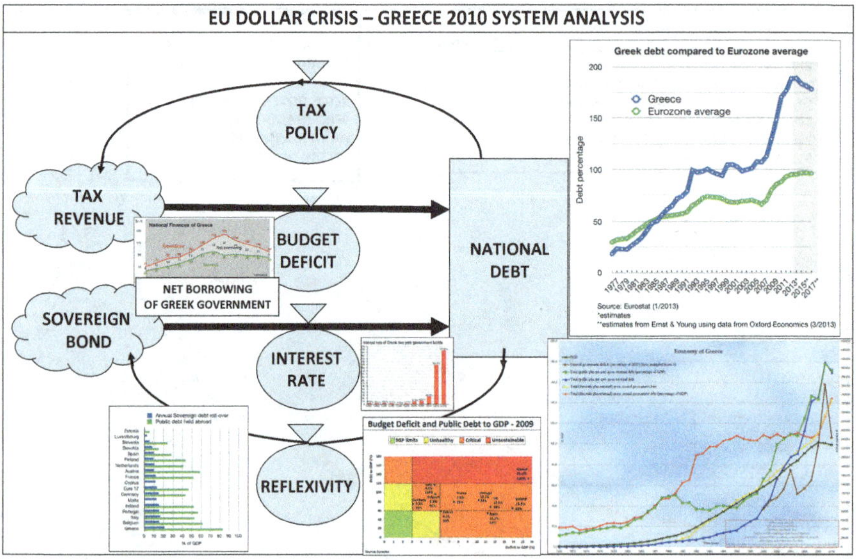

Fig. 3.10 Greece's fiscal policy displayed in a systems model

(that is to say 'pasting') empirical charts into the system model facilitates the understanding of how the system components interact—system valves, system feeds, and system feed-back loops.

In the case of Greek fiscal policy, the government's inability (unwillingness) to balance budgets, over time, accumulated increasing national debt, serviceable only by new issues of sovereign bonds to foreign investors. This 'feed-back loop' of national debt to international financial market operated over time—until perceptions in the bond market suddenly avoided future bond purchases—'reflexivity'. This market reflexivity triggered the fiscal crisis, but did not cause the crisis. There was no 'cause' of the crisis—only a system dynamics of bad fiscal policy over time, which finally led up to an instability—a 'Minsky moment' for the Greek government.

Unsound government policies can create government financial bubbles, as can excessive market speculation create stock market financial bubbles.

Austerity and Taxes

The Greek government response to the Greek fiscal crisis in 2010 was to seek outside help—rather than first trying to solve their own problem. Whether in government fiscal systems or financial market systems, it often happens in the 'Minsky moments of financial bubbles' that the 'speculators' seek 'bail-outs'. Earlier, this had happened in the U.S. Wall Street Bank Panic of 2008. In U.S. case, banks sought 'bail-out', and in the European case, both banks and governments sought 'bail-out'.

On April 23, 2010, the Prime Minister of Greece requested an emergency aid package from the European Union, European Central Bank and International Monetary Fund. On May 2, 2010, EU and IMF agreed to a 110 billion euro aid package, over the next 3 years. The Greek government agreed to austerity measures of decreasing government employment and pensions and increasing tax collection. Greek sovereign bond ratings continued to decline. In 2011, both Moody's and Fitch down-listed Greek bonds down to 'junk' status, likely to default. In November 2011, the Greek Prime Minister resigned.

As a condition of the aid package from the EU, the Greek government agreed to implement an austerity program. BBC News reported: "Greece is racing against time to enact profound changes to its economy, so as to reduce its debt mountain, clean up its public finances and avoid having to quit the eurozone. These changes are dictated by tough and controversial conditions set by the EU and IMF in return for two massive bailouts. The first (bailout) in May 2010, totaled 110bn euros (£89bn; $139bn). The second, in March this year, totals 130bn euros." (BBC News 2012a, b) The Greek budget deficit was cut to 9.2 % of GDP in 2011, down from 15.7 % in 2009. Yet the Greek economy shrank by 11 % over those 2 years.

Yet in tax reform, very little progress was actually made by the Greek government. Tax evasion and government corruption were not substantially addressed, as Phillip Inman reported: "Primary Greek tax evaders are the professional classes. Greece is riddled with corruption, but a study shows that banks, politicians and professional workers are largely to blame.... There is a political dimension that is centre stage at the moment, following proposals for closer union and control from Brussels and, in Greece's case, by the International Monetary Fund (IMF). Yet these economists ignore the challenges that beset a nation where very few people pay their taxes, where public-sector jobs are secured through family ties and where contracts for work, public or private, are rarely signed without someone in a position of power asking for a backhander. Greek banks are at the centre of the problem, as in Italy and Spain, where bankers perpetuate all the worst corrupt practices." (Inman 2012)

Inman was basing his reporting partly upon a study of bank records by Artavanis Nikolaos, Adair Morse, and Margarita Tsoutsoura, who had gained access to records of one of the large banks in Greece. From that data, Nikolaos, Morese, and Tsoutsoura estimated the level unreported tax bases of professionals in Greece: "We begin with the new observation that banks lend to tax-evading individuals based on the bank's perception of true income.... We use household micro-data from a large bank in Greece and replicate bank models of credit capacity, credit card limits, and mortgage payments to infer the bank's estimate of individuals' true income. From this, we estimated a lower bound of 28 billion euros of unreported income for Greece. This foregone government-revenues amounted to 31 % of the deficit for 2009. Primary tax evading occupations are doctors, engineers, private tutors, accountants, financial service agents, and lawyers." (Nikolaos et al. 2010)

From this study, the Economist reported: "Nikolaos, Morse, and Tsoutsoura found that, when professionals approached the bank for a loan or mortgage, their tax returns showed their debts almost exceeded their incomes (debt payments ate up 82 % of their incomes). For the beleaguered tax authority, this meant their income was too low to qualify for income tax. On average, they found the true income of self-employed people to be 1.92 times their reported income…. (About) €28bn (£22.4bn) of tax was evaded in 2009 by self-employed people alone. As GDP that year was €235bn and the total tax base was just €98bn, it is clear that this was a significant sum. At a tax rate of 40 %, it amounted to almost half the country's budget deficit in 2008, and 31 % in 2009." (Economist 2010) This sample was from one bank's records. But it indicated the scale of the problem of 'not-collected tax revenue'. Professionals had reported only about half their income; and that un-reported income could have contributed to (fixed) about one-half of the Greek annual budget deficit.

Data about uncollected taxes are difficult to obtain. In another study, one on the 'shadow economies' in Europe, Friedrich Schneider used electronic credit card data to estimate levels of unreported economies: "At an estimated €2 trillion, the shadow economy in Europe is significant—ranging from 10 % of gross domestic product (GDP) in the United Kingdom to almost 40 % in some Central and Eastern European countries. Governments have formulated clear objectives to reduce this "other" marketplace, but with a range of causes and drivers, finding a solution is a complex task." (Schneider 2008) In Fig. 3.11, The Economist used this report to chart an estimate of the underground economies Europe, including Greece (Economist 2010).

This estimate that the size of the unreported economy (and hence untaxed) was about 25 % of the reported Greek GDP. Adding the reported and unreported together indicated that 20 % of the total Greek economy was completely untaxed {(25 %/(100 %+25 %))=20 %}.

In Fig. 3.12, we next add this information as a chart into the systems model for assembling information on the Greek system of fiscal policy. This helps to understand the lack of reform in tax policy for the Greek economy.

Also next to the tax revenue and sovereign bond sources, we have placed a map indicating 'government instability' in Europe, as a result of that Euro crisis which began in 2010. Many governments changed under the EURO crisis beginning in 2010.

Summary

This systems-dynamics model of the Greek Fiscal Crisis in 2010 shows how to relate information (charts of data) one to another, to gain an explanation of the 'dynamics' of the crisis—how the price disequilibrium in Greek bond interest rates occurred in 2009. This is not of a simple 'causal' system; instead it is a 'functional' model of a socio-technical system—government budget funding. And this is in the spirit of the Keynes-Minsky model of a financial market as a 'dynamic' of the value of capital assets. Financial bubbles occur from 'perceptions'—cognitive 'reflexivity' in Soros' term—expectations of the future values in a financial market. The Minsky 'moment' occurs in the time when traders in a financial market have moved from speculative finance to the unstable reflexivity in Ponzi finance. The

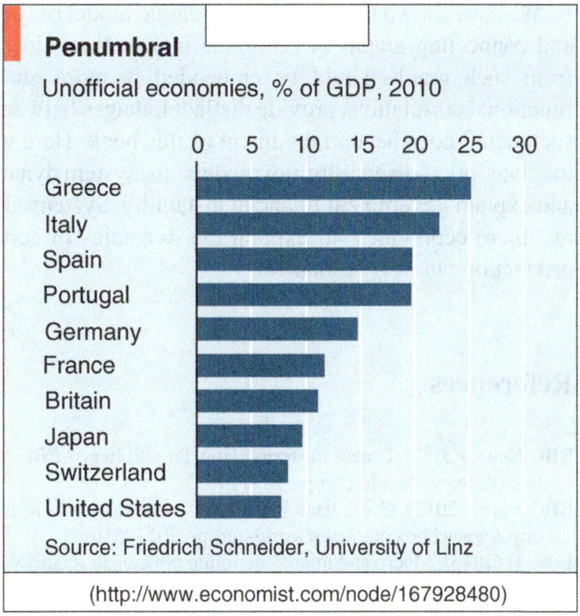

Fig. 3.11 Estimates of untaxed economy as percentage of GDP

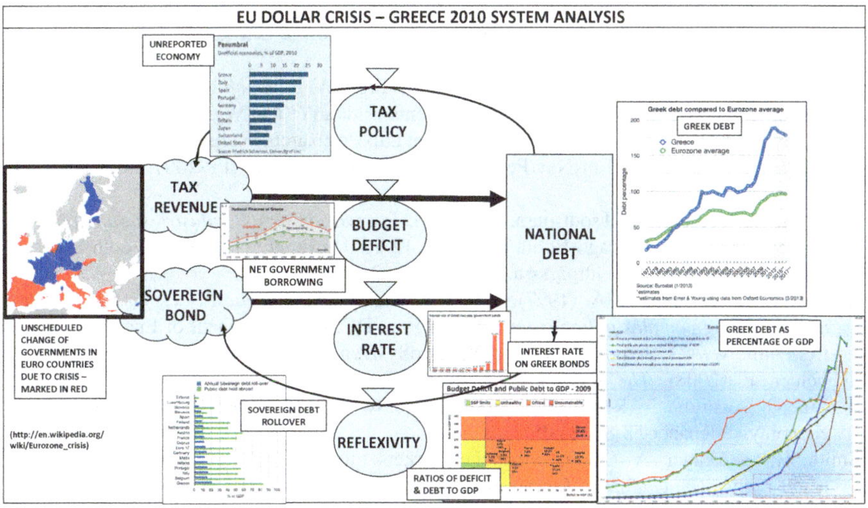

Fig. 3.12 Greek system analysis of fiscal policy leading to the euro crisis of 2009–2010

governments in Greece had indulged in the dynamics of a budget policy of 'Ponzi' finance. Unsound fiscal policy over many years had accumulated a very large and increasing government debt—until bond market 'reflexive cognition' triggered the Greek fiscal crisis in 2010. The 'reflexive perception' of bond traders was that either the Greek government must 'default' or be 'bailed out'.

We have shown that a systems dynamic model only as a technique for organizing and connecting graphs of economic information. However in future research, data from such graphs could be embedded in more quantitative expressions, when functional correlations provide distinct linkages between empirical phenomena. But such detail goes beyond the intent of this book. Here we only wished to show how to relate 'price-disequilibrium models' to 'system dynamic models' to both describe and explain government financial instability. Systems dynamics models can be used in 'micro-economics' to explain the dynamics of economic systems, not only of production but also of finance.

References

BBC News. (2012). Greece austerity: How far still to go? *BBC News*. Retrieved from http://www.bbc.com/news/world-europe-18511963

BBC News. (2012). Greek bank list editor Costas Vaxevanis acquitted. *BBC News*. Retrieved from http://www.bbc.com/news/world-europe-20172516

Betz, F. (2013). Macro and micro-economic policies in financial crises: Argentina 2000 and South Korea 1998. *Business and Management Research, 2*. Retrieved from www.sciedu.ca/bmr

Economist. (2010). Southern Europe will have trouble increasing its tax take. *The Economist*. Retrieved from http://www.economist.com/node/16792848

Inman, P. (2012) Primary Greek tax evaders are the professional classes. *The Guardian*. Retrieved from http://www.theguardian.com/world/2012/sep/09/greece-tax-evasion-professional-classes?CMP=twt_gu

Koenig, B. (2009). Fitch downgrades Greece to A—From A. *Bloomberg*. Retrieved from http://www.bloomberg.com/apps/news?pid=munievents&sid=a6Y6T3olWgX0

McCulley, P. (2007). *Teton remarks*. Retrieved from http://web.archive.org/web/20091124124300/http://www.pimco.com/LeftNav/Featured+Market+Commentary/FF/2007/GCBF+August-+September+2007.htm

Nikolaos, A., Morse, A., & Tsoutsoura, M. (2010). *Tax evasion across industries: Soft credit evidence from Greece*. Chicago Booth Paper No. 12-25. University of Chicago Booth School of Business. Retrieved from http://ssrn.com/abstract=2109500

Radzicki, M.J., & Taylor, R.A. (1997). *Introduction to system dynamics: A systems approach to understanding complex policy issues*. Washington, DC: US Department of Energy. Retrieved from http://www.systemdynamics.org/DL-IntroSysDyn/start.htm

Schneider, F. (2008). *The shadow economy in Europe*. Johannes Kepler Universitat Linz, Linz, Australia. Retrieved from http://www.visaeurope.fr/media/images/shadow-economywhitepaper-58-8752.pdf

Smith, H., & Seager, A. (2009). Financial markets tumble after fitch downgrades Greece's credit rating. *The Guardian*. Retrieved from http://www.theguardian.com/world/2009/dec/08/greece-credit-rating-lowest-eurozone

Soros, G. (1988). *The alchemy of finance*. New York: Simon & Schuster.

Chapter 4
Public and Private Debt Markets in Disequilibrium Theory

Introduction

We have modeled how financial markets trading capital assets can go into price disequilibrium and create financial bubbles. We next modeled how within an international financial grid, investment banks create the financial products of a financial market. And we saw how the unregulated networks in the grid produce and sell financial products of questionable quality and little public good. Next we modeled how the sovereign bonds of Greek nation went into price disequilibrium, triggering a financial crisis in Greece and a subsequent depression lasting over 5 years. But at the same time of the fiscal crisis in Greece, a fiscal crisis occurred in Spain. And after 2010, Spain's fiscal crisis was solved but Greece's was not solved. Why the difference between Spain's solution and Greece's lack of solution to their fiscal problems? It had to do with the different market sources of the crises, a private-debt market in Spain and a public debt-market in Greece.

Public and Private Debt in a Nation

In disequilibrium pricing of financial markets, excesses in either public debt or private debt can trigger a financial crisis, with attendant bank panics and recessions. In the 2010 Euro crisis, financial contagion in the sovereign bond market spread among four nations: Greece, Ireland, Cyprus, Portugal, and Spain. But the reasons for the contagion was initially different for the countries, due to either disequilibrium pricing in public debt markets or disequilibrium pricing in private debt markets. Figure 4.1 shows the relative debt levels of public and private debt, as percentages of GDP of the different nations in Europe and North America. Public debt is government debt, as shown in blue on the chart. Private debt is the sum of corporate and household debt as shown in green and brown on the chart.

F. Betz, *Stability in International Finance*, SpringerBriefs in Economics,
DOI 10.1007/978-3-319-26760-9_4

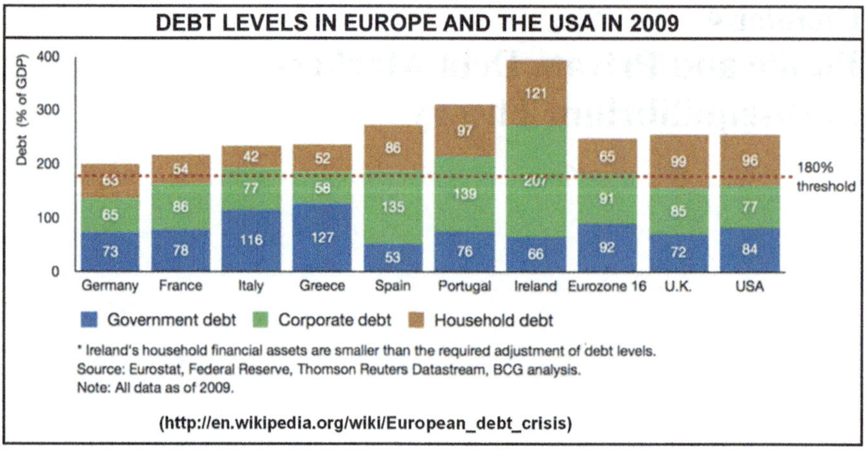

Fig. 4.1 Public and private debt (as % of GDP) in Europe and the U.S.

One notes that Greece had the largest public-debt-as-percentage-of-GDP at 127 % (PD/GDP), while Italy was close at 116 %. The difference was between Italy and Greece was tax policy. Greece had continuously run a government budget deficit, due to a reluctance to collect sufficient taxes. Martin Wolf expressed this: "What made the Greek fiscal position so bad was not that its spending was extraordinarily high by Eurozone standards, but rather that is revenue was so low, given the country's high spending." (Wolf 2014) The Greek tax policy was bad with tax collection continually deficient, never collecting sufficient revenue to fund its government services (in good economic times or bad). Greek governments used foreign borrowing (sovereign bonds) to fund their current expenses, covering perennial budget deficits. In 2009, Ireland at 66 % (PD/GDP) and Spain at 53 % (PD/GDP) and Portugal at 76 % (PD/GDP) were all cases first of private-debt market financial bubbles (and were not initially public-debt crises).

Yet in these cases of Ireland, Portugal, and Spain, their private-debt crises immediately triggered public-debt crises. Martin Wolf wrote: "… once (a private sector) crisis hit, the private-sector financial deficit disappeared swiftly, whereas the fiscal deficit soared. The explanation for the latter is that government revenue fell dramatically, and crisis-driven government spending automatically rose, as the banks were rescued…. When private spending collapses, as happened in Ireland and Spain, the fiscal deficit always rises more quickly than the external deficit falls…." (Wolf 2014) *Thus one needs to understand financial crises in both private and public debt markets to understand the Euro crisis of 2010–2015.*

In the financial contagion of the European sovereign bond market, contagion began with Greek bonds and next ran through Irish, Portuguese, Spanish bonds (while worrying the Italian and French bond market for a time). But the sources of the contagion differed in the different countries. In Greece, it was a financial contagion in the public debt market. In Ireland and Spain, it was contagion in private debt; and in Portugal, a contagion in both private and public debt. The contagions in the national private debt markets were due to housing booms, fueled by cheap Euro dollar credit.

Public Debt Market: Disequilibrium Systems Model in the Case of Spain 2010

In the Euro crisis of 2010, two different financial markets, public and private, had triggered Minsky moments in different national financial systems. In Greece, it was in the public debt (sovereign bond market for Greek bonds); but in Spain, it was private debt (housing market). Since 1984, private debt had risen in the Spanish housing market, until in 1999, housing prices began to climb into a 'bubble' (as shown in Fig. 4.2).

Residence ownership of houses was encouraged by the government and grew to 80 % occupancy. From 2001 through 2005, variable rate interest mortgages were used and property developments burgened. Over 500,000 residences were constructed in 2004, with about 300,000 purchased by Spanish citizens and 100,000 by foreign investors. When the housing bubble burst in 2007, housing sales immediately plunged 25 %. Housing prices continued to decline and, by 2012, had triggered a government crisis.

We next model this financial bubble (disequilibrium-price) in Spain from 2008–2010 to 2012. In the Spanish private-debt financial market for housing construction, interest rates and leverage were two controls on the flow of loans. Both leverage and interest rates were structural factors which could change over time. Until 2007, interest rates were low as Spanish banks borrowed in the Euro market; but interest rates in Spain jumped, after the 2007 U.S. fiscal bubble burst in U.S. mortgage-derivative market. Since structural features in a financial system change during the

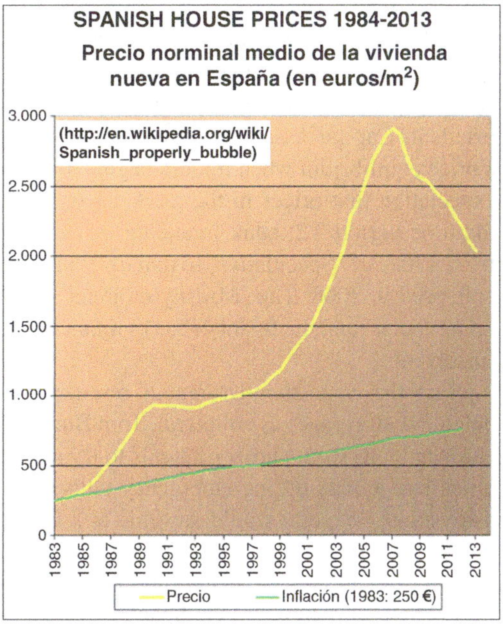

Fig. 4.2 Spanish house prices in the housing bubble 2000–2010

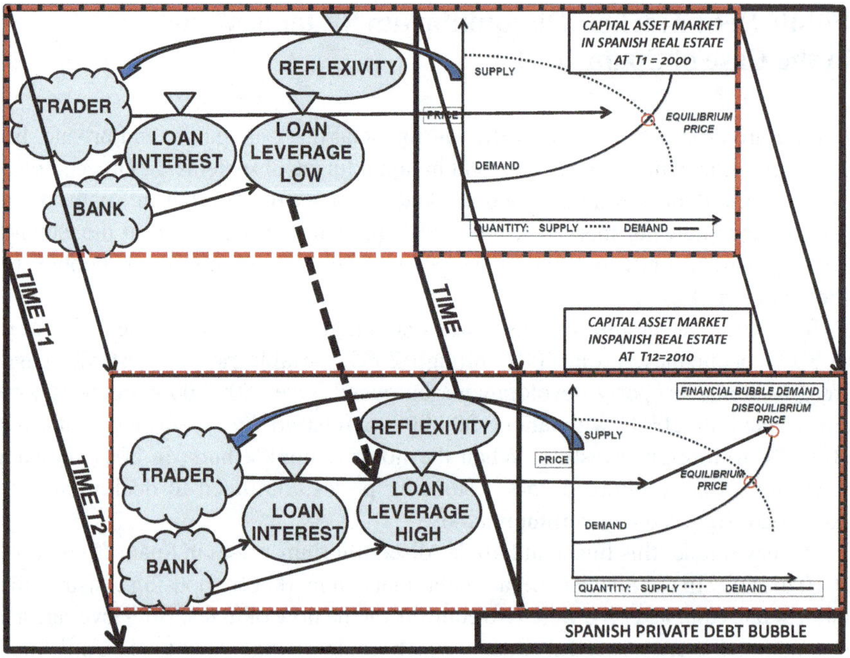

Fig. 4.3 Disequilibrium systems model of Spanish private debt bubble 2000–2010

speculation in the market leading up to a financial bubble, a disequilibrium systems model must explicitly display a dimension-of-time for the structural change—as shown in Fig. 4.3.

In this temporal model, a Trader obtains a Loan from a Bank with Leverage to purchase a capital asset in a Market in the time period **T1**. Rates on Interest and also Leverage are both necessary for the Trader to optimize profits, when the trader resells its Capital Asset purchase at the future time. The capital-asset market was in a price equilibrium when traders begin speculation in the market, with the reflexive expectation that prices in the market would rise above equilibrium price. Later in the time period **T2**, bank financing of trader loans changed the market financing from a state of 'Speculative' to that of 'Ponzi'—and then the global financial market collapsed in 2008. The 'Minsky moment' occurred when the real estate bubble in Spain 'burst' and the Spanish banks financing the real estate loans suddenly became 'insolvent'.

Next the Spanish government rescued the insolvent Spanish banks, holding defaulted mortgages as collateral. Tom Burridge wrote: "Spain is to get up to 100bn euros in loans from eurozone funds to try to help shore up its struggling banks. The move was agreed during emergency talks with eurozone finance ministers… Most analysts and experts would say this is a bailout…. and the money is going to be directed via the Spanish government using the Fund for Orderly Bank Restructuring (which is a bank restructuring fund in Spain). But it is a government institution, so the debt is going to be on the Spanish government's books. It is money that will be directed towards troubled Spanish banks, banks that lent heavily during the construction boom here—of course, the property market crashed and the loans turned bad." (Burridge 2012)

The government rescue of the private banks was necessary because of the insolvency of the banks. Floyd Norris had written: "The Spanish banks are bleeding from loans secured by raw real estate, and from loans for construction. The pain is made worse because such lending soared during the property boom. It is those loans that are now devastating bank balance sheets, as developers who borrowed to build offices, stores and neighborhoods saw demand dry up and now cannot pay the banks back. Just when markets were focused on the risks of a Greek default and the possibility of contagion to other countries, Spain's central bank reported this week that things were getting worse for that country's banks—but not because they held a lot of Greek debt or bonds issued by other troubled economies.... With Spain's economy weak and home prices falling, bad loans are growing. And the central bank thinks things are getting worse... It is impossible for Spanish banks to walk away from a collapsing bubble in Spanish real estate.... The Bank of Spain has created a program to force mergers of the smaller banks and to bring in better management. It has put about 11 billion euros into the banks to recapitalize them, and is putting in another 15 billion euros in a process.... (with) an estimate is that the overall number needed is closer to 50 billion euros." (Norris 2011)

The Spanish government had provided 62 billion euros to the Bank of Spain to distribute to Spanish banks. The funds were loaned to the government by the 'Troika' of the European Union and the International Monetary Fund. In return, the Spanish government agreed to reforms imposed as an austerity policy by the Troika institutions. The Spanish government debt did not soar until after the private-debt housing bubble burst, and the government stepped in as 'lender-of-last-resort' to save the Spanish banks. We next depict the role of the central bank of Spain in this connection between the financial system and production system in Spain at the time of the crisis in a time-explicit disequilibrium-systems model, Fig. 4.4.

The difference between this systems disequilibrium model (Fig. 4.4) and that of the preceding Fig. 4.3 is the intervention of the Spanish Central Bank—as the 'lender-of-last-resort' to prevent bank runs in Spanish banks. In banking literature, the role of a central bank in stopping bank runs is called the 'Baghot rule'. But this Bagehot role of the central bank rescuing the private banks then increased public debt of the Spanish government. Figure 4.5 compares Spanish public debt to average European pubic debt. The Spanish government debt was low, compared to the average government debt of EU countries—up until the time of saving the Spanish banks in 2008. Then the Spanish government debt rose to Eurozone averages.

Public Debt Market: Disequilibrium Systems Financial Model and Economic Recession in the Case of Spain 2010

Next the fiscal crisis in Spain triggered an economic crisis—a severe recession in the Spanish economy. This was again classical economic system behavior—a fiscal crisis triggered an economic crisis.

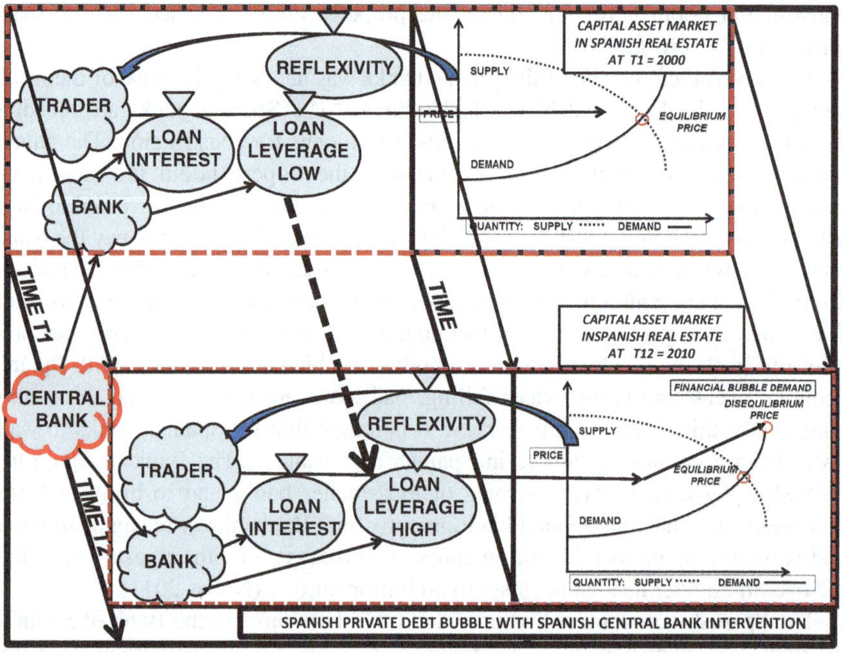

Fig. 4.4 Disequilibrium system model of Spanish real estate bubble with Spanish central bank bail-out

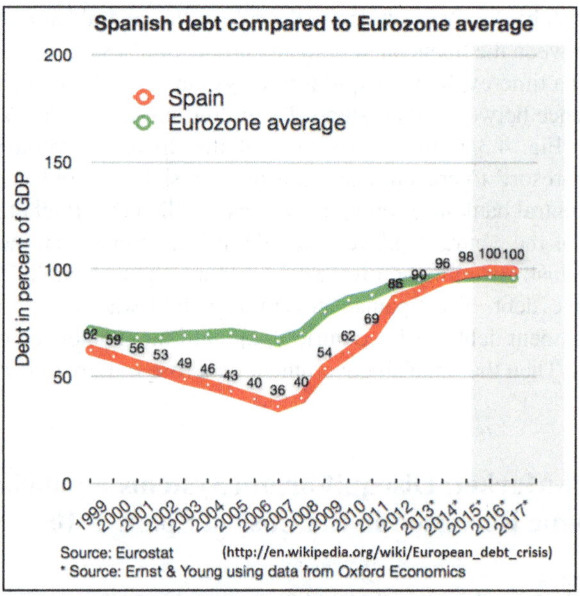

Fig. 4.5 Comparison of Spain's debt (% GDP) to eurozone average

We next connect the fiscal crisis in Spain to the economic crisis which followed, modeling the connection in a systems dynamics model of a society, as composed of the different subsystems: economic, cultural, political, and technological. (Betz 2013) In the production sub-system of a national economy, individual businesses, firms, produce goods within the industrial framework of an 'industrial value chain'. The firm can be modeled as a value-adding system; and the industrial context as an industrial value chain. All the firms and their industrial value chains operate in the production of commodities under an equilibrium pricing of supply–demand. Thus commodity products have a single economic value of 'consumption'—which is priced in equilibrium of supply and demand. In contrast, in the financial sub-system of a national economy, the buying-and-selling (trading) of capital assets need to be modeled in a time-dependent transactional process. Central to the profitability of capital asset trades is the 'leverage' in the loans—with higher leverage creating larger profits in the liquidity of an asset (and also higher risk). The time dependence in the financial market allows 'leverage' in financial transactions to increase over time with liquidity at higher and higher prices—a financial bubble.

A fiscal crisis in the financial system triggers an economic recession in the production plane. This occurs as bank failures stop the credit system of a nation; and business declines with unemployment rising. Banks provide the daily accounts and credit lines upon which businesses operate—manufacturing, services, and retail businesses. When bank accounts are frozen, the monetary system (currency and credit) stops and the economy seizes up. Businesses need daily credit lines with banks to operate on a daily schedule. Thus the monetary system is one of the societal sub-systems (in addition to energy sub-systems) which need to operate on a daily (and even hourly) basis for a modern economy to run continuously.

In Spain in 2011, this connection between financial and production systems was direct and swift. Spain's financial system plane (with its sudden *property-bubble/bank-failures*) and Spain's production system plane connected (with an immediate Spanish *economic-recession*). Unemployment in Spain jumped to 36 % in 2008 and, even as late as 2012, ran at 24 %. This connection is described in the disequilibrium systems model of Fig. 4.6.

In the *Financial Sector*, a price-disequilibrium systems model depicts the flow of loans from banks to traders (construction businesses and home owners) to develop, sell, and own residences. The reflexivity (market perception) was that housing prices would rise over time. And prices in the housing market did rise above an equilibrium price because new home construction was continually anticipating expanding demand. Thus in the growing home market, financial expectations (reflexivity) anticipated ever higher prices—driving the market from a price equilibrium to disequilibrium economic condition.

In the *Production Sector*, the loan collateral held by the banks in their funding of financial market speculation became worthless (unsellable) with the collapse of the housing market. Instantly, the banks became illiquid (and some insolvent). Bank runs began by depositors withdrawing their accounts. The illiquid/insolvent banks froze their accounts, and credit ceases in the economy. Businesses and employees unable to access their bank accounts and credit lines stop working.

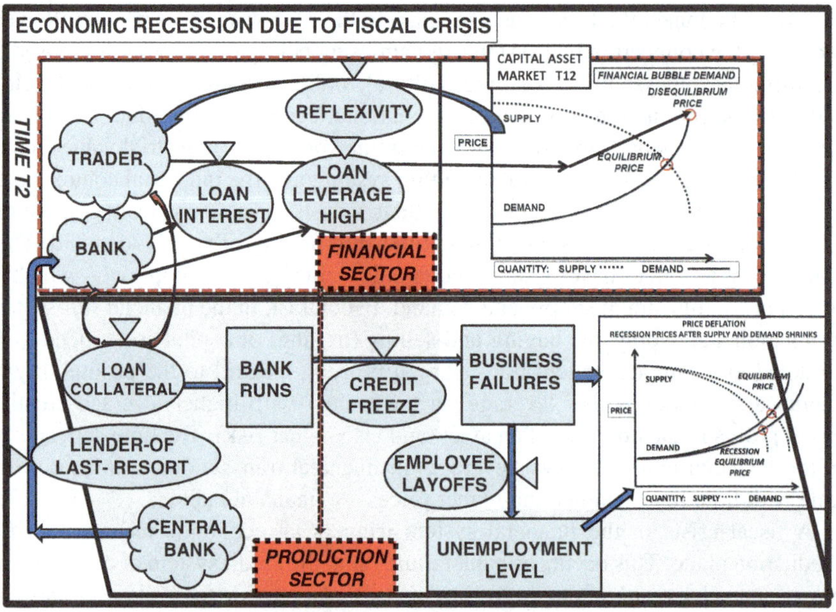

Fig. 4.6 Impact of financial crisis in Spanish economy

In providing construction loans and residence purchase mortgages as collateral the Spanish banks held highly-leveraged loans, with liens on the titles to the properties. When the housing bubble burst, the collateral could not be sold, and the Spanish banks became insolvent. They thus held long-term loans but funded by short-term borrowing from foreign banks and investors. Borrow short and lend long—is a basic way for banks to become insolvent. Thus from illiquid collateral, bank runs occurred on the insolvent banks. Insolvent, the banks could make no further loans and the credit market in Spain froze. Businesses operating daily upon credit lines with banks could no longer obtain cash and closed down production levels, laying off workers. Unemployed labor could not purchase commodities, so that prices in the commodity markets in Spain declined to recession/depression levels. And Spain was in a depression, with high unemployment, lowered production, and a financial crisis.

It was in May 2012 when the recession deepened, and the Spanish government began ‘bailing-out’ banks. David Jolly had reported: “Spanish retail sales fell in April by a record 9.8 % from a year earlier, the 22nd consecutive monthly decline, the government statistics institute said in Madrid. In a separate report, the Bank of Spain forecast that the economy would continue contracting throughout the first half of 2012, after shrinking by 0.3 % in the first 3 months of the year. Spain, with the highest jobless rate in Europe, is struggling to fix its financial sector, which was battered by the collapse of the credit bubble. The country has again become the subject of concern after Bankia, a real estate lender that the government is nationalizing, said Friday that it needed a total bailout of 23.5 billion euros, or $29.4 billion… The Spanish economy is shrinking as the central government and the regional authorities cut spending to meet budget targets. Making matters worse, the housing sector continues to decline and sales to other European countries, which have helped to sustain exporters, are likely to weaken as the bloc's economy stagnates. The banking sector's troubles could make it harder for even healthy companies to get credit." (Jolly 2012a)

As 'lender-of-last-resort', the central bank of Spain moved to 'bail out' the failing banks; and then the interest rate on Spanish sovereign bonds jumped higher. In June 2012, David Jolly reported: "...Government borrowing costs spiked to euro-era highs for Spain on Thursday, and Italy had to pay high rates again to complete a bond auction, as pressure mounted for a unified European response to the region's financial problems. The yield, or interest rate, on Spain's 10-year bonds reached 7 %, the level that has set off full international bailouts of some other euro zone members, after Moody's Investors Service downgraded the nation's credit rating late Wednesday... Italy's Prime Minister, Mario Monti, said Thursday that more steps needed to be taken at a European level to protect the euro union from the onslaught of the financial markets. It was an assessment shared by the new French president, François Hollande, who appeared with Mr. Monti at a news conference after they met for 2 hours in Rome." (Jolly 2012b)

In July 2012, Raphael Minder and Stephen Castle reported: "Struggling to meet euro zone financial targets, Prime Minister Mariano Rajoy of Spain introduced his latest package of tough austerity measures Wednesday, including a rise in the sales tax, reversing his previous stance. The package, Mr. Rajoy's fourth set of budget measures in 7 months, is intended to reduce the budget deficit by €65 billion, or $80 billion, over two and a half years. It follows a decision by European Union finance ministers Tuesday to relax Spain's deficit target for this year to 6.3 % of gross domestic product, rather than the 5.3 % target that was set only 4 months ago. But the finance ministers also said they expected Madrid to continue showing progress on its deficit cutting. The new austerity plan came as Finland's prime minister, Jyrki Katainen, issued a warning Wednesday that the euro's predicament was as perilous as at any time in the past 2 years. "This situation is dangerous, very dangerous," he said in an interview with Finland's biggest daily, Helsingin Sanomat. One of the main elements of the new round of Spanish austerity measures is a rise in the value-added tax to 21 % from 18 %." (Minder and Castle 2012)

In 2012, the austerity pressure on Spanish people was heavy and many exported savings and/or also left Spain. In September 2012, Landon Thomas reported: "After working 6 years as a senior executive for a multinational payroll-processing company in Barcelona, Spain, Mr. Vildosola is cutting his professional and financial ties with his troubled homeland. He has moved his family to a village near Cambridge, England, where he will take the reins at a small software company, and he has transferred his savings from Spanish banks to British banks. "The macro situation in Spain is getting worse and worse," Mr. Vildosola, 38, said last week just hours before boarding a plane to London with his wife and two small children. "There is just too much risk. Spain is going to be next after Greece, and I just don't want to end up holding devalued pesetas." Mr. Vildosola is among many who worry that Spain's economic tailspin could eventually force the country's withdrawal from the euro and a return to its former currency, the peseta. That dire outcome is still considered a long shot, even if Spain might eventually require a Greek-style bailout. But there is no doubt that many of those in a position to do so are taking their money—and in some cases themselves—out of Spain." (Thomas 2012)

Public Debt Market: Disequilibrium Systems Model in the Case of Greece 2010

When we compare this to the Greek case, which we previously modeled, we recall that the fiscal crisis in Greece arose originally from government borrowing to cover annual budge deficits—public debt market. We show this again in Fig. 4.7.

In this public-debt bubble, Greek governments had issued new sovereign bonds each year to fund annual budget deficits. Over time, this continual funding of budget deficits built up the national debt of the country. The Greek national debt as a percentage of GDP (%ND/GDP) rose about the Eurozone average of 50 %ND/GDP in 1985 to 100 % in 1993 and then (after 2007) jumped to 180 % in the crisis year of 2011. Then Greece needed to annually roll-over 20 % (ND/GDP), with its 80 % of sovereign debt held by foreigners. This need (1) for annual roll-over mostly to foreigners along with (2) the need to annually continue to add debt to cover budget deficits—spooked the bond market—'market reflexivity'. From 2009 to 2012, interest rates on new Greek bonds demanded by the market jumped from 3.7 to 177.37 %. The Greek government was bankrupt in 2010—desperately needing a EU 'bail out'. And in 2010, the European Union and International Monetary Fund (Troika) began bail-outs—coupled to an Austerity policy.

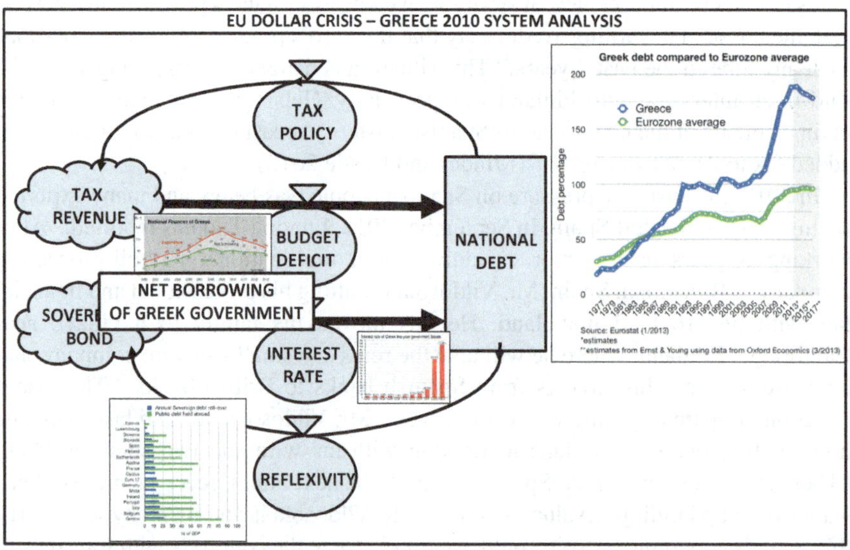

Fig. 4.7 Disequilibrium systems model of Greek fiscal policy

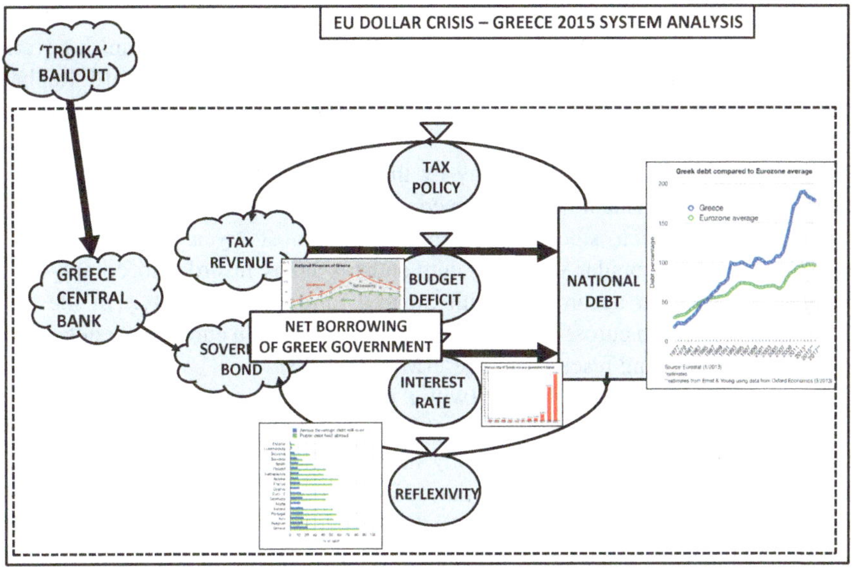

Fig. 4.8 Europe begins bail-out of Greece in 2010

Thus a structural change occurred in the systems model of the Greek fiscal system, with the addition of 'bailout' funding from the 'Troika'; and this is shown in Fig. 4.8. One needs to add a central bank source (Greece Central Bank) to receive funds from outside Greece as the 'bailout' loans from the Troika. From T1 (2009) to T2 (2015). Greek fiscal policy was on a Troika financial 'life-line' (bail-out), unable to handle its debt load—while also having to begin paying back IMF loans.

In the next chapter, we will examine how well this policy of austerity worked. It didn't. Even 5 years after 2010, the Greek government was still in fiscal crisis and the Greek economy was still in depression,

Summary

In modeling different countries crises in the Eurozone, one observes different debt markets triggering the financial bubbles—either as public-debt (sovereign bond markets) or as private-debt (e.g. residential markets). Greece was a pure economic case of a public-debt bubble, and Spain was a pure economic case of a private-debt bubble. All the other countries impacted by the Euro crisis (such as Ireland, Portugal, Italy were cases of one or the other or a mixture of both). The importance of distinguishing the market source of a disequilibrium price crisis is that different policies are needed to solve crisis problem 'fix' a crisis.

In the case of Spain (with a private debt crisis) the economy could be fixed by preventing bank runs and regulating the bank system—recapitalizing the illiquid banks, and closing down the insolvent banks. The Spanish central bank was able to accomplish this with the 'bail-out' of European Union loans to the Spanish government. And Spain began to emerge from the 2010 crisis 3 years later in 2013. Raphael Minder reported: "Spain pulled out of a 2-year recession in the third quarter (October 2013), with its economy growing 0.1 % from the previous quarter, according to preliminary data released Wednesday by the Spanish central bank… The growth news will likely provide a fillip for the conservative government of Prime Minister Mariano Rajoy, which, since coming into office almost 2 years ago, has pushed through deeply unpopular spending cuts and tax hikes in order to comply with budgetary targets in accordance with Spain's European partners…. In the end, Spain used 41 billion euros, or $56 billion, of the 100 billion euros that it negotiated in a European banking rescue package." (Minder 2013)

In contrast in the case of Greece (with a public debt crisis), the Greek economy continued in crisis and depression from 2010 into 2015—still with no 'fix' (despite sizable loans from the European Union). In 2015, Hugo Dixon wrote: "The debt is still huge—313 billion euros, or about $353 billion—175 % of the Greek gross domestic product. But the bulk, about €184 billion, is now owed to eurozone governments and pays low interest. What is more, Greece doesn't have to start repaying it until 2020 and then has over 30 years to finish. The so-called present value of this debt, what it is worth today, is therefore much lower than its official face value. Unfortunately, this isn't the full story. Greece has four other sources of borrowing: €27 billion owed to the European Central Bank; €20 billion owed to the International Monetary Fund; debt owed to private investors; and short-term treasury bills. The private debt isn't an immediate problem, because most of it has also been stretched out over a long period. Nor are the treasury bills, as Athens is still able to roll them over as they come due. But the ECB and IMF debt is problematic because most of it comes due in the next 5 years. In fact, there is a crunch in the next few months, with over €10 billion in repayments due by the end of September. The snag is that IMF and ECB debt cannot be rescheduled without breaching rules and treaties. This is why the focus of the current talks is about lending Greece more money, so that it can meet these obligations…. The eurozone will also be under pressure to provide yet more loans to Athens because the money left in the current bailout program won't be sufficient to cover all the repayments due to the E.C.B. and I.M.F. What is more, the country has other needs, such as paying overdue bills to suppliers, recapitalizing Greek banks and repaying the loans it has forcibly extracted from local authorities within Greece." (Dixon 2015)

The Eurodollar crises of 2009–2010 have provided empirical evidence about policies for dealing with two different debt markets, private and public. Disequilibrium-systems models of how private and public financial markets can move toward price disequilibrium are useful for identifying (1) how fiscal policies can create fiscal crises and (2) how central bank policies can help or not-help to solve fiscal crises.

What is particularly interesting in this comparison is that the European Union (including its European Central Bank and the IMF) was able to help solve the Spanish financial crisis but not the Greek financial crisis. This difference in 'crisis solvability' depended upon the underlying fiscal models of private-debt markets compared to the public-debt markets. Accordingly, the two disequilibrium-systems models of financial markets in the empirical case of the Eurodollar crises suggests the following hypothesis: Central banks can solve crisis-problems of private-debt but not crises of public debt.

References

Betz, F. (2013, November). *Why bank panics matter*. New York: Springer. ISBN 978-3-319-01757-0.

Burridge, T. (2012). Spanish banks to get up to 100bn euros in rescue loans. *BBC NEWS*. Retrieved June 12, from http://www.bbc.com/news/business-18382659

Dixon, H. (2015). Financial engineering to Athen's rescue. *New York Times*. Retrieved June 14, from http://www.nytimes.com/2015/06/15/business/international/financial-engineering-to-athenss-rescue.html?_r=0

Jolly, D. (2012a). Spanish data point to further decline. *New York Times*. Retrieved May 29, from http://www.nytimes.com/2012/05/30/business/global/daily-euro-zone-watch.html?_r=0

Jolly, D. (2012b). Spanish cost of borrowing soars after rating cut. *New York Times*. Retrieved June 14, from http://www.nytimes.com/2012/06/15/business/global/daily-euro-zone-watch.html

Minder, R. (2013). Spain emerges from two year recession. *New York Times*. Retrieved October 23, from http://www.nytimes.com/2013/10/24/business/international/spain-emerges-from-two-year-recession.html

Minder, R., & Castle, S. (2012). Spain plans new round of tough austerity measures. *New York Times*. Retrieved July 11, from http://www.nytimes.com/2012/07/12/business/global/daily-euro-zone-watch.html

Norris, F. (2011). Spain's banking mess. *New York Times*. Retrieved September 22, from http://www.nytimes.com/2011/09/23/business/spains-banking-mess.html

Thomas, L. (2012). Fears rising Spaniards pull out their cash and get out of Spain. *New York Times*. Retrieved September 3, from http://www.nytimes.com/2012/09/04/business/global/money-and-people-leave-spain-as-economic-gloom-deepens.html

Wolf, M. (2014). *The Shifts and the Shocks: What we've learned-and have still to learn-from the financial crisis*. London: Penguin Press.

Chapter 5
Why 'Austerity' Failed in Greece: Testing the Validity of Macro-Economic Models

Introduction

Models have always been important to informed policy making. In the formulation of policy, models can provide information about the situation and the problem which a policy intends to address; and in the execution of policy, models can provide information about the consequences (and unintended consequences) of a policy. Models are used for the formulation and assessment of policies, as in Fig. 5.1. Each model has a specific form, specific dynamics, specific content, and specifically formatted data input and information output.

All models require some simplification of reality; but proper simplicity captures the primary essences of reality. A modeling methodology needs to have an efficient modeling procedure—capturing the empirical reality of a system.

Testing a social science theory for empirical validity (such as the macro-economic theory underlying 'austerity'), one needs first to methodologically formulate a specific 'model' within the principles of the theory—in order to test in the empirical context of a historical event of a society the validity of the model. Models can be directly empirically verified or invalidated. Theory and theoretical principles of a theory are only indirectly validated/invalidated by implications of the validity of their models.

In the previous chapter, we reviewed how European Austerity policy facilitated the fixing of the Spanish Euro crisis but not the Greek crisis. This different response was due to the initial crisis in Spain occurring in a private-debt market, while the initial crisis in Greece was in the public-debt market. The European austerity policy fixed a fiscal crisis due to private-debt financial bubble but not one due to a public-debt financial bubble. We next examine the Greek fiscal crisis to see in detail why the Austerity policy did not solve the Greek crisis.

Earlier in the history of the International Monetary Fund (IMF) it had been established that the IMF 'austerity policy' approach to solving national fiscal crises was based upon a macro-model of a national economy called the 'Polak Model' (Stiglitz 2002;

F. Betz, *Stability in International Finance*, SpringerBriefs in Economics,
DOI 10.1007/978-3-319-26760-9_5

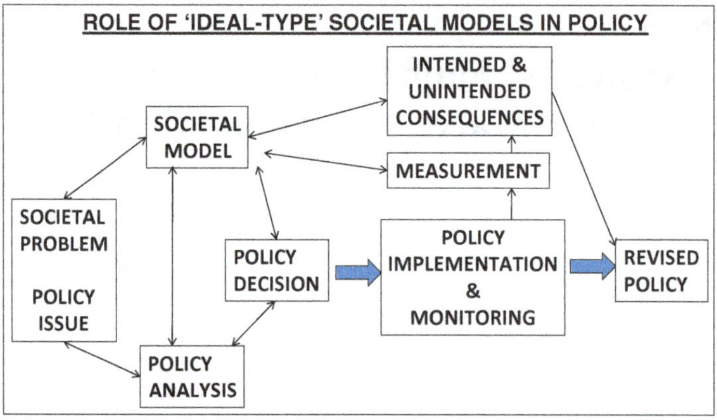

Fig. 5.1 Role of models in policy formulation and implementation

Woods 2006). While there is no direct evidence that in the European crisis, the 'Troika' (European Union, European Central Bank, and the International Monetary Fund) explicitly based their Austerity Policy upon the macro-economic model of Polak, we will assume some such thinking might have been behind the Troika's persistent use of 'Austerity Policy' which they applied to Greek fiscal assistance from 2010 through 2015. But historically, the IMF had explicitly justified their austerity-and-loan policy upon the 'Polak Model'. We will compare the Polak model to an alternative macro-economic fiscal model (based upon the theory of disequilibrium-pricing and systems-dynamics modeling techniques). We examine the validity of each model in the empirical case of Greece—in order to understand why austerity failed.

From 2010 through 2015, 'fiscal austerity' had been imposed upon the Greek governments as the price of EU bailouts of bankrupt Greece. But after 5 years, the EU austerity policy was judged by many as a failure. Greece continued to struggle at the bottom of a depression.

Fiscal Policy

Since the fiscal crises of the U.S. in 2008 and the European Euro-dollar crisis from 2009, much attention is being paid to 'fiscal policy' and macro-economic models underlying policy. There are many widely respected economists who have written about this. Nouriel Roubini emphasized that several economic questions need to be restudied. These include the appropriate relation of public debt to economic growth, the causes of large continuous debts in government budgets, and how a large government debt can be reduced without throwing a nation into depression. Also Roubini cautioned about a policy of 'austerity' for quickly reducing debt (front-loading) by immediately and simultaneously increasing taxes and reducing government employment and pensions (Roubini 2014). Paul Krugman wrote that the Greek fiscal crisis came as a shock to European Union officials, as previous Greek Governments had falsified debt information: "As the news sank in with investors, first Greece, then much of Europe, found itself in a new kind of crisis—one not of failing banks but of failing governments, unable to borrow on world markets." (Krugman 2013) Such consequences did occur in Greece and other EU countries, which had the 'front-loaded' EU austerity policy applied to them in exchange for EU bail-out assistance.

In Greece, even by 2015, the empirical result was that Greece had not grown out of a depression during 4 years of the austerity program. Describing this, Mark Blyth wrote: "In line with such (austerity) thinking, and following the shock of the recent financial crisis, which caused public debt to balloon, much of Europe has been pursuing austerity consistently for the past 4 years. The results of the experiment are now in, and they are equally consistent: austerity doesn't work. Most of the economies on the periphery of the eurozone have been in free fall since 2009, and in the fourth quarter of 2012, the euro-zone as a whole contracted for the first time ever. Portugal's economy shrank by 1.8 %, Italy's fell by 0.9 %, and even the supposed powerhouse of the region, Germany, saw its economy contract by 0.6 %. The United Kingdom, despite not being in the euro-zone, only barely escaped having the developed world's first-ever triple-dip recession." (Blyth 2013) This report emphasized that the front-loaded austerity policy had only triggered recessions, without immediate relief of debt.

Austerity Program and IMF Macro-Fiscal Model: Polak Model

The Polak model had long been used by the IMF in justifying its policy of 'austerity' for assisting an economically troubled nation. Ngaire Woods explained: "Crucially, the Polak model linked a country's domestic economic policies to its balance of payments position. This opened the door for IMF conditionality (conditions for making an IMF loan to a country)….The starting point of the Polak model is what was known (in macro-economic theory) as the 'absorption approach' to the balance of payments—that a country with a balance of payments deficit was absorbing too many resources in consumption and investment, relative to what that country can produce. With a couple of simplifying assumptions, it will follow that a country which increases domestic credit too rapidly will encounter increasing balance of payments deficits reflected in a loss in central bank reserves… On the basis of this analysis, when a country has a balance of payments deficit, the Fund's prescription focuses on reducing government spending, increasing taxes, and reducing domestic credit creation." (Woods 2006)

In 1989 and 1998, J. J. Polak had published his model, and his paper was reprinted later as collected essays. (Polak 1989) The Polak Model consisted of four equations:

1. **I = k P**
   Imports (**I**) are proportional (**k**) to GDP (**P**).
2. **E − I = (ΔR − C)**
   Exports (**E**) minus Imports (**I**) are equal to (Change-in-Reserves (**ΔR**) minus Net-Capital-Inflow (**C**) of the non-banking sector).
3. **ΔM = k ΔP**
   Change-in-Money-Supply (**ΔM**) is proportional (**k**) to Change-in-Gross-Domestic-Product (**ΔP**).
4. **ΔR = (ΔM − ΔD)**
   Change-in-Reserves (**ΔR**) equals (Change-in-Money-Supply (**ΔM**) minus Change-in-Domestic-Credit (**ΔD**).

The first equation is about imports (I) and exports (E) in a nation, asserting that: *Imports (I) are proportional to the total revenue (P) in a nation.* In the case of Greece, this was a questionable assumption. In any nation, what-is-imported and what-is-exported depends upon what-cannot-be-produced-in-a-nation *(Imports)* and what-can-be-produced *(Exports).* But what-can-be-produced and what-needs-to-be-imported bears no relation to the total revenue. Instead, what-can-be-produced depends upon the industrial technology in a nation and the resources of a nation. For example by 2009, Greece did not produce automobiles, and many Mercedes and other automobiles manufactured in Germany were purchased by Greek citizens, under the low interest rates available then in Euro dollar countries. The import of German cars into Greece had less to do with GDP than with interest rates on car loans (with low rates due to Greece's participation in the Eurodollar). One of Greece's primary 'exports' then lay in the 'import' of tourists (a service industry rather than a manufacturing industry). Greece received German and other European tourists who enjoyed the climate and beauties of the Aegean Sea—with tourism contributing at least 18 % to GDP.

Thus for Greece, the first equation **(I = kP)** was not true. Imports (I) in Greece was not at that time directly related to the Gross Domestic Product (P). The level of imports was financed not by the level of GDP but by the availability of inexpensive foreign credit. It was excessive borrowing of money (foreign loans) which increased the level of national imports, far more than did their GDP. Polak's first macro-economic assumption about imports and GDP was not historically correct in Greece in the Euro crisis.

The second equation was about imports (I) and exports (E) in a nation: **E − I = (ΔR − C).** It assumed that the difference between Exports (E) and Imports (I) depended upon changes-in-money-reserves (ΔR) in the central bank of the nation and upon the inflow of capital (C) into the non-banking sectors. Did exports increase over imports when the central bank reserve of money increased in Greece? No. Imports were principally dependent upon the international financial community buying Greek sovereign bonds, which subsidized government employment. The difference of exports-to-imports bore little relation to the amount of gold held by the Greek central bank, instead reflecting the sales of Greek sovereign bonds.

Also the second equation **(E – I = ΔR – C)** assumed that the difference between Exports (E) and Imports **(I)** depended negatively upon the inflow of capital (**C**) into the non-banking sectors. This meant if companies in the nation borrow less in foreign loans, then exports will increase over imports. Certainly financial strength in a nation could increase exports—but only if financial strength is used to invest in more manufacturing capability in the nation. Thus Polak's second macro-economic assumption is contextually dependent on how a country uses its wealth, upon its micro-economic structure. In Greece, the inflow of capital (**C**) did not finance manufacturing development but financed the employment of government workers. The difference of exports and imports had no direct relationship to decrease in foreign loans. This macro-economic assumption was not historically true in Greece.

For the third equation **ΔM = k ΔP**, the assumption was that Change-in-Money-Supply (**ΔM**) is proportional (**k**) to Change-in-Gross-Domestic-Product (**ΔP**). In Greece, this also was not true. As a member of the EU Euro dollar currency, Greece had no control over its currency. It could not inflate its supply of money to lower the costs of servicing national debt. Polak's third equation was not true in Greece, in the times leading up to and during its fiscal crisis.

For the fourth equation **(ΔR = ΔM – ΔD),** the Change-Reserves (**ΔR**) did not in Greece actually equal the Change-in-Money-Supply (**ΔM**) minus Change-in-Domestic-Credit (**ΔD**). Domestic Credit froze up as banks stopped lending because of their insolvency when Greece was unable to issue new sovereign bonds in 2010. The central bank reserves did not increase; instead, the economy stopped. The Change-in-Money-Supply was controlled by the European Union provision of Euro dollars. Change in bank reserves (**ΔR**) was dependent upon capital flight from Greek banks to Swiss banks; and Change-in-Domestic-Credit (**ΔD**) was dependent upon solvency of Greek banks. The empirical reality about Reserves (**R**) of Euro dollars was quite different from Polak's assumption.

Criticism of the IMF's use of the Polak model has been made earlier by several economists. After the Asian Financial Crisis, Joseph Stiglitz had criticized IMF austerity policy: "The IMF combined the money with conditions....higher interest rates...cutbacks in government spending and increases in taxes. The IMF would claim that imposing these conditions was the responsible thing to do...The IMF programs, with all of their conditions and with all of their money, failed....As a crisis progressed, unemployment soared, GDP plummeted, banks closed...The crisis economies...were clearly threatened with a major downturn and needed stimulation. The IMF programs pushed exactly the opposite course....Today, the IMF admits that the fiscal policy it recommended was excessively austere." (Stiglitz 2002)

Ngaire Woods also wrote: "In defining its craft, the IMF is heavily constrained both by its capacity and by the limits put upon it by its most powerful members. Within these constraints for a long time, the Polak model (and successive financial programming models) made life relatively easy for the Fund....That said, financial programming was severely challenged during the 1980s as the IMF sought an appropriate response to the debt crises that afflicted so many developing countries... The downside of professionalism for the IMF (and the World Bank) is that there is very little room for local knowledge. Local knowledge is messy, political, intractable, and very difficult to make judgments about." (Woods 2006) This meant that micro-economic information was not properly used to modify macro-economic models. As a macro-economic model, the Polak four equations were used by IMF policy to justify austerity. Reducing government expenditure could force people into the private sector, thereby lowering wages for reducing cost-of-production (raising productivity) and increasing exports by lower prices of manufactured goods.

In this paper, we are not criticizing the IMF generally but only demonstrating that the Polak model (if the IMF was still using it to justify austerity policy) was not empirically true in the case of Greece. Austerity policy focuses both upon raising taxes and reducing government employment, immediately and at the same time—'front-loading' government cuts to stimulate the economy.

The Polak macro-economic model assumed a direct connection (1) between imports and GDP and (2) between export–import ratios and central bank monetary reserves minus next capital inflows. Why these assumptions? And if the Polak model were empirically accurate, then one might expect IMF policy based upon it to be effective. But the policy was ineffective in Greece; and any model, underpinning the austerity policy, was invalid. (Earlier, one of the authors analyzed the IMF Polak model when it was applied by IMF austerity policy to the Argentine fiscal crisis in 2000; and the empirical evidence was that the model had also been invalid in the case of Argentina (Betz 2013)).

Some form of an economic model involving the economic concept of 'productivity' (export–import balances and perhaps similar to the Polak model) did underlie economic thinking by EU economists in 2009–2015. This is evidenced by the EU emphasis, all during this crisis, upon the 'productivity' in the affected nations. EU economists emphasized the importance of the 'cost-of-labor' as a major factor in 'economic competitiveness' and this appeared in the EU publication in 2011, entitled: "*Conclusions of The Heads of State or Government of The Euro Area*" *(Brussels, March 11,* 2011*)*. Under the topic of *Foster Competitiveness*, the document stated: "Progress will be assessed on the basis of wage and productivity developments and competitiveness adjustment needs. To assess whether wages are evolving in line with productivity, unit labor costs (ULC) will be monitored over a period of time, by comparing with developments in other Euro area countries and in the main comparable trading partners. For each country, ULCs will be assessed for the economy as a whole and for each major sector (manufacturing; services; as well as tradable and non-tradable sectors). Large and sustained increases (in labor wages) may lead to the erosion of competitiveness, especially if combined with a widening current account deficit and declining market shares for exports." (EU Brussels 2011) One sees in this prescription of the EU commission that there was an assumption that increasing 'labor wages' lowers a 'national productivity'.

Economically, 'productivity' is judged as 'good' because it leads to higher exports by a nation (more competitiveness); and the Polak model was constructed explicitly upon a difference between exports and imports of a nation. But this is not an obvious assumption. In management theory, an increase in labor wages decreases business profitability but not necessarily business productivity. Automation is a more important factor in increasing productivity because it multiples labor productivity. This economic concept of 'wages' as directly coupled to 'productivity' is at odds with the management concept of 'automation' as being more directly coupled to 'productivity'.

Yet Polak was an able economist. Why did Polak make these assumptions? Why has the assumptions (about exports-imports and the productivity-of-labor) as the major factors in economic stability continued to influence so much economic thinking? The author can only suppose that the economic idea connecting labor-costs-and-exports traces back to traditional economics in the early history of the industrial revolution. Karl Polyani had traced the history of ideas in economic thinking in 1800s (Polyani 1944). At that time, economic thinking had focused upon exports, because what industrial technology was doing was producing too-much-product-to-be-consumed-locally.

Then English economic thinking had focused upon exports and imports. More exports were good! More imports were bad. A positive ratio of exports to imports created prosperity and wealth in England. A negative ratio created economic recession in England. Economic recession was bad because capitalists lost wealth and labor lost employment. What could management do to increase exports and decrease imports? The economic thinking then was to increase unemployment—as a way to reduce labor prices thus reducing production costs and thus decreasing export products prices—thereby increasing exports and profits. This was a solution. Management can control employment. Firing labor increased exports by reducing prices. When exports increased, labor could be rehired.

Looking back historically, labor cost had been a major factor in production. In the 1800s, manufacturing automation was not yet a technology and would occur only later in the 1900s. In the 1800s, manufacturing needed many people to run the machines, as industrial labor. In the time of the English industrial revolution, labor had been a large part of production costs—roughly 50 % of production costs was in labor and 50 % in materials. (Then the costs-of-production did not include the cost of factory investment, because manufacturing machinery was directly purchased and not financed by loans). Accordingly, while material costs could not be controlled by English capital, labor costs could be controlled by increasing unemployment and making people more willing to work at lower wages.

But in the modern twenty-first century, labor costs in most manufacturing are no longer large costs. Computerization and automation has taken most of the labor costs out of manufacturing. Labor costs are now around only 5 % of direct production costs; while material costs are still high, around 35 % and overhead is the remainder of the 60 % of direct costs. (The exception to this is the cost of labor in clothing assembly, as labor costs are still at least 35 %, with material costs 35 % and overhead 30 %.) The difference in manufacturing costs between the nineteenth and twenty-first century has been in the technologies of manufacturing automation. Automation progressed rapidly all through the twentieth century. For this reason economic thinking about an industrialized economy in the 1800s is not appropriate for modern economic thinking about present industrialization. *The Polak model constituted economic thinking by IMF officials, which was 100 years out of date about technology.*

Yet in 2011, European Union macro-economic policy advisors were still assuming that it was the 'high-price' of labor which reduces 'competitiveness' in an economy and that the price of labor can be reduced through unemployment. Government employees are assumed not to be productive to the economy. Fire government employees, and they will be forced to find lower-paying-but-productive employment in the private economy. This was the thinking in the earlier quoted EU Commission report. Apparently, historical technological progress in 'automation' was ignored in EU macro-economic thinking.

Sometimes models are used which are convenient to policy. About the IMF Polak model, Ngaire Woods wrote: "The Polak model offered staff a way to diagnose and prescribe conditions for any economy facing a balance of payments crisis ... The original model required few data. It focused attention on a key variable that governments could control—domestic credit creation." (Woods 2006) In the 4 years of the EU austerity policy, there had been no public expression of an underlying macro-economic model. However, IMF had long used the Polak model to underpin its austerity policies; and if the Polak model had lain behind the austerity policy, one could test its validity in the Greek context.

On empirically validating macro-economic models, sometimes econometrics is methodologically appropriate and sometimes institutional analysis is appropriate. Econometrics provides correlations between factors, which may be included in a model. A model depicts the empirical correlations as kinds of variables whose relations can be tested. Econometric analysis was not as appropriate a methodology for testing the Polak model, as were the methodologies of institutional and micro-economic analysis. The validity of the kinds of variables in the Polak macroeconomic model depended on the situation of the microeconomics of Greece, its institutional infrastructure. The microeconomics was that Greece was not a major manufacturing export nation and only had principle industries in shipping and tourism. Also as a member of the EU monetary union, Greece had no control over a national currency exchange rate and could not use central bank interest rates to deflate or stimulate the Greek economy. The macro-economic assumptions in Polak's model were not met by the micro-economic situation in Greece.

Disequilibrium Theory and a Dynamic Model of Greek Euro Crisis

Earlier, we had modeled the Greek fiscal policy in a disequilibrium systems model, which we show again in Fig. 5.2.

By July 2010, sovereign bond traders had connected information about the budget deficit to information about Greek tax policy. Then the market reflexivity about reliability of Greek bond jumped rates to 9.7 %. Martin Wolf wrote: "What made the Greek fiscal position so bad was not that its spending was extraordinarily high by Eurozone standards, but rather that its revenue was so low, given the country's high spending.... It was the gulf between the Greek embrace of high public spending

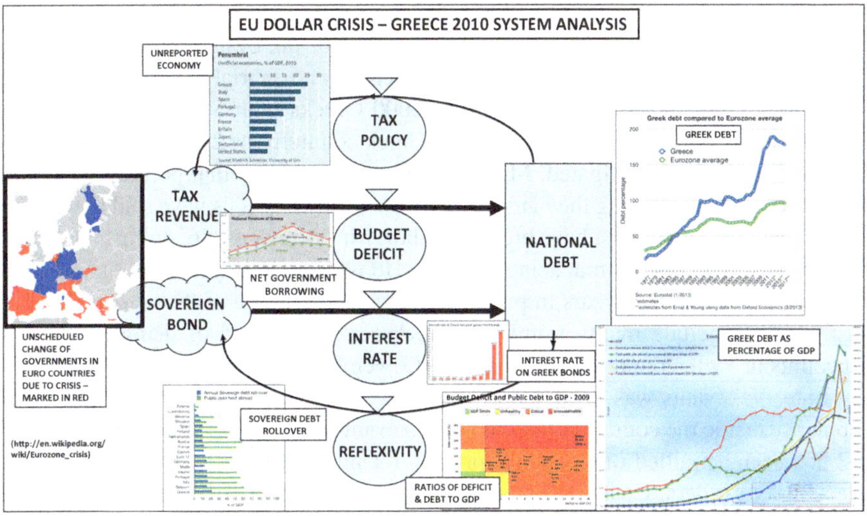

Fig. 5.2 Disequilibrium systems model of Greek fiscal policy up to 2010

(much of it relatively wasteful) and the country's inability or unwillingness to raise taxes that lay at the root of its fiscal difficulties. This was ultimately a political failure more than an economic one, though a failure that membership of the Eurozone helped." (Wolf 2014)

In the functional relations, the systems model clearly points out that the major factor in the Greek fiscal crisis was poor taxation policy. The systems model is not just a display of charts and data but also how these charts of information relate to one another as system components, such as sources, flows, stocks, feedback loops, etc. The difference between information displays and models are the relationships between information (system variables).

As a macro-economic fiscal model in the Greek fiscal crisis, a price-disequilibrium systems dynamics model highlights 'tax policy' as the key to solving the fiscal policy.

Only when sufficient taxes are collected to fund annual government budgets can government debt stop increasing.

There is no way out of the macro-fiscal-policy trap (continually-accumulating-debt funded by annual-issues-of-sovereign-bonds) except by collecting sufficient taxes to fund essential governmental operations.

Austerity and Tax Policy

Let us again review the austerity program, but this time focusing upon tax policy. In 2010 in Greece, the European Union began a bail-out of the Greek government, imposing economic conditions of 'austerity' on the Greek government. But even the EU's 'austerity' program for Greece, there occurred very little real 'reform' of

Greek tax policy and collection. An indication of this was the arrest and trial of a Greek journalist who dared to make public a list of tax evaders in Greece. Mark Lowen reported: "Journalist Costas Vaxevanis has gone on trial in Athens for breach of privacy after publishing the names of 2000 Greeks with Swiss bank accounts. French authorities gave the names to their Greek counterparts 2 years ago, but documents were never investigated. Mr. Vaxevanis told the BBC that politicians should be prosecuted for keeping the names secret. But Greek officials have said there is no proof that those on the list have broken the law. Mr. Vaxevanis, 46, published the list in Hot Doc, the weekly magazine he edits. He is accused of breaking private data rules and faces up to 2 years in prison if convicted.... Some of those named in the list, said to include many prominent Greeks, are suspected of using the HSBC accounts in Switzerland for tax evasion." (Lowen 2012)

Later Vaxevanis was acquitted of the charge. BBC News reported: "There was applause inside the court building as Mr. Vaxevanis was acquitted. A Greek journalist has been acquitted of breaching privacy for publishing the names of 2000 suspected tax evaders. Costas Vaxevanis published a list of Greeks with Swiss bank accounts, including a government minister and other prominent figures in public life. Lawyers for Mr. Vaxevanis, 46, argued that the charges were outrageous and said no-one on the list had actually complained of a breach of privacy. After a 1-day trial, a court in Athens found Mr. Vaxevanis innocent.... The BBC's Mark Lowen in Athens says the swift ruling will be an embarrassment to the Greek government. Greece is being urged by international lenders to crack down on tax evasion as part of far-reaching reforms demanded in exchange for billions of euros of bailout money. The list of suspected evaders was reportedly leaked by an employee at the HSBC bank and passed to IMF chief Christine Lagarde when she was French finance minister in 2010. Ms. Lagarde apparently handed the list to the Greek authorities, but they took no action. Two of Greece's former finance ministers have acknowledged seeing copies of the list. However, Yannis Stournaras, who took office in June, has told parliament he has not seen it. Mr. Vaxevanis said he had published the list because it was his job as a journalist to reveal the truth. 'The three last governments have lied and have made a mockery of the Greek people with this list,' he said." (BBC News 2012)

Although tax reform was called for in the EU austerity program and also highlighted in the disequilibrium fiscal systems model, yet little progress had been made by the Greek governments. Tax evasion and government corruption were not substantially addressed. We recall that Phillip Inman had reported that professional classes were the principle tax evaders in Greece (Inman 2012). And we recall that Artavanis Nikolaos, Adair Morse, and Margarita Tsoutsoura had gained access to records of one of the large banks in Greece and found that people made nearly twice as much as they reported on their taxes (Nikolaos et al. 2010).

Thus even in 2012, the EU Troika had been aware of the corruption in Greek tax policy but still funded the bailout of Greece. The Greek government deficit continued, even under severe cuts in public spending. By 2013, there was still a government deficit of nine billion euros (the difference between the budget of 94 billion and the tax revenues of 85 billion). The 'feed-back-loop' of tax policy is the critical loop for sound government policy versus unsound government fiscal policy. *If over time, tax revenues cannot support needed government services, then the financial system of a nation will be unstable in the long run.*

Conclusion

Although we have discussed the IMF focus upon the net exports (exports minus imports), there was a similar macro-balance in the minds of many economists as relevant to the Euro-dollar fiscal crisis. This was the current-account balances in the EU countries. For example about current-account balances, Martin Wolf wrote: "Indeed, the single most important lesson of the crisis is that the balance of payments continues to matter just as much within a currency union as outside one.... Once a country inside a currency union becomes dependent on large net capital inflows, a sudden turnaround in these flows will cause an economic crisis. Such a crisis will be marked by a financial shock, as external funding is withdrawn, and a deep recession, as the imports on which the economy had come to rely can no longer be financed." (Wolf 2014) This again describes the economic result of a 'front-loaded' austerity policy, as earlier emphasized by (Roubini 2014)

A current account balance of a nation is earnings on foreign investments minus payments made to foreign investors. In 2007, the current-account-balances-as-percentages-of GDP of the crisis EU nations were negative (with Greece a negative 14.4 %, Portugal a negative 10.1 %, and Spain a negative 10.0 %). In contrast, the EU nations not in crisis had positive balances (with Germany with a positive 7.5 %, Netherlands positive 6.7 %, Finland positive 4.3 %, Austria positive 4.1 %, Belgium positive 1.6 %, and the close-to-crisis France had a small negative balance of 1.0 %).

Some economists have focused upon current-account-balances as a primary explanation of the Euro-Dollar crisis. Martin Wolf is an example, and he wrote: "These huge current-account surpluses and deficits can be viewed in three mutually consistent ways. First, they reflected private-sector capital flows towards what were mistakenly believed to be higher-return opportunities in more dynamic economies, such as construction in Spain.... The second way in which the current-account deficits and surpluses can be viewed is as an excess of income over spending—or a surplus of savings over investment—in surplus countries and the opposite in deficit countries.... Because they are jointly determined, it is logically impossible to say that countries in deficit are responsible for their plight while those in surplus are guiltless.... The third way is that the surpluses and deficits reflected strengthening external competitiveness in surplus countries and declining competitiveness in deficit countries. Real unit labor costs in the former group of countries, especially in Germany, stagnated and real unit labor costs in the latter soared from the beginning of the euro." (Wolf 2014)

Competitiveness is one of the main reasons why current-account balances are seen as decisive factors in a financial crisis. Although Martin Wolf did not approve of the EU austerity policy, yet competitiveness was (the third way, 'productivity') was still prominent in Wolf's explanation of the crisis. Wolf assumed that labor costs are an important factor in economic competitiveness; but as we earlier noted, because of automation, labor cost in modern manufacturing is not significant for productivity. In a manufacturing firm, labor cost more impacts 'profits' than 'competitiveness'. This does not mean that nations need not be economically competitive. They do need to be competitive; but also they need to have a government which 'lives within national means'. Year after year after year, governments should not use foreign borrowing to pay for current services, covering over continuous budget deficits. Tax policy is an important factor for national fiscal policy and needs first to be attended. But in the macro-economic explanations of EU economists, the high-cost of labor had been focused upon again and again—assuming high wages causes low productivity.

Particularly when in a time of fiscal crisis, unemployment by itself cannot create a positive current-account-balance, as unemployment may not only lower prices but also reduces demand. Reduction in aggregate demand by unemployment is recognized by economists; as for example, Martin Wolf also wrote: "A clash … arises within this low-inflation Eurozone, between improving competitiveness and managing the debt overhang. This is because a rapid restoration in competitiveness of countries like Italy or Spain requires falling wages and prices. But falling wages and prices also raise the real burden of debt. The relatively high interest rates on both private and public debt that characterize these economies make the problem of managing debt even harder. This is 'debt deflation'—a condition in which debtors are forced to save an ever higher share of their incomes in order to pay down debt, because the latter's real value is rising over time." (Wolf 2014) Certainly, it is difficult for labor to save 'an ever higher share of their incomes in order to pay down debt' when they have no income as unemployed workers. A share of 'zero' is still zero. But Martin Wolf, an outstanding financial reporter, knows this; as all economists know that any share of zero is still zero. Thus why the continual economic references to 'productivity' as an explanation for the Euro-crisis in Greece? This has been particularly striking, since the principle reason for the Greek negative current-account-balance was not due to 'productivity' but to government 'profligacy' (continuous unbalanced government budgets, even in good economic times, funded by sovereign bond issues).

Perhaps, the fiscal policy focus on productivity has occurred because the variables of 'employment', 'competiveness', 'productivity' (while important aspects of macro-fiscal policy) have seldom appeared in fiscal models (such as the Polak model). And this kind of fiscal policy issue still needs to be addressed. Who benefits from and who pays for a fiscal austerity policy? As an example of economists who do emphasize employment, Paul Krugman discussed this: "So is the 'austerian' impulse all a matter of psychology? No, there's also a fair bit of self-interest involved. As many observers have noted, the turn away from fiscal and monetary stimulus can be interpreted, if you like, as giving creditors priority over workers. Inflation and low interest rates are bad for creditors even if they promote job creation; slashing government deficits in the face of mass unemployment may deepen a depression, but it increases the certainty of bondholders that they'll be repaid in full. I don't think someone like Trichet was consciously, cynically serving class interests at the expense of overall welfare; but it certainly didn't hurt that his sense of economic morality dovetailed so perfectly with the priorities of creditors. It's also worth noting that while economic policy since the financial crisis looks like a dismal failure by most measures, it hasn't been so bad for the wealthy. Profits have recovered strongly even as unprecedented long-term unemployment persists; stock indices on both sides of the Atlantic have rebounded to pre-crisis highs even as median income languishes. It might be too much to say that those in the top 1 % actually benefit from a continuing depression, but they certainly aren't feeling much pain, and that probably has something to do with policymakers' willingness to stay the austerity course." (Krugman 2013) Although in 2011, European banks holding Greek bonds did have to take a 'hair cut', a 50 % loss in the value of the bonds. Yet from 2011 to 2015, the result of debt was transfer the holding of Greek debt from private banks to Troika banking.

Here are two kinds of public and private interests, of which any policy formulated upon a macro-economic model needs to be aware. One 'private interest' is that of 'creditors' (bondholders), and another other 'private interest' is that of 'labor' (Greek employment). If the EU Troika identified the 'public interest' of the European Union as those of the 'creditors', then EU austerity policy was in the public interest of the EU. If, on the other side, the public interest of Greece lay in the private interest of Greek labor (employment), then EU austerity was not in the public interest of Greece. In the application of social science to policy, different private-public interests arise. (One notes that the economic measure of 'employment' did not appear in Polak's macro-economic model.) EU Troika policy appears to have focused more upon creditors benefit as the EU 'public good' than upon the Greek nation's employment as a 'public good'. *This implies that macro-economic models need to have explicit in their models the factors of 'employment' and 'fiscal responsibility'.*

Summary

Using a conceptual model to depict underlying economic policy is important to clarify the validity or invalidity of the model assumptions upon which a policy rests. We have compared the macro-economic Polak model to an alternative model of the Greek fiscal crisis as 'disequilibrium-pricing' in financial markets. An empirically invalid model can suggest bad policy, which may not solve an economic problem but can even deepen a crisis. An empirically valid model can provide a realistic basis for formulating effective policy. This research highlighted the deficiency of an economic model, which might have been used in justifying macro-economic fiscal policies of the European Union in dealing with the Greek Fiscal Crisis. The Polak model was a model focused on macro-exchange-rate policy. The disequilibrium-systems model is focused on macro-fiscal policy. The fiscal crisis in Greece was not one of monetary-exchange-rate but one of fiscal policy. The disequilibrium-systems model is more empirically-valid for the Greek Euro-dollar crisis. The two different models underpin different economic policies. The Polak model led to an austerity policy which did not immediately solve the fiscal problem but only deepened the Greek fiscal crisis into unemployment, recession, and government instability. *An empirically-invalid economic model can influence bad economic policy, which can intensify and not solve an economic crisis.*

What kind of economic policy might have a disequilibrium-systems model suggested for fiscal policy? In the case of the Greek Euro Crisis, tax policy is more important than export–import measures for contributing to national financial stability. (But tax policy had not been sufficiently emphasized in the EU austerity program.) Therefore, there could have been an alternate policy to 'austerity' which would have emphasized making 'tax reform' the immediate focus—before cutting government employment and privatizing government services. A solution to the Greek fiscal crisis might lie in (1) immediate tax reform and anti-corruption measures, but (2) placing debt repayment into the future, and also (3) incurring no new fiscal indebtedness, even from the IMF. The solving of the problem of the enormous debt (of prior Greek governments) could have been 'kicked-down-the-road'. Instead of loaning more money to Greece (increasing the national debt), the EU might better have paid (subsidized) the interest-service on Greek debt, while also forbidding the Greek government to incur new debt from the bond market—even from the EU Central Bank, the World Bank and the IMF.

In fact, the opposite was occurring. The IMF loaned money to Greece and then insisted Greece pay it back, even while the Greek crisis continued. In April 2015, Greece and the EU Troika were still haggling over continuing the bailout, as the BBC News reported: "Greece has ordered its public sector bodies to hand over any reserve cash to help it meet a payment due to the International Monetary Fund (IMF). The country is running out of cash and must repay the IMF nearly €1bn in May… Negotiators are trying to strike a deal ahead of a meeting of eurozone finance ministers on Friday (24 April 2015). There are mounting fears that Greece could default on its debts and exit the eurozone. Prime Minister Alexis Tsipras urgently needs money to pay government salaries as well as the country's debt repayments…." (BBC News 2015) In May 2015, government continued to pay back IMF loans, while still teetering on bankruptcy.

So the EU policy was the opposite of what might have repaired the Greek fiscal situation. While structural reform was going on in Greece, the EU did not help Greece service its debt and loaned still more money to Greece—deepening a spiral of national debt, which can be impossible to climb out.

> *In contrast, a policy suggested by a disequilibrium-systems model would suggest differently—reform now and pay back debt later—when the reforms begin to work.*

Of course, Greece would have to cut government spending, but not immediately—if the EU had extended all debt over more time, paying thc interest on the Greek debt, until it could be 'restructured' and paid at a future debt. More immediate for Greece to begin to emerge from the fiscal crisis is the need for a complete overhaul of Greek government tax policy and an anti-corruption campaign. This could have gotten the budget into a current balance—as long as Greece did not have to, at the same time, service its enormous international debt.

A valid macro-fiscal model can suggest practical remedies to a fiscal crisis—and even help prevent such occurrence.

Joseph Stiglitz wrote: "As the Greek crisis proceeds to its next stage, Germany, Greece and the triumvirate of the International Monetary Fund, the European Central Bank and the European Commission (now better known as the troika) have all faced serious criticism. While there is plenty of blame to share, we shouldn't lose sight of what is really going on. I've been watching this Greek tragedy closely for 5 years, engaged with those on all sides. Having spent the last week in Athens talking to ordinary citizens, young and old, as well as current and past officials, I've come to the view that this is about far more than just Greece and the euro. Some of the basic laws demanded by the troika deal with taxes and expenditures and the balance between the two, and some deal with the rules and regulations affecting specific markets. What is striking about the new program (called "the third memorandum") is that on both scores it makes no sense either for Greece or for its creditors .... I believe strongly that the policies being imposed will not work, that they will result in depression without end, unacceptable levels of unemployment and ever growing inequality. But I also believe strongly in democratic processes—that the way to achieve whatever framework one thinks is good for the economy is through persuasion, not compulsion. The force of ideas is so much against what is being inflicted on and demanded of Greece. Austerity is contractionary; inclusive capitalism—the antithesis of what the troika is creating—is the only way to create shared and sustainable prosperity. For now, the Greek government has capitulated. Perhaps, as the lost half decade becomes the lost decade, as the politics get uglier, as the evidence mounts that these policies have failed, the troika will come to its senses. Greece needs debt restructuring, better structural reforms and more reasonable primary budget surplus targets. More likely than not, though, the troika will do what it has done for the last 5 years: Blame the victim." (Stiglitz 2015)

Under the austerity program, the firing of Greek government employees and reduction of government services had reduced the budget deficit (before debt service) to a 'budget surplus. This indicates that the reforms in the Greek government budget could pay for government operations, yet not still service debt. This is evidence that an alternative policy could have aimed at a budget-balancing-program in Greece—subsidizing debt service without adding new debt. And such an alternative policy would have been indicated by a disequilibrium dynamics model of Greek macro-fiscal policy. Yet the Troika policy was still to loan Greece more money, increasing Greece's debt load. Giving a country more debt when its basic problem is too much debt is not a practical solution.

References

BBC NEWS. (2012). Greek bank list editor Costas Vaxevanis acquitted. Retrieved November 1, 2012, from http://www.bbc.com/news/world-europe-20172516

BBC NEWS. (2015). Greece debt deal reforms will combat tax evasion. *BBC NEWS*. Retrieved February 22, 2015, from http://www.bbc.com/news/business-31574868

Betz, F. (2013). Macro and micro-economic policies in financial crises: Argentina 2000 and South Korea 1998. *Business and Management Research*, 2(4). Retrieved from www.sciedu.ca/bmr

Blyth, M. (2013). The austerity delusion: Why a bad idea won over the west. *Foreign Affairs*. Retrieved May/June, from http://www.foreignaffairs.com/articles/139105/mark-blyth/the-austerity-delusion

EU Brussels. (2011). *Conclusions of the Heads of State or Government of the Euro Area*. Brussels: European Union. Retrieved March 11, 2011, from http://www.consilium.europa.eu/uedocs/cms_data/docs/pressdata/en/ec/119809.pdf

Inman, P. (2012). Primary Greek tax evaders are the professional classes. *The Guardian*. Retrieved September 9, 2012, from http://www.theguardian.com/world/2012/sep/09/greece-tax-evasion-professional-classes?CMP=twt_gu

Krugman, P. (2013). How the case for austerity has crumbled. *The New York Review of Books*. Retrieved June 6, 2013 Issue, from http://www.nybooks.com/articles/archives/2013/jun/06/how-case-austerity-has-crumbled/

Lowen, M. (2012). Greek journalist Costas Vaxevanis on trial over bank list. *BBC NEWS*. Retrieved November 1, 2012, from http://www.bbc.com/news/world-europe-20163430

Nikolaos, A., Morse, A., & Tsoutsoura, M. (2010). *Tax evasion across industries: Soft credit evidence from Greece*. Chicago Booth Paper No. 12-25. University of Chicago Booth School of Business. Retrieved from http://ssrn.com/abstract=2109500

Polak, J. J. (1989). *Financial policies and development*. Paris: Organization for Economic Co-operation and Development.

Polyani, K. (1944). *The great transformation*. Boston: Beacon Press (reprinted in 2001).

Roubini, N. (2014). Fiscal policy. In G. A. Akerlof, O. J. Blanchard, D. Romer, & J. E. Stiglitz (Eds.), *What have we learned?* Cambridge, MA: International Monetary Fund, Massachusetts Institute of Technology.

Stiglitz, J. E. (2002). *Globalization and its discontents*. New York: W. W. Norton and Company.

Stiglitz, J. E. (2015). Greece, the sacrificial lamb. *New York Times*. Retrieved July 25, from http://www.nytimes.com/2015/07/26/opinion/greece-the-sacrificial-lamb.html?_r=0

Wolf, M. (2014). *The Shifts and the Shocks: What we've learned—and have still to learn—from the financial crisis*. London: Penguin Books.

Woods, N. (2006). *The globalizers: The IMF, the World Bank, and their borrowers*. Ithaca, NY: Cornell University Press.

Chapter 6
Financial Hegemony: Dutch Republic

Introduction

We have been examining the theory of instability in financial markets. Instability arises from the time dimension in financial markets—which allows for both current rents and future liquidity, in valuing the capital assets traded in a market. Since the value of a capital asset continues over time from purchase at time T_1 to sale at T_2, profitability can be increased by using debt to purchase the asset. The percentage of the purchase price financed by debt is called 'leverage'; and the higher the leverage the greater the profit. This allows 'speculation' in trading in the market, using higher and higher leverage to drive up the prices of assets in a 'hot' market. As speculators move from financing the purchase of an asset with conservative leverage to speculative leverage to Ponzi leverage, the financial market moves into a financial bubble, bursting in the 'Minsky moment' of Ponzi leverage. Leverage in private markets creates instability in stock and real estate markets; and leverage in government budgets creates national fiscal instability.

But what about a stable financial system? Given the endogenous nature of financial markets with an inherent tendency to instability, is it possible to construct a stable financial system? Yes, because historically there have been two periods in modern history, when stable financial systems have existed internationally. These were under the financial leadership of the Dutch Republic in the 1600s and the British Empire in the 1800s; and a stable international trading and currency system has been called a 'liberal financial hegemony'—'liberal' for freedom of trade across countries, 'financial' for an international currency, and 'hegemony' for national leadership in international trade and finance. We now review the concept of a liberal hegemon in international finance.

This political-economic concept of 'liberal hegemony' is a complicated idea. It is both economic and political; and it requires particular institutional requirements to implement and sustain its stability. By examining the historical periods in which liberal hegemony existed, we can learn about the interaction of economy

F. Betz, *Stability in International Finance*, SpringerBriefs in Economics,
DOI 10.1007/978-3-319-26760-9_6

and politics for the conditions of hegemony, and we can learn about the institutional requirements for a financial hegemony. In Europe, the first financial hegmon was established by the Dutch in the 1600s. Later in the 1700s, Great Britain began replacing the Netherlands as the 'liberal hegemon' in international trade and finance, maintaining that leadership through the 1800s. But it was the war of 1914 that destroyed Great Britain's place as financial leader. Britain had large war debts and a shrunken market, with one quarter of its male youth dead and not available to begin new families. Britain took its currency off the gold standard.

Although the U.S. might have inherited hegemonic leadership with its strong gold-backed 'dollar' after that First World War, yet a stock-market instability in the U.S. in 1929 broke the U.S. economic system—dropping the country into a decade-long depression in the 1930s. Europe soon followed in 1931 into a world depression. It was only after World War II that the US was capable of acting as the 'liberal hegemon' in international trade and finance. This was in competition against the USSR and other communist countries. But after the fall of the Soviet Union, the twenty-first century began as a new 'global economy', with no one nation able to act in the old tradition of a 'liberal hegemon'.

The contempory political-economic issue is whether an how a stable international financial system can be constructed, without any national liberal hegemon.

Dutch Financial Hegemony

Any economic theory of stability of international finance needs to be implemented in an institutional framework (or as sociologists would call this, in the 'institutionalization' of the system). Studies in economic history about 'hegemony' have provided a 'prototype' about the institutional framework need for financial stability. We review the history of how in the 1600s the Dutch created the first hegemony (leadership) of a stable international financial system; and the Dutch Republic was the center of international banking in Europe.

Andrew Sobel wrote: "Dutch finance came to dominate international commercial and financial relations in the 1600s and for most of the 1700s.... Financial innovations, fiscal responsibility, respect for property rights and contracts, and Dutch adherence to the rule of law engendered confidence in the Dutch system and thus contributed to an increasing return dynamic that brought new capital to the Dutch financial markets from domestic and foreign savers." (Sobel 2012) Before this in Europe, trade was impeded by the lack of 'good' money and the tendency of sovereigns to default on their debts to merchants (Fig. 6.1).

Sobel summarized Kindleberger's description of a 'liberal hegemon': "Kindleberger suggests that a political economy acting as the (financial) system leader provides five key collective goods: 'maintaining a relatively open market for distress goods, providing countercyclical, or at least stable, long-term lending; policing a relatively stable system of exchange rates; ensuring the coordination of

Fig. 6.1 Courtyard of the Amsterdam Stock Exchange in 1653 (By Emanuel de Witte, in the Museum Boijmans Van Beuningen)

macroeconomic policies; and acting as a lender of last resort by discounting or otherwise providing liquidity in financial crisis.... The historical record appears consistent with Kindleberger's explanation that the provision of collective goods (in the political operation of an international economic system) creates the essential scaffolding for productive liberal exchange and globalization of (economic trade)." (Sobel 2012) Sobel was emphasizing that financial history does provide evidence that an 'essential scaffolding' (a proper institutionalization of international finance) facilitates international trade. Such an 'essential scaffolding' for finance was constructed in the Dutch republic around a reliable currency, 'good money'. Good money needs the institutional features of the integrity of a central bank and a sound governmental fiscal policy

For a 'reliable currency', Sobel wrote about the financial innovation of the Bank of Amsterdam: "The creation of the Bank of Amsterdam by the provincial government of Holland helped address the currency confusion.... First, the provincial government minted and supported two good coinages, the guilder and stuiver, ... The Bank willingly served as a clearinghouse for currencies. It accepted deposits of any currency, ... assessed the gold and silver content of such currencies and gave the depositors an equivalent value in guilder and stuivers... The bank became a financial clearinghouse…. The guilder and stuiver became the preferred currency for international exchange." (Sobel 2012) Other currencies then in use were deposited in accounts of the Bank of Amsterdam and translated into the preferred 'guilder and stuiver'.

From Dutch history, we will see that the first requirement of a financial hegemon is to establish a 'reliable currency for international exchange'—good money universally accepted. Two institutional forms are needed to do this—banking integrity and a fiscally-prudent government.

Thus the second requirement for fiscal stability is for a government with a financially sound policy which practices a fair and sufficient taxation policy to fund public services. Sobel wrote: "Taxation affects a society's capacity to provide public services, such as national security, infrastructure… Taxation is an incredibly difficult task… Ultimately, a good tax system is one of the foundations of a hegemon's capacity to exercise leadership, as it is a means of extracting surplus and providing liquidity. … Productive taxation spills over into another critical aspect of public finance, borrowing by public authorities. It contributes to a government's ability to borrow by providing a mechanism to finance debt, adding to a government's credibility in its promises to repay its debt obligations. Even successful governments face emergencies…, such as a war, that are too immense to pay-as-you-go, in the short term." (Sobel 2012)

A financially-sound government is needed to mint 'good' money (good in the sense that 'bad' money drives out good); and a central-bank must act as an honest clearing house for good money.

Trade and the Cities of the Low Countries

Since history is instructive but not repetitive, one needs to understand the unique economic and political situation in which the Dutch Republic came to establish the financial innovations of a central bank and fiscally-sound government, both of which are needed for stable financial systems.

The history of the Netherlands (Low Countries) is a complicated history. In the mid-1500s, there were 17 provinces, ruled by but enjoying some autonomy under the Hapsburg Emperor, Charles V. But when inherited by Charles's son, Phillip II, the provinces rebelled and united against the Spanish Hapsburg rule and gained independence after 50 years of war. It was in rebellion that the Dutch methods of government, commerce and finance developed. In the rebellion, the provinces developed self-governance and a political-economics infrastructure around 'mercantile interests'. Sobel wrote: "By the mid-1500s, the Dutch were already one of the more industrious and commercially busy societies in Europe. Cities in the Hapsburg Netherlands were some of the most densely populated in Europe and the inhabitants among the best educated, but the Dutch lacked significant agricultural capacity and natural resources…." (Sobel 2012)

What had made the provinces unique in Europe was that they had a different feudal history than most provinces in medieval Europe, having developed principally as independent cities based upon trade. Those provinces constitute now the modern nations of Netherlands, Belgium and Luxembourg. But in the Middle Ages, they were called the 'Low Countries' and were small territories around cities, politically recognized as duchies, counties, or bishoprics; and they were under the rule of the Holy Roman Empire (with the exception of the county of Flanders under the Kingdom of France).

The Low Countries were trading centers in northern Europe. Maarten Prak wrote: "Since the twelfth century, Flanders and later Brabant had been developing into the most important commercial centres in north-west Europe. In Bruges, Italian merchants sold luxury goods such as spices and silk, which they acquired from their agents in the Middle East. At first such trade was conducted overland, and merchants met at the annual fairs held in the Champagne region of France. From around 1300, however, there was also a direct maritime route between Bruges and the most important centres of trade in Italy of Venice and Genoa. These trade routes encouraged the emergence of industrial centres which developed in such cities as Bruges and Ghent. In the Flemish countryside as well, spinning and weaving thrived and provided exports. The Flemish textile centres also functioned as processing points for English cloth, imported as semi-finished goods to Flanders, there to be dressed and dyed and finally sold. It was this finishing stage in the manufacturing process that yielded the greatest profits." (Prak 2005)

The environmental conditions of the Low Countries encouraged the development of trade as a livelihood complementary to agriculture. There were many waterways to transport goods, facilitating trade. Some of the provinces, such as Holland, lands were too wet to grow grain, needing imports of wheat. Moreover, land was built from the marches by draining them. The land reclamation had begun in the middle ages and by the 1600s, a large portion of the western lands were new land. Maarten Prak wrote: "The grain trade, which now became the lifeblood of the Dutch economy, had not been a viable alternative before the fourteenth century, when the high cost of transport had limited long-distance trade mainly to luxury products, which combined small volume with large profits. Many areas of the Republic were self-supporting, meaning that most of their food came from the surrounding countryside (except for Holland)…At first Holland acquired its grain from adjoining regions in the Low Countries: Zeeland, and probably Utrecht and Gelderland as well, shipped their surpluses to Holland. England and especially northern France were equally important suppliers. Finally, there was the Baltic, which in the mid-fifteenth century was a relatively minor source of grain—though the Hollanders were involved in Scandinavian wars aimed at keeping the Danish Sound open to their shipping traffic—since at least three and perhaps even four times as much grain was imported from France…(In contrast) agriculture in Zeeland had been highly commercialised since the Middle Ages…(but) farming in Zeeland was far from easy. Maintenance of the seawalls was costly, the groundwater was often brackish, and frequent shortages of drinking water made it difficult to breed cattle. The profitability of farming in this region was boosted, however, by the proximity of urban markets." (Prak 2005)

Thus agriculture was not a profitable economic basis for the Low Countries, with much land reclaimed from marshes and ocean. Trade became the major economic activity of the 17 provinces even in the middle ages. For example in Flanders, trade in wool with England became its basis for the growth of it cities. Weavers made light woolen goods from imported English wool which was widely traded in Europe. In turn, Flanders exported French wine to England.

Next in the 1400s, a new ocean technology was innovated in the south of Europe by the Portuguese, a boat called the caravel. The caravel changed the trade routes between Europe and the Mediterranean and then between Europe and the world. The caravel was designed by Portuguese ship makers to sail in the Atlantic, adapted from the form of the Portuguese fishing boats. It has a high stern to sail down-wind in a following sea, and it had a lateen sail to sail to windward. In 1451, Prince Henry the Navigator of Portugal funded its design to voyage around Africa to the East Indies. Its purpose was to enable Portugal to engage in the spice trade.

Until then spices reached Europe, transported by the Arabs to the Mediterranean and then sold to Viennese traders for sale in Europe. Maarten Prak wrote: "Since the discovery of a direct sea route to the East Indies and the European conquest of Central and South America, the focal point of international trade had shifted more and more from the Mediterranean to the Atlantic. Until that time, the cities of Italy had been the arrival point of spices coming from the Middle East, which were then shipped by land or sea to the other markets of Europe. Shortly after 1500, Antwerp became the official entrepôt for Portuguese spices, which meant that all spices shipped by Portugal from the East Indies were first unloaded at Antwerp and then transported to other parts of Europe. By the mid-sixteenth century, Antwerp was handling around 80 % of all the trade conducted by the Habsburg Netherlands." (Prak 2005) (Fig. 6.2)

Fig. 6.2 Caravela de armada of João Serrão in 1502 and a Brazillian Navy copy of a caravel

Friesland and Flanders had evolved as centers of trade; and in the 1300s, also the country of Holland developed as center of trade, focused upon shipping. By the late 1400s, Holland had one of the largest merchant fleets in Europe. By 1600, Dutch traders operated worldwide, to the East Indies for spices and to the West Indies for sugar. The trade was organized in a corporate form, with the Dutch East India Company founded in 1602, and the Dutch West India Company in 1621. In January of 1609, the Amsterdam Exchange Bank was founded to facilitate the financing of Dutch trading. Thus the history of the Low Countries were in trade and in the merchants operating and financing the trade.

History of the Politics and Cities of the Low Countries

In the history of the financial innovations of the Dutch Republic, both economy and politics were important. We next briefly review the politics.

In the 1400s, the cities of the Low Countries began having periodic meetings of their provincial states, including the largest cities of Dordrecht, Haarlem, Delft, Gouda, Leiden and Amsterdam. But there were conflicts, as Maarten Prak wrote: "Gelderland endangered the transport of goods to Holland via the Zuider Zee, which was the only supply route serving all the cities to the north of Amsterdam. This threat was underscored in 1508, 1517 and 1528 when troops from Gelderland made predatory raids through Holland. The Habsburgs were in a position to do something about this, but only at a price." (Prak 2005)

The price of peace between the provinces was in Charles V taking control of the Netherlands. He suppressed quarrels among the provinces but also raised taxes. Maarten Prak wrote: "In 1521–1523, Holland lent aid to the (Hapsburgs') campaigns in Friesland, and in 1527–1528, when it assisted in the capture of Utrecht, Holland's contribution to the central coffers in Brussels rose to fourfold that of a normal year. Around the mid-sixteenth century, Holland was paying 10–15 times more to Charles V's war budget than it had 30 years before." (Prak 2005) The price that the Hapsburgs extracted to bring peace among the Dutch provincial states was sovereignty; and with sovereignty came taxes.

In 1549 Charles had consolidated his rule over the provinces, issuing the law of the 'Pragmatic Sanction', which proclaimed all the 17 Low Country provinces under his rule. Charles' tax burdens on the provinces were significant. Maarten Prak wrote: "The tax burden increased dramatically and , with it, complaints were voiced by the citizens (especially the merchants and entrepreneurs who held most of the power in the cities and were witnessing the erosion of their competitive position). In an effort to alleviate the tax burden, the States of Holland developed a new debt instrument, the annuity bond, in which the local elites avidly invested. This gave rise in the cities to an awareness, largely lacking until this time, of common interests and responsibilities." (Prak 2005) Thus the perception of unity among the Low Country provinces increased under the tax burdens of their rule by the Hapsburgs; and in this unity a new debt instrument was invented by Holland, the annuity bond. (This is an example of phenomenon in 'political economy'—the intersection of economics and political science.)

In 1555, Charles abdicated and gave the Netherlands to his son, Phillip II. About the transition of rule from Charles to his son, Maarten Prak wrote: "On Friday, 25 October, at around 3 o'clock in the afternoon, an important gathering was convened at Brussels. Representatives of the 17 provinces of the Netherlands had been summoned to the palace to assemble in the great hall .... When the guests of honor had taken their places, the door to the hall opened and Emperor Charles V hobbled in, leaning on the arm of William, the young prince of Orange. They were followed by Charles's son, Philip II, and the emperor's sister, Mary of Hungary, regent of the Netherlands. Even though Charles was only 55 years old, he could barely walk without support. Born in Ghent in 1500, he had been forced at the age of 15 to assume the reins of government, not only of the Netherlands but also of the Spanish and Austrian possessions of the House of Habsburg. King of Spain since 1516 and Holy Roman Emperor since 1519, Charles V had been compelled to crisscross Europe dozens of times, waging war repeatedly at the head of his troops. Charles had not succeeded in suppressing the Reformation, which had broken out at the beginning of his reign, nor in restoring the authority of the Catholic Church. Deeply disillusioned and plagued by gout and other ailments, Charles, decided that he could rule no longer and abdicated in favor of his son Philip." (Prak 2005) (Fig. 6.3)

Fig. 6.3 Portrait of Charles V by Lambert Sustris (in Alte Pinakothek in Munich) and Portrait of Phillip II of Spain by Sofonisba Anguissola (in Prado Museum in Madrid)

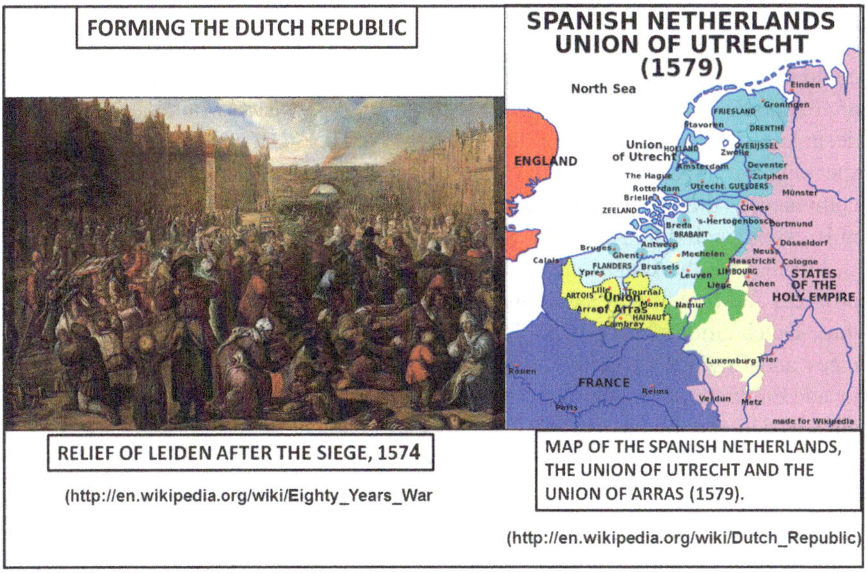

Fig. 6.4 Painting of relief of Leiden by Otto van Veen (in the Reijksmuseum, Netherlands) and map of the Spanish Netherlands in 1579

Charles V had been born in Ghent and identified with the Netherlanders (Low Countries). But Phillip II had been born and raised in Spain, not identifying with the Netherlanders. He used force to control the Spanish Netherlands. Also he felt justified in using force, as the merchants were heretics, adopting Protestantism while the Spanish remained catholic. For both religious and economic reasons, both nobles and merchants of the Netherlands wished to throw off Spanish rule.

One rebellious Dutch noble was William of Orange. Although he had been born in Germany, he had a noble title (Duke of Orange) inherited from a French province. He possessed estates in Holland, Brabant, and Luxemburg; and he identified as a Netherlander, leading the revolt against the Spanish. In 1579, some of the northern provinces united and signed the 'Union of Utrecht'; and in 1581, they passed an 'Act of Abjuration', declaring independence from Philip II, after 25 years of his rule (Fig. 6.4).

With 10,000 Spanish troops, Philip sent the Duke of Alba to crush the rebellion. Alba prosecuted rebels, sentencing 1000 people to death and confiscating their estates and wealth. But he was not able to capture William of Orange. Alba levied new taxes and billeted his soldiers in Dutch homes, treating all Netherlanders as heretics. When the town of Mechelen rebelled, it was captured and plundered by Spanish troops, and all of the inhabitants of Mechelen were slaughtered.

The protestant northern provinces next asked the Duke of Anjou (the younger brother of the King of France) to be formally the ruler of the Dutch States General, formally rejecting Phillip's authority over the States. The Duke of Anjou had no real authority over the Dutch States General and also happened to die 3 years later.

Meanwhile the provinces of Holland and Zeeland had given the reins of their government to William of Orange, as 'stadholder'. (In the middle ages, a stadholder could manage an estate for a noble but did not feudally rule the estate.) But a month after Anjou's death, William of Orange also died of a gunshot wound; and William's death left a leadership crisis for the rebellious Netherlanders. Next from the French-speaking provinces in the south (Walloon provinces), the Duke of Parma assumed command, as the highest representative of the Spanish king. Parma conquered cities in Brussels, including Antwerp.

In England, the Protestant Queen Elizabeth worried about the Catholic Parma's progress and brutality in subduing the Dutch. She sent English troops to assist the three Dutch cities of Vlissingen, Rammekens and Den Griell. Then the Dutch provinces and England formally formed a Protestant Alliance, and Spain decided to invade England. In the summer of 1588, Phillip's Spanish Armada sailed to England but was defeated by the English fleet and bad weather.

In 1590, Phillip next ordered Parma to attack France; but Parma's forces were too few to battle both the Dutch Netherlands and France. Maurits, the son of William of Orange, led the Dutch, taking back cities, such as Zutphen, Deventer, Steenwijk, Coevorden, Geetriuidenberb, and Groningen. But he still faced Spanish troops in Newupoort and was almost defeated there. The struggle between Spain and the Dutch Republic continued until 1609, when finally a 12 year truce was signed.

About the condition of the Netherlands in 1609, Maartem Pak summarized: "In 1609, at the beginning of the 12 Years' Truce, the young Republic was still a country with a split personality. The coastal provinces, which were experiencing spectacular economic growth, were overrun with immigrants, fleeing the violence elsewhere or in search of a better life. Ever since the Spanish had vacated Geertruidenberg after the Dutch recaptured it in 1593, the violence of war had been nothing more than a frightening memory and a financial burden to the people of Holland. The inhabitants of Friesland and Zeeland could also reckon themselves safe. In the inland provinces, however, people were still suffering from the ravages of war. Twente was in Spanish hands and would remain so for years to come. Groenlo was still Spanish, whereas the rest of the county of Zutphen had already surrendered to the States General.... The west had made an amazingly quick recovery from the trauma of war. Leiden's textile industry had been in serious trouble before the Revolt, but by 1586 the civic authorities were already worrying about the housing shortage. Between 1582 and 1609 the population of Leiden had tripled, owing mainly to the immigration of textile workers and manufacturers from Flanders... The population of Amsterdam, like that of Leiden, had grown sharply, increasing from over 30,000 in 1585 to approximately 70,000 in 1609. Here, too, the influx of immigrants had been the main cause of the population explosion." (Prak 2005)

Dutch Republic Financial Innovations

Thus it was in the 'forge of war' that the Dutch provinces formed themselves into a mercantile nation, creating a financial structure to lead in finance and trade—a liberal hegemon—leadership in free trade and sound finances. After independence, the Dutch would extend their empire into Southeast Asia and the new world of the Americas. Earlier we noted that a significant Dutch innovation was a central bank, the Bank of Amsterdam. Sobel wrote: "All modern political economies… have some organization (a central bank) that acts as a lender-of-last-resort for its economy….(A central bank) develops a reliable currency that others in the system are willing to use as an international transactional currency to settle accounts across national borders (or hold as a storehouse of value over time)…." (Sobel 2012)

We recall also that Sobel emphasized that both public and private institutions are needed for financial leadership by a nation. Sobel wrote: "A hegemon's private financial markets are critical to the accumulation, formation, and reallocation of capital that underpins the pro-cyclical provision of liquidity in the system. This liquidity promotes new economic enterprise and the creation of employment….To sit at the hub of a network of global finance, a political economy must be relatively porous to international flows of capital….Amsterdam emerged at the heart of a (financial) network….The relative transparency, predictability, efficiency, reliability, and adherence to the rule-of-law by Dutch governance and finance engendered confidence in Dutch financial markets and merchants." (Sobel 2012)

Thus in Sobel's description of the financial hegemony in the Dutch Republic, one sees the need for both public and private institutional partnerships and rules for system performance (with 'transparency, predictability, efficiency, reliability, and rule-of-law'). We depict this in the graphic form of societal dynamics, Fig. 6.5.

GROUP—The groups involved in the events were the Dutch Provincial Government and the Bank of Amsterdam. Also classes of Dutch merchants, peasants, and leaders brought together to oppose foreign governance and establish a prosperous trading society.

PROCESS—The process involved was establishing a liberal hegemony for Holland in international finance and trade.

ACTION—The actions occurred during the Dutch rebellion from Spanish rule. They included the creation of a fair and stable tax base in the Dutch Netherlands provincial governments. Also the Dutch Provincial Government minted good currency. The Bank of Amsterdam was established as a financial clearing house.

REASON—The reasoning of the Dutch were (1) to create a sound tax base to fund the wars of overthrowing Spanish rule and (2) to create a sound financial system for facilitating Dutch trade and a merchant class.

SOCIETY—The societies involved were the provinces of the Netherlands, which united into the Dutch nation.

INDIVIDUAL—Individuals involved were the Charles V and Phillip of Spain. William of Organge an his son, Marutis, and the Elizabeth I, Queen of England.

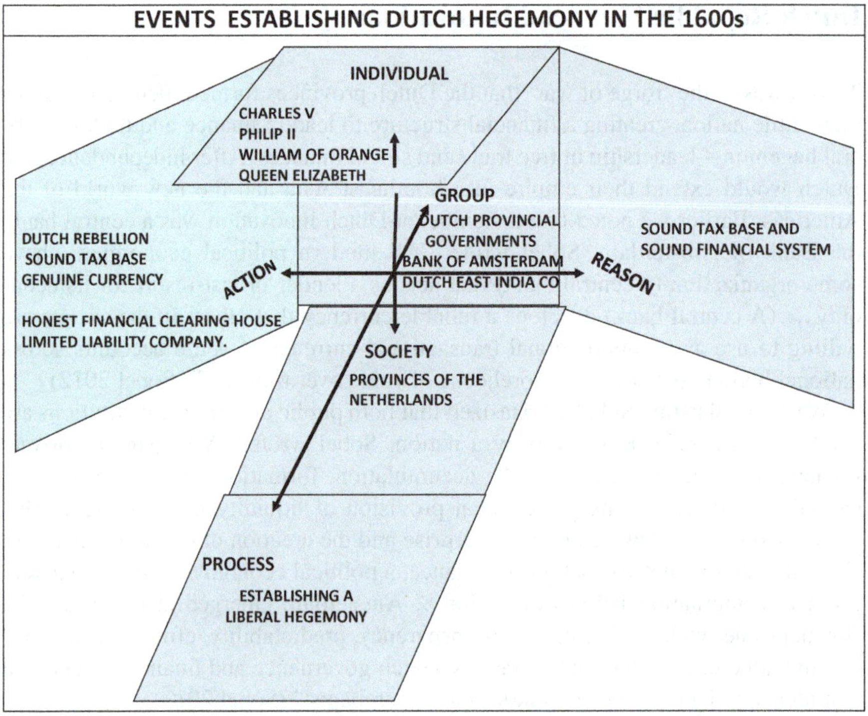

Fig. 6.5 Events establish Dutch hegemony

Historical Lesson of the Dutch Hegemony

What this perceptual-space-analysis of the event of financial innovation in the Dutch Republic emphasizes are two major points about the historical context.

1. The political and economic contexts of the formation of the Dutch Republic occurred with the merchant-trader class as the dominant group in the political activities; and the political unity in the group was forged in the opposition to Spanish rule and taxation;
2. The two financial innovations (of central banks to ensure sound currency and of appropriate taxation to ensure sound national fiscal policy) were invented by the merchant-trader class.

It takes two kinds of societal factors in group processes to accomplish both a political union and a financial progress—political unity and merchant experience (politics and economics). The historical lesson in this is that the merchant class is the key to reform (innovation) for economic progress—due to the depth their experience in trade. This economic experience of 'trade' focuses financial innovation upon 'private good' of merchants in earning profits. However, the political experience of 'unity' focuses financial innovation upon the 'public good' of effectiveness and justice in government. In the war against foreign rule and taxation, the merchant-trader group were motivated to tax themselves sufficiently to fund their war for liberation. Unless there is a political reason for unity, a group such as the merchant-trader class will most likely emphasize only the private-good of their actions and not the public-good.

Groups which are not bound together in political union (public good) and devoted to the effectiveness of economic activity (private good) are hindered in achieving both public justice and private wealth.

This political unity among the merchants focused the group upon the public good as well as their private good. For their public good, they regulated their currency as 'good money' supervised by a central bank.

Institutional Control of Financial Innovation

We can next use the societal perceptual space to analysis the system conditions for the Dutch hegemon of the 1600s. The connections between the dimensional factors form a graph with 15 kinds of explanations in historical events, Fig. 6.5. Partitioning the societal graph into upper and lower pyramids identifies the kinds of system control possible in a societal event: (1) control of managed systems, (2) control of socio-technical systems, and (3) control of self-organizing systems. See Betz (2012) (Fig. 6.6).

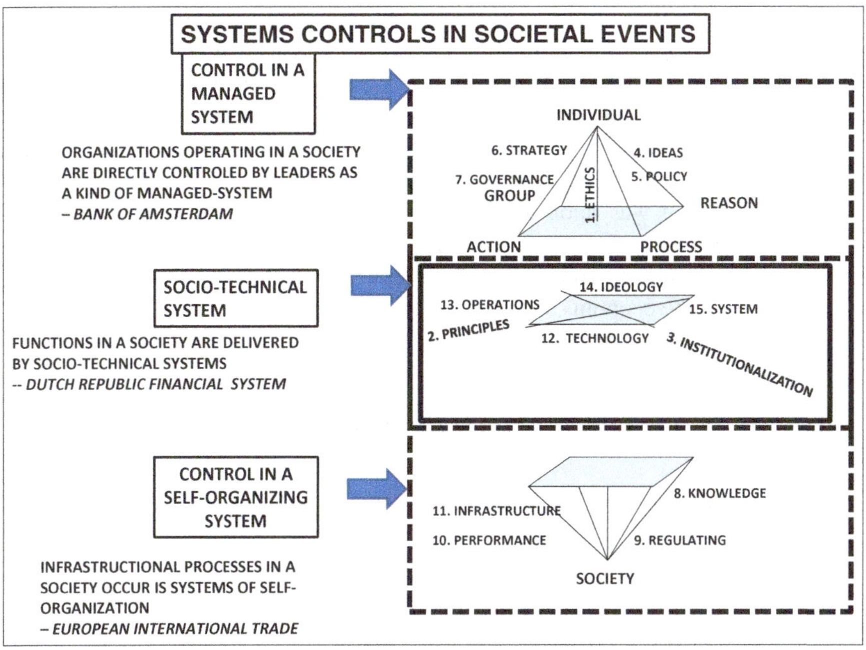

Fig. 6.6 Kinds of control systems in a society

An analysis of a society in terms of control processes in the society distinguishes three kinds of control: control of organizations as a manage system, control of a functional system as a socio-technical system, and control of self-organization infrastructures in a society. For a full description of this approach to societal control see (Betz 2011).

Since two organization are important to the explanation of Dutch hegemony, we will graphically analyze this event with two managed systems (Dutch government and Bank of Amsterdam), and a self-organizing system of the Dutch economy, Fig. 6.7.

A financially-sound-government needs a sufficient and fair tax base to finance public needs, create fiscal credibility, and issue sound money. A central bank needs to act as an honest clearing house for private financial transactions. This graphic analysis emphasizes that three kinds of systems were involved: (1) a public financial system of the Dutch provinces, (2) a private financial system around the Bank of Amsterdam, and (3) an international financial system, in which the Bank of Amsterdam played a role of a national central bank.

Managed System Control in the Dutch Government

The *Groups* involved in the Dutch Republic were *provincial governments* of the Netherlands provinces. The *Individuals* involved in managing the government were *Dutch officials*. Their *Reasons* principally thought about upon facilitating *trade*. The *strategy* of the Dutch government officials was to attain national *independence*. Their *ideas* focused government as a *rule-of-law*; and their *policies* focused upon *fairness*. Their *Action* was to level sufficient *taxes* to finance their war of independence; and a means of increasing government revenue was through the *Process* of issuing *sovereign bonds*. The function of the government socio-technical system *operated* by issuing *currency* in a *system* of *public finance*. The *principles* of the currency operation was upon a *gold standard*, so that Dutch money was 'good money'. The *technology* of issuing money was *minting* coin. And the *institutionalization* of the finance was through a representative *parliament*. The *ideology* of the government for the economy was efficient *capitalism*.

Managed System Control in the Bank of Amsterdam

The *Group* involved was the *Bank of Amsterdam*. The *Individuals* involved in managing the bank were *bank officials*. Their *Reason* principally were thoughts about upon facilitating *profits* in trading. The *strategy* of the bank officials was to ensure *transparency* in financial *transactions*. Their *ideas* focused on honest transactions; and their *policies* focused upon *exchange*. Their *Action* was to facilitate *financial transactions*, through the *Process* of facilitating *private lending*. The function of the

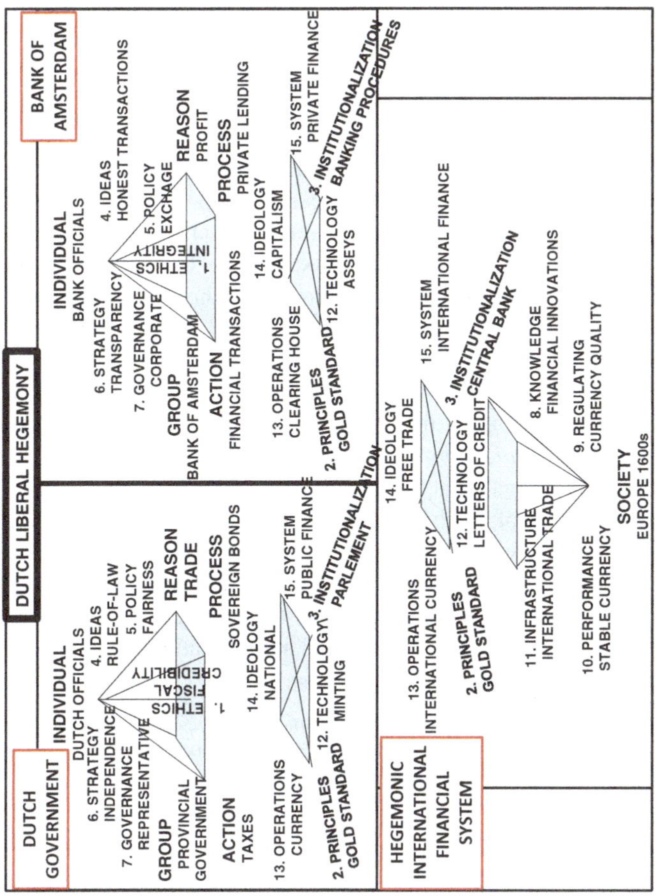

Fig. 6.7 Control analysis of the institution of the Dutch liberal hegemony

bank socio-technical system *operated* as a *clearing house* for private financial transactions. The *principles* of the clearing house was to maintain a *gold standard* in the different currencies deposited in the bank. The *technology* of recording the value of currency was *assaying* money for gold content. And the *institutionalization* of the clearing house operation was through establishing proper *banking procedures*. The *ideology* of the bank about finance was for an efficient *capitalism*.

Self-Organizing System Control of Finance-Trade in the Dutch Republic

The *Society* impacted by Dutch hegemonic financial system involved *European states in the 1600s*; and the *infrastructure* of the self-organization was *international trade*. The *performance* of the financial infrastructure provided *stable currency. Regulation* of currency exchanges by the clearing house operations of the Bank of Amsterdam established the *quality of the different monetary coins*. The *knowledge* involved in establishing Dutch financial hegemony were *financial innovations* to establish a sound international currency, good money. The *operations* of the self-organizing international financial system involved the use of an *international currency* (guilders); of which the currency value was based upon the *principles* of a *gold standard*. The *institutionalization* of the system of international finance occurred through the clearing house operations of a *central bank* (Bank of Amsterdam). The *technology* of financial transactions used *letters-of-credit* issued by private banks; and the *ideology* of the self-organizing international financial system was to facilitate international *free trade*.

One sees in this 'control' analysis of the Dutch Liberal Hegemony of Finance, is that international financial control was not a single nor simple issue. Instead societal control of international finance in required several kinds of cooperating controls—a set of properly interacting controls between the managed systems of the Dutch Government and the Bank of Amsterdam and an international self-organizing system of international trade.

Control for the stability and integrity of an international financial system is a complicated issue involving not a single institution but a set of institutions and policies—government fiscal policies, national central bank policies, and a stable international currency.

Summary

We recall that Sobel argued that 'institutional foundations' are necessary for a stable international financial system. Sobel wrote: "The following micro-foundations are critical to the ability to provide such collective services: (1) a political economy's governance arrangements, (2) its public and private financial arrangements,

(3) credibility of those arrangements, and (4) development of a global financial network around those arrangements." (Sobel 2012) The graphic analysis clarifies the following points:

1. The *governance* arrangements of the Dutch political economy as the provincial governments of the Netherlands in the 1600s,
2. Public financial arrangements in the form of *taxes* and *currency* of the Dutch Provincial Government and the private financial arrangements of the Bank of Amsterdam as a *clearing house* for transactions,
3. The *fiscal credibility* of the government public finance and the *integrity* of bank private finance in their *respective Ethics*, and
4. The development of a *self-organizing hegemonic international financial system*.

   The graphic analysis adds more necessary institutional connections:

5. Proper *governance* in a nation for hegemonic leadership, in terms of a *strategy* of independence, *ideas* of a rule-of-law, and *policies* for fairness,
6. Proper fiscal responsibility in public finance, in terms of the need for *adequate taxes* and *representation* in assignment of taxes.
7. Proper *credibility* in public and private financial systems in terms of no government-debt defaults nor coinage debasement and also honest private financial transactions.
8. A system of international finance, based upon the *principles* of a gold standard with an international Dutch currency, whose quality was regulated by a 'central bank' of the Dutch government.

References

Prak, M. (2005). *The Dutch Republic in the seventeenth century: The golden age*. Cambridge: Cambridge University Press.

Sobel, A. C. (2012). *Birth of hegemony*. Chicago: University of Chicago Press.

Betz, F. (2011). *Societal Dynamics (New York, Springer, 2011)* ISBN 978-1-4614-1278-6.

Betz, F. (2012). Control in knowledge economies. *Journal of Knowledge Economy, 5*(4), 761–783. doi:10.1007/s13132-012-0100-0.

Chapter 7
Financial Hegemony: British Empire

Introduction

There is a second example in economic history of hegemony in international finance. After the Dutch Republic established a liberal hegemony in finance in the 1600s, they were replaced in the 1700s by the British Empire, which provided as subsequent stable financial system for international trade. Andrew Sobel wrote: "The British gradually replaced the Dutch as the commercial and financial hegemon, emerging at the center of the global political economy by the middle to late 1700s. The transition was relatively peaceful, at least between the Dutch and the British. The movement of surplus Dutch capital and Dutch financial skills and innovations to the financial markets in London were important contributors to London's becoming the preeminent international financial and commercial center. The baton of global leadership passed gradually during the 1700s, and British hegemony lasted until the First World War." (Sobel 2012)

The movement of capital and financial skills to the British was assisted by a major event in British history, the 'Glorious Revolution'. In 1688, William III of Orange (the great grandson of William of Orange who had led the revolt of the Spanish Netherlands from the Spanish Empire) invaded England, laying a claim to the English throne jointly with his wife, Mary, daughter of King James II. They deposed her father from the English throne.

English Throne: William and Mary

In 1685, James Stuart became the next King of England, James II, succeeding his brother King Charles II. But James II favored Catholicism and was disliked by Protestant English Parliament. In the Dutch Republic, William III of Orange was stadholder of the protestant Dutch Republic, and the Protestant Republic was at war

F. Betz, *Stability in International Finance*, SpringerBriefs in Economics,
DOI 10.1007/978-3-319-26760-9_7

Fig. 7.1 Prince of orange landing In England in 1688

with Catholic France. Before James' coronation, his daughter Mary had married William III. William's mother (also named Mary Stuart) had been the sister of James II and Charles II. Thus William had a claim to the British throne through his mother as daughter of Charles I; and his wife, Mary II, had a claim to the English throne as daughter to the present monarch, James II.

With the connivance of the British Parliament, William III planned to invade England and, with his wife, seize the British throne. In November 1688, William's Dutch army landed in England at Torbay (Fig. 7.1).

William III had been born in 1650 as the Prince of Orange of the House of Orange-Nassau. His great grandfather had been William of Orange, who led the Dutch rebellion against Phillip II of Spain. His grandfather was Frederick Henry of Orange; and his father was William II of Orange. In 1672 during the war in between the Dutch and the French, French forces overran the Dutch provinces of Gelderland and Utrecht. The Dutch army under William III retreated into Holland, had the Dutch flood the fields and stopped the French advance on the eighth of June in 1672. But a large French army still remained in the Dutch Republic, and States of Holland appointed William III as 'stadtholder' to lead the Republic. William III continued to battle the French, which had joined with James II as another catholic monarch. In 1673, the Dutch navy defeated a combined Anglo-French fleet attempting to invade Holland. And Charles II ended English participation in the Dutch-French war. Then Louis XIV of France withdrew French forces from Holland. William III was regarded by English protestants as a staunch opponent to catholic rulers, such as Louis XIV and James II.

Earlier William III had proposed to Mary Stuart, before James became King. Mary was William's cousin and 11 years younger. At the time, the King of England, Charles II (who was James brother), had approved of the match, and James yielded his consent. Charles II had become king of England after the protestant Oliver Cromwell had defeated his father, Charles I (and had him beheaded). After Cromwell's death, the English Parliament restored the throne to Charles' son, as Charles II. The condition of restoration was that Charles II was to act as a constitutionally-limited monarch and not try to restore the Catholic Church in England. But James II was perceived by Parliament as intent upon restoring Catholicism in England; and the English Parliament sided with William's claim to the throne. William's army defeated James' army, and James II fled England to France. Then Parliament passed a British law naming William III and his wife Mary as joint monarchs of England (Fig. 7.2).

We analyze the event of William and Mary's ascention, as shown in Fig. 7.3.

ACTION—The Dutch leader, William III marries Mary Stuart, the daughter of James Stuart. Later James becomes king of England. The Dutch fleet invades England, and James' forces are defeated by William's army, and James II flees England. The British Parliament passes a law, establishing William and Mary as joint constitutional monarchs of Britain.

Fig. 7.2 Portraits of William and Mary

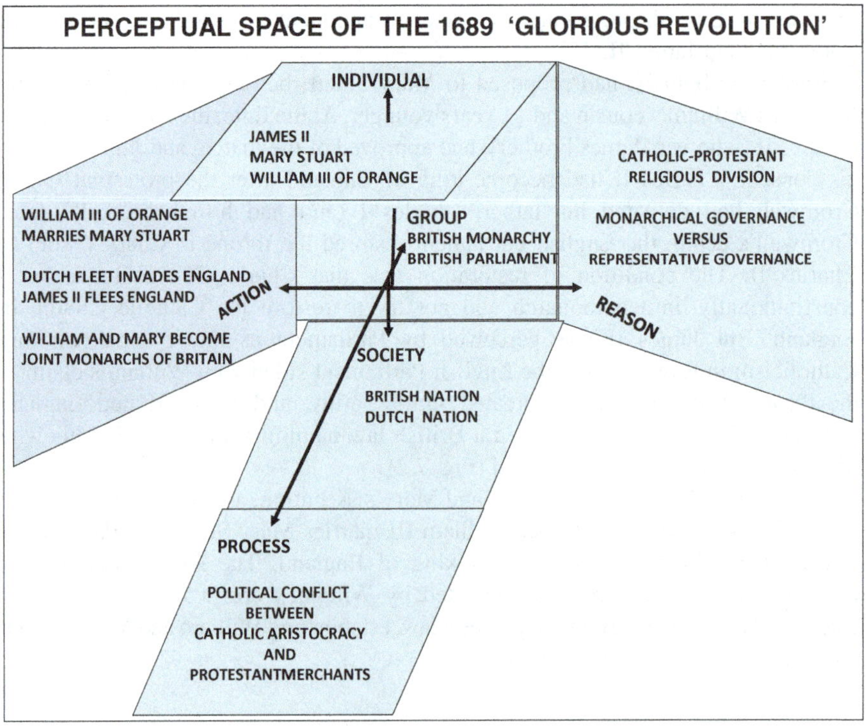

Fig. 7.3 Perceptual space of the English event of the 'Glorious Revolution'

REASON—There is ongoing religious conflict in Europe between Catholics and Protestants during the seventeenth and eighteenth centuries. And there is a conflict over governance in England in the seventeenth century about monarchical or representative governments—the Crown versus Parliament.

INDIVIDUALS—The individuals involved in the event were James II, King of England, his daughter, Mary Stuart, and her husband, William of Orange.

SOCIETY—The two societies involved were the British and Dutch nations.

GROUP—The two groups involved were the British Parliament versus the British Monarchy and the Catholic Aristocracy versus the Protestant Merchants.

PROCESS—The process was civil war in England between Parliament and Monarchy.

The reign of William & Mary assisted in the transfer of Dutch fiscal practices to Britain. Andrew Sobel wrote: "The Dutch conquest of the British Isles, the replacement of James II by William and Mary, and the Glorious Revolution brought important changes in the relationship between the Crown, Parliament and society. These changes… would empower reforms that transformed British governance, public and private finance, and the United Kingdom's position in the global arena." (Sobel 2012)

British Financial Hegemony

Over the eighteenth century (1700s), financial hegemony in Europe transferred from the Dutch to the British. There were three interacting factors for this financial success of the British in assuming financial leadership in international trade: industrial technology, financial systems, and government reform. Sobel wrote: "As the reforms that began with the Glorious Revolution took hold and gained credibility, the costs of financing public and private endeavors declined—whether war, domestic governance, or commercial enterprise. Financial markets grew in volume, capacity, and sophistication. These markets stimulated British commercial enterprise and economic growth, funded English overseas exploration and expansion, and financed a century of warfare with France. They led to London's rise as the center of global finance and commerce and eventually made the pound the dominant currency for pricing international transactions and settling international accounts." (Sobel 2012)

Also Peter Termin and Hans-Joachim summarized the time: "The dynastic wars that had wracked England during the previous century and before ended with the Glorious Revolution of 1688, and Parliament gained new powers. Taxation increased, and the taxes collected, in addition to increased borrowing, financed the wars fought by King William and his successors. The changes we now call the Industrial Revolution were well under way by the end of the century, growing out of the fertile soil of this tranquil economy." (Temin and Voth 2012)

The industrial revolution began in England toward the end of that century, based upon the new technologies of the steam engine, textile machinery and factories, and coke-fueled steel production. The economic expansion required financing as the technologies and factories were expensive; but the industrial investments produced wealth, which further extended the financial function. Thus both in Britain and following closely in Europe and America, industrialization and financial expansion drove the great economic developments over the nineteenth and into the twentieth centuries. Sobel wrote: "London's financial markets provided capital for the Industrial Revolution that started in the United Kingdom and then spread to other nations of the Atlantic economy. London's capital markets financed canals, railroads, and economic enterprise in the United States; Argentinean infrastructure and development; colonial expansion; Italian and German political unification; and other public and private activities around the world." (Sobel 2012)

It was not just the financial institutions developing in Britain but also new industrial technology of the Industrial Revolution which together drove the emergence of Britain as a financial hegemon in the nineteenth century. Sobel wrote: "Only after the British economy embarked on the Industrial Revolution did British output and economic prowess actually exceed that of France and other nations. This absolute lead in economic size lasted but a short time, for the United States and Germany, industrializing later than the United Kingdom, both passed the British in the late 1800s. By 1900, the United States had become the largest economy in the world. Yet the British remained the commercial and financial hegemon of the system until World War I, influencing the rules of exchange, financing economic activity, and managing economic or financial stress in the system." (Sobel 2012)

Drawing of Marshall's Mills, Holbeck showing operators at their machines. From the Penny Magazine Supplement, December 1843 "A Day at a Leeds Flax Mill".
Date: 1919, original image from 1843

(https://en.wikipedia.org/wiki/File:Marshall's_flax-mill,_Holbeck,_Leeds_-_interior_-_c.1800.jpg)

Fig. 7.4 Industrial revolution in England—Leeds Flax Mill in 1843

Figure 7.4 shows the sketch of a textile factory in 1843.

Government reforms in finance began under William and Mary. Sobel wrote: "…the succession of William and Mary to the English throne came bundled with the reforms of the Glorious Revolution. These reforms held the prospect for redefining state-society relations in a manner that restrained the power of the Crown and established the foundations for parliamentary dominance and governance by rule of law, transforming public and private finance in England and increasing the influence of civil society in England." (Sobel 2012)

Sobel wrote: "Adherence to a rule-of-law signals a government's reliability to follow the rules that the government helped lay out in social, political, and economic interactions, even as that government has the capacity to renege on such rules. Rule-of-law delineates the constraints on government actions and arbitrariness, forming a foundation for expectations that influence choices of the participants in a society. In the economic sphere, rule-of-law underpins the credibility and reliability of contracts, as well as a government's willingness to exercise self-restraint, avoid arbitrary choices, and adhere to stable rules of the game, all of which encourages private economic actors to extend their time horizons, enter into contracts, and take risks over time and space. The rule-of-law that emerged from the Glorious Revolution underpinned the credibility of English government activities and commitments, promoted greater fairness in sharing the burden as well as the distribution of gains, and encouraged stake-holding among a broader swath of English society." (Sobel 2012)

The establishment of a 'rule-of-law' by the English Parliament occurred over time through several laws, among which was the famous 'Bill-of-Rights'. Sobel wrote: "The most important part of this new state-society contract was what has become known as the English Bill of Rights. In 1689 Parliament passed An Act Declaring the Rights and Liberties of the Subject and Settling the Succession of the Crown. The act provided the framework for a constitutional monarchy and cataloged the basic political and civil rights of the English people and the responsibilities of the Crown to those people." (Sobel 2012)

Other acts were passed by Parliament, and the Bank of England was established. Sobel wrote: "In the same year (of 1689 in passing the Bill of Rights), Parliament passed the Act of Toleration, which provided for freedom of worship.... The Bank of England was next established in 1694 and awarded a royal charter with the passage of the Tonnage Act of 1695... This addressed dilemmas in public finance." (Sobel 2012)

Peter Temin and Hans-Joachim Voth described the political conflict in England in the reign of William and Mary: "The Glorious Revolution was not a revolution in property rights; instead, it was part of an ongoing contest between groups. One group, associated with the Tories, thought the country should advance by territorial acquisition. The other group, associated with the Whigs, thought that commerce and manufacturing were the way forward for England. King William paradoxically represented a victory for both sides. He engaged in a series of wars on the continent of Europe, following a Tory program. The wars, however, required the construction of a tax system in England to finance them, and Whigs dominated the design of the nascent fiscal and financial system. The Bank of England in particular was a Whig creation in the face of Tory resistance." (Temin and Voth 2012)

The political conflict during England's Glorious Revolution (between Tory and Whigs) centered on differing views on the sources 'wealth' in a society. Peter Temin and Hans-Joachim Voth wrote: "The difference between the Whigs and Tories can be summarized by reference to their implicit worldviews. Tories saw wealth as a zero-sum game, that is, one where total wealth was fixed and one nation's gain could only come about when another nation loses. It was natural for them to emphasize the role of land, since its supply is fixed, and to support wars of conquest. Whigs, by contrast, based their policies on a view of expanding wealth based on the earnings of labor instead of land.... The change in trade policy was gradual, taking longer than the eighteenth century, but the Whig view was dominant in the development of English financial capability after the Glorious Revolution." (Temin and Voth 2012)

Tories based their political interests upon the value of land, producing 'rents'; whereas Whig's wanted the policies favoring manufacturing and free trade. The Tories wanted wars-of-conquest to increase territory; whereas the Whigs wanted markets for trade. Tory and Whig policies coincided when in 1689 England went to a long war with France, lasting two decades. Public expenditures jumped from two million pounds annually to five million pounds. The need to borrow funds for the war was pressing; and efforts to solve the government's financial problem stimulated the financial revolution in Britain.

Under the financial reforms over time by the British Parliament, fiscal stability was attained over time. Sobel wrote: "The English tax structure prior to the Glorious Revolution... was strongly deficient compared with the Dutch tax system. England's tax structure was burdened by inequities that favored the rich, the nobility, and landed property holders but penalized the commercial and working classes. This limited government revenues had increased the difficulty in financing its debt obligations. The incentives in the tax structure were misaligned with the economic activities that would eventually transform the British political economy and produce a stronger, richer, and healthier United Kingdom." (Sobel 2012)

This illustrates an important and basic point about sound fiscal policy needed for a stable national fiscal policy.

What activities produce wealth in a society, and how should these activities contribute to the support of government (pay taxes)?

What public good occurs from the private accumulation of wealth, and what is the tax responsibility of private wealth to contribute taxes back to the public good?

Taxation policy is not just an 'economic issue' but a 'political-economic issue'—involving not only economic efficiency but also political justice. A fair-and-adequate tax policy is part of a larger concept in government often called the 'rule of law'. A society which is governed by just laws is also part of a social contract which both provides legal stability in a society and legitimacy as perceived by the governed. A 'rule of law' means that government will not be conducted by the whims and prejudice of the ruler, but restrained by law—both the governed and the governor are restrained.

Peter Temin and Hans-Joachim Voth described the fiscal challenges to the English Parliament: "Sovereigns had borrowed for centuries, but there had been little sustained borrowing in England before the Glorious Revolution. The fumbling efforts by Parliament to supply resources for William's wars gave rise to a financial revolution in the years following the political revolution. Initial attempts to institute steady borrowing included annuities, tontines, lotteries, and lots of short-term loans. The system was chaotic and expensive for the government. The Bank of England was established in 1694 and introduced some order into the process of gathering resources for the government, but it too was in learning mode." (Temin and Voth 2012)

The understanding of proper fiscal policy did not come easily nor particularly swiftly for the new Bank of England. Peter Temin and Hans-Joachim Voth wrote: "Patterned after the Bank of Amsterdam, the Bank of England was run by bourgeois directors rather than parliamentary members. Government borrowing remained expensive, and the government was not above grasping at straws in the early years of the eighteenth century." (Temin and Voth 2012)

The infrastructure of a sound financial system for Britain continued as a work-in-progress throughout the 1700s. The infrastructure needed an effective central bank to issue and regulate currency and a fiscally-responsible government which collected taxes to pay its debts.

Sobel was arguing that a proper tax structure of a nation is essential to the strength of a nation, both economic strength and military strength. Unfair and inadequate tax systems weaken a country, sometimes to disaster. For example much later in Europe in the twenty-first century, the union of European nations (European Union) came

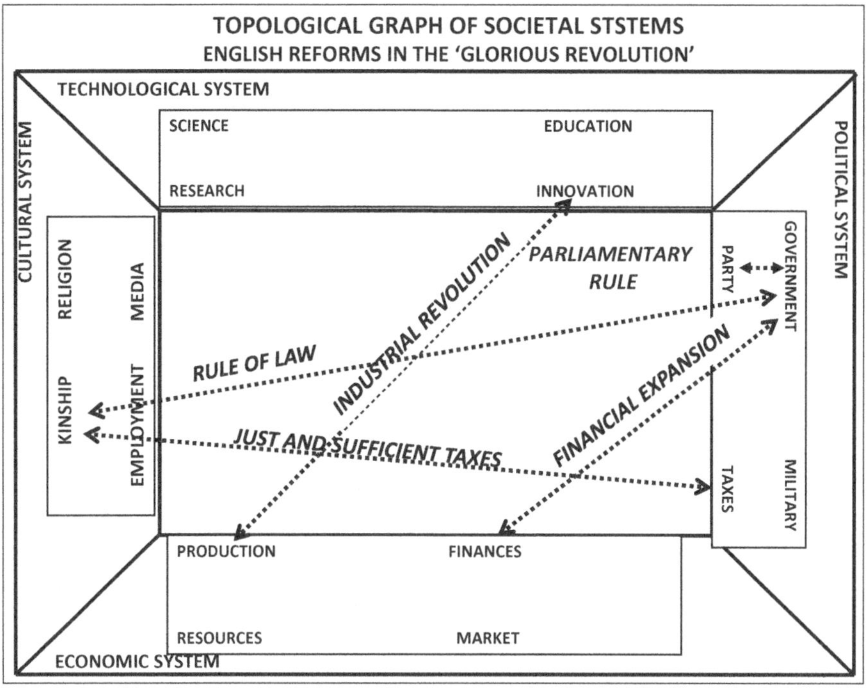

Fig. 7.5 Political, economic, technological, cultural subsystems of British society in 1900s

close to collapsing in 2009—precisely because of ineffective and unfair tax systems in some of its nations (including Greece, Italy, Spain, and Portugal). Sobel commented: "Unfair and unreliable tax systems, reneging on public debts, and arbitrariness had restrained activities in private financial markets and limited commercial development.... A government that adopts (tax) reforms is the same entity that 'controls the tools of coercion' in society and can unilaterally change the rules of the game (from financial instability toward fiscal stability)." (Sobel 2012)

A societal system can be topologically modeled in a taxonomy of systems: technological, political, economic, cultural (Betz 2014). We can analyze the connections in political-economy in a societal model, Fig. 7.5.

The technologies of the 'industrial revolution' provided the British society with extraordinary increases in production efficiency and capacity, making England a leading manufacturer in the world through the early era of the 1800s. 'Financial expansion' of the British financial system was facilitated by prudent fiscal policies of the British government. The prudent policies were underpinned by 'just-and-sufficient-taxes' collected by a 'parliamentary government', operating under a 'rule-of-law'. Thus international financial leadership is dependent not only on technological and economic factors but also governmental factors of representative rule, rule-of-law, and just taxation.

Loss of Financial Hegemony: Financial Instability in the 1930s World Depression

World War I ended the British financial hegemony of the nineteenth century, when the British pound sterling ruled international finance. The departure of British currency from an international gold standard occurred in the world depression of the 1930. Charles Kindleberger explained that depression, not in terms of 'causality' but in terms of 'systems failure'. Kindleberger wrote: "The explanation … is that the 1929 depression was so wide, so deep and so long because the international economic system was rendered unstable by British inability and United States unwillingness to assume responsibility for stabilizing it…" (1973)

There were different circumstances in each country, which were connected together through different government policies and through unstable flows in international finance and trade. Germany's repatriations to France contributed to German societal instability, while Germany had also lost traditional governance. Austria had lost its monarch and empire. Britain and France had lost one-quarter of their young men in the war (which would have formed new families and contributed to market growth and demand). Also financially, they had large war debts to the U.S. European nations were unstable from consequences of the First World War.

Andrew Sobel wrote: "During the war, Germany's currency base expanded its money supply by 350 %, and prices increased by more than threefold. In Great Britain, the money supply more than doubled… with a 250 % increase in prices…. On top of the problem of inflated currencies by the war's conclusion, the European governments were left with huge outstanding debt or reparation obligations and drained national treasuries… The Germans were shackled with excessive reparations…. The end of the war presented all governments with the dilemma of constraining inflated money supply, restoring the gold standard, and meeting debt or reparation obligations. These demands proved incompatible…." (Sobel 2012)

Monetary policy destabilized Germany society and prepared the way for the Nazi revolution in the 1930s. Sobel wrote: "The interaction of Germany's economic circumstances at the end of the war and the burden of reparations placed German policy makers in an extremely difficult position. Addressing inflation and paying reparations were almost mutually impossible policy objectives without causing severe economic hardship and massive unemployment within Germany and feeding revolutionary political upheaval. Instead the Reichsbank chose to continue to expand the money supply to provide what the government needed to finance its budget, to make reparation payments and to avoid inflation. This led to the well-documented hyperinflation that struck Germany in the early 1920s…. Without the burden of excessive reparations, Germany would not have fallen into arrears on its payments and French and Belgian troops would not have occupied the Ruhr Valley in lieu of payment. Certainly, this would have influenced extremist, nationalistic politics in Germany, maybe altering the dynamic that led to the success of Hitler's National Socialist Party." (Sobel 2012)

Another deflationary factor was a decline in commodity prices. The price of wheat dropped from $1.5 per bushel in June 1929 to $1.05 in June 1930. All other commodity prices declined world-wide in 1930. Kindleberger wrote: "The essential truth is found in the conventional wisdom that price declines are deflationary in so far as they 'check confidence, provoke bank failures, encourage hoarding and in various ways discourage investment'." (Kindleberger 1973)

Government policies about international trade also contributed to deflation. A U.S. tariff act, the Smoot-Hawley Tariff Bill in June 1930, raised tariffs on US imports. Charles Kindleberger wrote: "While other countries had raised tariffs before the Smoot-Hawley Bill became law, the course of the legislation through Congress had been followed with close attention.... There were 34 formal foreign governmental protests. (The bill) let loose a wave of retaliation.... This was a failure in leadership." (Kindleberger 1973) Andrew Sobel wrote: "The trade process is another means to push liquidity into the international system.... (There was a) downward spiral in international trade, a reduction of approximately 60 % from 1929 to 1933." (Sobel 2012)

About Germany, Kindleberger wrote: "When Germany restricted long-term borrowing abroad in the late 1920s, it failed to limit short-term.... Germany was subject to the outflow of foreign funds.... A crisis occurred in March 1930 because of unemployment.... By early 1930, unemployment was at 1.9 million people,... (creating) a budget deficit.... Bruning took over the government.... Deflation was called for German obligations under the Young Plan, by the fear of inflation, which persisted from 1923, and by the notion that profits could be restored by pushing wages down.... The budget had to be balanced: old taxes were raised... new ones imposed... Expenditures were reduced. The deflationary policy was followed for two fateful years.... (Unemployment rose) from 176,000 in 1929 to 2,800,000 in 1931." (Kindleberger 1973) Elections were held in September 1930, and the Nazi party went from 12 to 107 seats in the parliament. There was a withdrawal of foreign funds. In 1933, the Nazi party won more seats, and President Hindenburg appointed Adolf Hitler as chancellor. Hitler began his reign of terror in Germany.

Capital flows also played an important factor in the international deflation. Kindleberger wrote: "With the tension growing among Germany France and Britain, the crack, when it came, appeared in Austria. In the early spring of 1931, a Dutch bank wrote a polite letter to the Credit-Anstalt in Vienna saying that it was obligated to raise the charge on its acceptance credits from 1/4 a month to 3/8 %.... Credit-Anstalt chose to pay off the loan.... (Three months later the Credit Anstalt could have used the money.) The Austrian banking system, hurt by both the break-up of the Austro-Hungarian Empire and inflation, had adjusted haphazardly, placing heavy reliance on short-term credit from abroad." (Kindleberger 1973) Credit-Anstalt had fused with Bodenkerdianstalt and gained 80 million of capita but 140 million of losses. It needed help and requested assistance from the National Bank. But when announcement of support was made in May 1931, a run on the bank began.

The Credit-Anstalt failure triggered other bank runs. Then the bank runs triggered a currency crisis. Investors turned to gold, upon which the British currency was based. This began a run on the British pound. Kindleberger wrote: "At the end of May 1931, Austrian financial difficulties ramified widely and led to runs in the banks of Hungary, Czechoslovakia, Romania, Poland, and Germany.... There were new bankruptcies in Germany, which communicated tension to Amsterdam, which in turn drew funds from London....The pace of withdrawal (in London) accelerated. On 21 September, Great Britain left the gold standard." (Kindleberger 1973) This illustrated how interconnected were the banking systems in Europe.

Bank runs in the instability of the financial systems, nationally and internationally, were important contributors to the world depression. When economies decline, produced goods are under stress (distressed) as they cannot find markets and cannot be sold. Stimulating markets in depression aids the sales of consumer goods. Thus politics, money, trade instabilities—all contributed to the world depression.

The world depression of 1930 was triggered by the US depression, which in turn had been triggered by the 1929 US stock market crash. In a previous paper, the author had applied graphical analysis to the US depression (2013). That depression began with the bad banking practice of excessive funding of stock speculation. The US stock market rose to a financial bubble due to extensive purchase of stock through bank loans (stocks purchased on margin). When the market collapsed, such margined stock reverted to banks as collateral—but of decreasing value as the market continued to collapse. The banks which had made large amounts of broker loans then became insolvent, and bank runs on them occurred. Sobel wrote: "As important as were the reparations-war-debt-connection, and the trade-area, neither fed the fundamental problems leading to the 1929 stock market crash, nor the insolvency and liquidity problems underpinning the US banking crisis, that festered after 1929 and culminated in 1933. US financial practices and processes were nontransparent, lacked credible monitoring and accountability, were excessively vulnerable to manipulation, corruption, and cronyism, and lacked sufficient public and private regulatory oversight to address ills before they could overwhelm the confidence of those engaged in financial exchange." (Sobel 2012) Bad banking practices tipped an unstable US financial system into crisis.

Now we apply the graphical analysis to understanding the dynamics of the world depression, as shown in Fig. 7.6.

SOCIETY—The societies involved in the 1930s world depression were the nations of the U.S. and Europe, and included Japan.

INDIVIDUAL—The individuals involved were key decision makers of the U.S. presidency and European presidents and prime ministers.

GROUP—The organizations were principally central banks of a nation, which oversaw the financial stability of a nation.

PROCESS—The processes involved were financial in the forms of national debts and budgets, international capital flows and exchange rates, and Britain removing its currency from the traditional 'gold standard'.

ACTION—Actions in the events, which contributed to the world depression, were many. They included the 1929 New York Stock Market crash, which was followed by 3 years of U.S. bank panics in 1930–1933. Contributing to destabilizing the European government budgets were the large British and French war debts to the U.S. and large German war reparations to France and Britain. Government funding of German reparations triggered hyperinflation in Germany and the French

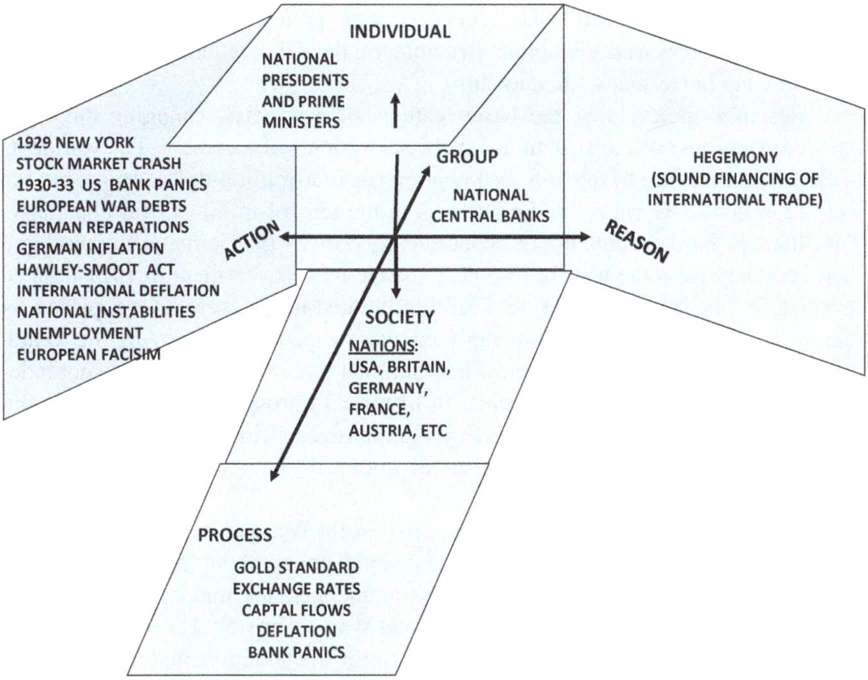

Fig. 7.6 Events triggering 1939s world depression

occupation of the Germany's Ruhr Valley. The inflation and French occupation increased the political influence of the Nazi political party in Germany. The U.S. Smoot-Hawley Act triggered retaliatory trade tariffs in European nations, diminishing world trade and contributing to deflation of international commodity prices. Bank runs froze credit—contributing to declines in production and raising unemployment in the US and Europe. European fascism in Italy and in Germany enabled dictators who began the Second World War in Europe.

REASON—Prior to the First World War, liberal hegemony in the British governmental and financial systems had made Britain the financial center of the world. The British pound was backed by gold, then international currency standard. But Britain was unable to continue to play this international hegemonic role—after the casualties and financial burden from the First World War. Without such leadership, the financial system of the world became unstable.

Explanations in Institutional Economics

This analytic form highlights the explanations of the world depression, which lay in institutional factors—institutional economics. Institutional arrangements are significant but none is ever a single 'cause' of societal events. The crises in the US and

Europe in their financial and economic and political systems resulted in changes—the depressed economic structure of the US (deflation) and the Nazi political coup in Germany (dictatorship).

Crises in a society alter the basic features of a society—changing the stasis (stable operations) of the structural-functional systems of a society. The war debts of Britain and France to the U.S. had been in the four-million-dollar range, but the war reparation of Germany to France was in the tens-of-millions-of-dollar range. This financial burden could not be economically born by the Germans, in rebuilding their economy from the war. In response, the German government in 1921 inflated its currency, the 'mark'. In 1 year a million-inflated-marks were later replaced by one 'new mark'. All mortgages in Germany were wiped out, destroying the wealth of people and banks who lent money. International financial systems were not independent of national financial policies. In historical retrospective (and graphically viewed), one can see that, as Kindleberger emphasized (Kindleberger 1973), it was 'policy' that contributed to the destabilization of the international economic situation.

Among historians of the period of the First World War and its aftermath, there is no exact consensus on a 'normative judgment' about policy, about 'blame' for the war. But there is agreement that it was a terrible war and, perhaps, unnecessary. It created the societal disruptions, from which the Second World War would emerge.

As to my opinion, I think it was bad policy for the governmental leaders of the USA to insist upon the repayment of these war debts by Britain and France. If the US really believed in the Allies' side of the war story, then perhaps the US should have forgiven the debts, so the US allies of Britain and France could have more rapidly recovered. I think it was also bad policy for the French leaders to impose and insist upon German reparations. After all, it had been the 'balance-of-power' international alliances which had actually precipitated the war. In this policy framework, all the European nations were equally to blame, since they had all entered into alliances. At the time of the assassination of the Austrian-Serb affair, all nations mobilized—the Russian, the German, the French, the Austrian armies. Thus no single nation was to blame for the war—not the Germans, not the Austrians, not the Russians, not the French, not the British. It was (as Kindleberger emphasized in the factors of history) an 'accident'. It was an accident of 'mobilization', an accident of 'policy', an accident of 'national leaders not really thinking though the consequences of their decisions', an accident in 'misunderstanding' the major changes in war technology.

Leaders (political and military) did not understand the increased destructiveness of military technology. Frontal assaults by masses of infantry were not possible against the then new machine gun and steel artillery. The French launched a massive assault in 1915, failing with 50,000 casualties. In 1916, the British launched a massive assault, failing with enormous casualties. In the spring of 1918, the Germans launched their massive assault, failing and (with the addition of fresh American troops) resulting in the German surrender. The people who paid the price in the war were not the leaders, but the soldiers and civilians. They were the soldiers slaughtered in a new mechanized war of destructive steel artillery, machine guns, and poison gases. Images from the war are memorable, Fig. 7.7.

Clockwise from the top: The aftermath of shelling during the Battle of the Somme, Mark V tanks cross the Hindenburg Line, HMS Irresistible sinks after hitting a mine in the Dardanelles, a British Vickers machine gun crew wears gas masks during the Battle of the Somme, Albatros D.III fighters of Jagdstaffel 11.

(http://en.wikipedia.org/wiki/World_War_I)

Fig. 7.7 Images from World War I

Great Britain established its empire in the 1700s and dominated world trade and finance through the 1800s. It was the war of 1914 that destroyed Great Britain's place as financial leader. Britain had large war debts, a shrunken market with one quarter of its male youth dead and not able to begin new families. Britain took its currency off the gold standard.

With modern technologies, ignorant policies can create great havoc in modern societies—societal catastrophes

Summary

The importance of an institutional approach to regulation of international finance was nicely summarized in a recent commentary by the economist Paul Krugman: "For it's now clear that the flood of money into emerging markets—which briefly drove Brazil's currency up by almost 40 %, a rise that has now been completely reversed—was yet another in the long list of financial bubbles over the past generation. There was the housing bubble, of course. But before that there was the dot-com bubble; before that the Asian bubble of the mid-1990s; before that the commercial real estate bubble of the 1980s. That last bubble, by the way, imposed a huge cost on taxpayers, who had to bail out failed savings-and-loan institutions.

The thing is, it wasn't always thus. The 1950s, the 1960s, even the troubled 1970s, weren't nearly as bubble-prone. So what changed? O.K., the … obvious culprit is financial deregulation—not just in the United States but around the world, and including the removal of most controls on the international movement of capital. Banks gone wild were at the heart of the commercial real estate bubble of the 1980s and the housing bubble that burst in 2007. Cross-border flows of hot money were at the heart of the Asian crisis of 1997–1998 and the crisis now erupting in emerging markets—and were central to the ongoing crisis in Europe, too. In short, the main lesson of this age of bubbles—a lesson that India, Brazil, and others are learning once again—is that when the financial industry is set loose to do its thing, it lurches from crisis to crisis." (2013)

References

Betz, F. (2014). Patrimonialism in political economy—A graphic analysis. *Business and Management Research, 3*(3), 1. ISSN 1927-6001 (Print) ISSN 1927-601X (Online).

Kindleberger, C. P. (1973). *The world in depression*. Berkeley, CA: University of California Press.

Sobel, A. C. (2012). *Birth of hegemony*. Chicago: University of Chicago Press.

Temin, P., & Voth, H.-J. (2012). *Prometheus shackled: Goldsmith banks and England's financial revolution after 1700*. Oxford: Oxford University Press.

Chapter 8
Design of an International Central Bank

Introduction

What kind of international structure could properly regulate the whole of the international financial grid? We analyze whether and how such a proper banking institution might be an international central bank which regulates national central banks. Then we compare this ideal model to the present reality of the European Central Bank and the Bank of International Settlements.

European Central Bank and Financial Contagion 2009–2015

In 2015, the only presently existent form of an *international central bank* is the European Central Bank (ECB). But it is international only for the European Union—and not for the global economy. Yet the role of the ECB, in the Euro crisis of 2010–2015, is instructive about what kind of regulatory roles international central banks need fulfill. We analyze how the European Central Bank played its institutional role in the Euro crisis. What functions evolved in its role, as the European Central Bank assisted in solutions to the European crisis?

We recall that the Euro crisis, the European Central Bank supported European central banks—including the National Bank of Greece (Greek central bank), from 2010 even into the summer of 2015. On 21 June 2015, in the climatic months of the Greek crisis, Landon Thomas Jr. and Peter Eavis reported: "Europe's central bank has been the lender of last resort for Greece, keeping its banking system, if not the country itself, from collapse. But the ECB has also been among the most recalcitrant of its creditors, pushing Greece to the verge of default by refusing to offer relief on its heavy debts." (Thomas and Eavis 2015)

We also recall that on 5 July 2015, the Greek government scheduled a national referendum on whether or not Greece should remain in the European Monetary

F. Betz, *Stability in International Finance*, SpringerBriefs in Economics,
DOI 10.1007/978-3-319-26760-9_8

Union (whether or not to continue to use the Euro as a national currency). Paul Kirby wrote: "Greek banks have been closed and strict limits placed on cash withdrawals as Greece's government is set to default on a debt repayment to the IMF on 30 June of €1.5bn. Months of negotiations on a deal have collapsed and Prime Minister Alexis Tsipras has called a referendum for 5 July, asking Greeks to reject reform proposals from the IMF and EU, which he says are against European values." (Kirby 2015) The whole week before the referendum, Greek banks had closed, when the ECB stopped lending money to the National Bank of Greece (Greek central bank).

The role of the European Central Bank in assisting Europe to impose 'austerity' upon the Greek economy had been important—but not worked. The reason was a system problem. The problem in the Euro Crisis was that the monetary union had been constructed only partially as a sound financial system, as it was without a complete political and fiscal union. Jean-Claude Trichet was president of the European Central Bank from 2003 to 2011 and afterwards wrote: "The epicenter of the worst financial crisis since World War II was located in the United States in 2007 and crossed the Atlantic at the beginning of 2010….(In these) we observed a global crisis of the advanced economies—not only a European crisis. Some have argued that the subprime crisis and post-Lehman Brothers developments were an American crisis. We learned the hard way that the financial crisis was global, even if its epicenter was in the United States….The euro zone is indeed at the epicenter of sovereign risk tensions because its specific economic and fiscal governance has revealed four major weaknesses. First, the rules of the Stability and Growth Pact in the euro union (which was the core of fiscal governance and the quid pro quo for the absence of a federal state in the euro area) were not respected. Second, there was no established surveillance of the evolution of national competitiveness, and of national external imbalances. Third, there was no banking union. Fourth, there was no stabilization mechanism to cope with dramatic financial circumstances." (Trichet 2013)

The euro (€) was supposed to be an international currency; but currency is only one part of a monetary system. Currency and credit together compose a monetary system. For example, the designation of 'M2' is an economic measure of money in a nation, with currency and credit added together to determine the supply of money (M2). Thus the euro was the currency part of the European Union (EU) but without the credit part; and so it was not the M2 (money) of the EU. Also currency has traditionally been 'money' issued by a nation; but the European Union was not a nation, nor a confederacy, nor a federation of nations. For this reason there was no effective macro-fiscal policy of the EU to control its currency union. Thus Trichet's four 'rules' (fiscal governance, balance of nations' competitiveness, banking union, financial stabilization mechanism) were not implemented in the EU monetary union.

Historically, the European Union had been founded after World War II, principally as a mechanism to prevent a 'third world war' in Europe between France and Germany. In 1948, a European Movement International was established in a meeting, called the Hague Congress. In 1957, a European Economic Community (EEC) was established in a Treaty of Rome, signed by Belgium, France, Italy, Luxembourg, the Netherlands, and West Germany. In 1993, the European Union (EU) was established by a Maastricht Treaty, led principally in Germany by Helmut Kohl (Chancellor of West Germany from 1982 to 1990 and of Germany from 1990 to 1998) and in France by Francois Mitterrand (President of France, from 1981 until 1995).

A creation of a single currency for Europe was one objective of the EU and was accomplished in 1999, with the European Central Bank established to administer the euro. In signing onto the monetary union, member companies agreed to be legally bound by 'convergence criteria'. This required a member country to reduce its public debt to 60 % of GDP and any annual budget deficits to 3 % of GDP. But these criteria were not always followed by member countries.

Barry Eichengreen wrote: "While the European Community seemed on the road to solving its exchange rate problem, other more fundamental difficulties remained. Unemployment was disturbingly high, often in the double digits, and policymakers felt hamstrung by their commitment to peg the exchange rate .... This led them to contemplate a radical acceleration of the process of European integration as a way of injecting the chill winds of competition into the European economy and helping producers to better exploit economies of scale and scope .... The attempt to create a single European market in merchandise and factors of production accelerated the momentum of monetary integration. Eliminating currency conversion costs was the only way of removing hidden barriers to internal economic flows, of forging a truly integrated market. Abolishing the opportunity for countries to manipulate their exchange rates was necessary to defuse protectionist opposition to the liberalization of trade .... The initiative (of a single currency) turned out to have profound and not wholly anticipated consequences for the evolution of the European Monetary System." (Eichengreen 2008)

There were two major goals in the concept of the Euro monetary Union, which were sometimes complementary and sometimes contradictory. One goal was to improve trade and enlarge the European market (the liberalization of trade); a second goal was to encourage full employment in member nations. Neither of the goals were accomplished in the monetary union of the euro. It was late in 2009, when these contradictory economic threads (of trade and employment) unraveled.

First these problems appeared in Greek bonds. Early in 2010, the international bond market refused to buy more Greek sovereign bonds except at a jump to very higher interest rates; and this problem continued for Greece onward through 2015, as the Greek-Euro fiscal crisis, putting Greece continually on the edge of an exit from the Eurodollar monetary system. In April 2015, Liz Alderman wrote: "Greece, the weak link in the eurozone, is struggling to pay its debt as its people and its creditors grow more restive .... The so-called troika—the International Monetary Fund, the European Central Bank and the European Commission—issued the first of two international bailouts for Greece, which would eventually total 240 billion euros, or about $264 billion at today's exchange rates. The bailouts came with conditions. Lenders imposed harsh austerity terms, requiring deep budget cuts and steep tax increases." (Alderman 2015)

The European Central Bank (along with the other two members of the 'Troika', the European Commission and International Monetary Fund) provided funds for the 'bail out' of the nations in the contagion of the Euro monetary union.

The European Central Bank had been playing a significant role—but both as *lender-of-last resort* to the Central Bank of Greece and also as a *discipliner-of-national-fiscal-policy* over the Greek government's fiscal irresponsibility. Landon Thomas Jr. and Peter Eavis summarized this conflict: "As Greece's standoff with its creditors enters the final stretch, the European Central Bank finds itself in the awkward position of being both the country's savior and its scold. Europe's central bank has been the lender of last resort for Greece, keeping its banking system, if not the country itself, from collapse. But the European Central Bank has also been among the most recalcitrant of its creditors, pushing Greece to the verge of default by refusing to offer relief on its heavy debts." (Thomas and Eavis 2015)

But the ECB had not been established with this kind of the full responsibilities of a national central bank. Thomas Jr. and Eavis described: "Unlike central banks in the United States, Britain and Japan, the ECB's status as a lender-of-last resort is circumscribed and conditional, the result of strict European rules that outlaw money printing as a means to bail out broke governments. That means the central bank leadership in Frankfurt can quickly shift from a stance of propping up a banking system to allowing it to implode… " (Thomas and Eavis 2015)

And the European Central Bank assumed more responsibility over the banks in the EU. Jack Ewing wrote: "Only a few years ago, the European Central Bank was regarded as relatively powerless when compared with its counterpart in the United States. But as it has struggled to hold the eurozone together, the bank has become more like the Federal Reserve." (Ewing 2015)

A reform that was to have the European Central Bank provide regulatory supervision over large banks in Europe. Large European banks were in jeopardy in both the U.S. derivative market failure in 2007 and in the sovereign bond market failures in the Euro crisis of 2010. Melissa Eddy wrote: "Europe inched closer Wednesday to establishing a European banking union for the Continent's largest lenders after the German cabinet approved legislation that would grant to the European Central Bank oversight of such institutions…. As part of efforts to help resolve the debt crisis in the euro zone, E.U. leaders agreed last year to establish a banking union with the aim of preventing overly indebted states from having to bail out failing banks." (Eddy 2013)

In 2012, a press release by the European Commission stated: "The Commission has today received the report prepared by the High-level Expert Group on reforming the structure of the EU banking sector (MEMO/12/129). The Group chaired by Erkki Liikanen presented the main findings to Michel Barnier, Commissioner for internal market and services. Governor Erkki Liikanen said "The report contains the Group's recommendations for further reforms of the banking sector, including structural reform. Building on the substantial measures already under way, I believe that the Group's recommendations would if implemented provide for a safer, more stable and efficient banking system serving the needs of citizens, the EU economy and the internal market." In brief, the Group recommends actions in the five following areas:

- Mandatory separation of proprietary trading and other high-risk trading activities,
- Possible additional separation of activities conditional on the recovery and resolution plan,
- Possible amendments to the use of bail-in instruments as a resolution tool,
- A review of capital requirements on trading assets and real estate related loans, and
- A strengthening of the governance and control of banks." (European Commission 2012)

These structural reforms were recommended to the European Union in order to make "a stable and efficient banking system serving the needs of citizens, the economy and the internal market." (European Commission 2012)

The Central Bank of Europe was given the authority to shut down insolvent banks in any member country. The central banks in the different member nations had not been doing their proper regulatory job, partly because large banks crossed international borders. Andrews Higgins and David Jolly wrote: "Battling to defend its credibility after a series of troubled bank failures across the Continent, European finance officials finally reached a deal on how to plug a gaping hole in Europe's economic defenses, agreeing to a centralized system to shut down sickly banks in the 17 member nations that use the euro." (Higgins and Jolly 2013) Gaining the responsibility and authority to regulate European banks was not easy, as James Kanter wrote: "European leaders gathering here on Thursday for their year-end summit meeting hailed an agreement to place euro zone banks under a single supervisor, calling it a concrete measure to maintain the viability of the currency as well as a step in laying the groundwork for a broader economic union.... Under the agreement, 100–200 large banks in the euro zone will fall under the direct supervision of the European Central Bank." (Kanter 2012a, b)

Analysis of European Central Bank Events in the Euro Crisis

For the actions in the event of the European Central Bank in the European monetary crisis of 2009–2015, we next identify these factors on a perceptual-space event box, as shown in Fig. 8.1.

ACTION—European Central Bank was established to administer the euro, controlling the currency in the Eurozone to prevent monetary inflation. In the 2010–2015 Eurocrisis, the European Central Bank had its authority expanded to (1) regulate the financial solvency of European banks and (2) to provide lender-of-last-resort to the Greece Central Bank.

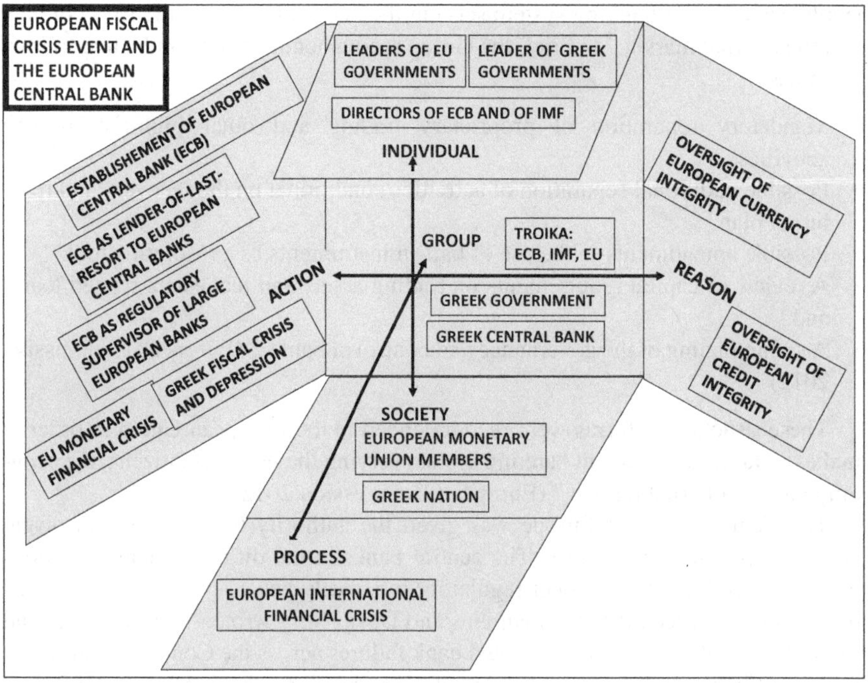

Fig. 8.1 Perceptual space analysis of European Central Bank action in the Euro crisis

REASON—The reason for expanding the authority of the European Central Bank was to oversee not only the currency of the European monetary union but also the credit integrity of the union. Money in a financial system includes both currency and credit.

GROUP—The Monetary Union of the European nations was the principal group in the event, organized into a shared currency. The Central Bank of Europe was established to administer the euro currency. In addition to the Central Bank of Europe, the European Stability Fund, and the International Monetary Fund had together been providing 'bail-out' funds to the contagious government in the crisis, including Greece. Also the central banks of these illiquid European member governments were involved. And large international private banks which had held sovereign bonds were involved.

PROCESS—The financial processes in the Euro Crisis was financial bubbles in private debt markets and in public debt markets. The first private debt financial bubble began in the derivatives market of the U.S. Wall Street institutions in 2007, with billions of dollars of bank money frozen in the securitization of illiquid U.S. mortgage bonds (toxic assets) and spread to European banks which had purchased some of the toxic derivatives. The second financial bubble burst in 2009 in the public debt market of Greek sovereign bonds. Then further public debt contagion spread to the governments of Ireland, Portugal, and Spain—as their respective central banks 'bailed-out' their private banks, which had had funded real-estate bubbles in each country.

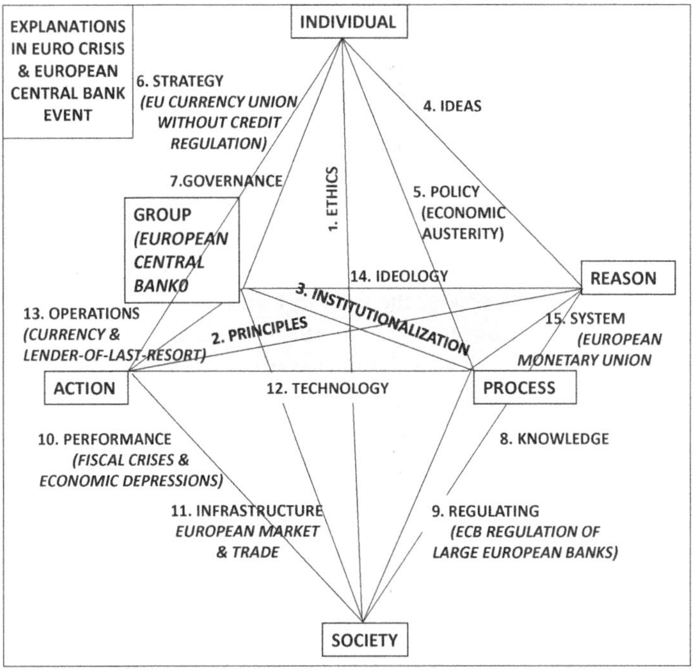

Fig. 8.2 Explanations of the activities of the European Central Bank in the Euro crisis

SOCIETY—The societies involved in the Euro crisis were the member nations of the European Union.

INDIVIUALS—The individuals involved were the Director of the European Central Bank, the Managing Director of the International Monetary Funds (Christine Lagarde in 2015) and the heads of governments of member states of the European Union. German Chancellor Angela Merkel, Greek Prime Minister Alexis Tsipras

We next use the societal dynamics theory to identify important relationships between these factors to explain the event. We recall that societal dynamics perceptual space provides kinds of explanations in societal events, as shown in Fig. 8.2. The *Group* we are focusing upon in this economic case analysis is the *European Central Bank*. The *Society* is the *European Union*. To understand the role of the European Central in the event of the Euro crisis, we next analyze the key explanatory relations in the event: *(6) Strategy, (5) Policy, (15) System, (13) Operations, (10) Performance, (9) Regulating, (11) Infrastructure.*

The explanatory relationship between the *Individual* and *Action* is (6) *strategy*; and strategy in the Euro crisis had been for the European Union to form a monetary union which controlled currency but not credit. This restricted economic policy in member nations from inflating or deflating their euro currency. But it did not restrict national credit policy, and several nations used EU credit conditions to fund financial bubbles in private or public debt (or both).

The explanatory relationship between the *Individual and Process* is *(5) policy*; and policy in the Euro crisis was to impose economic austerity upon fiscally defaulting nations. 'Austerity' is policy of imposing reduction in government spending and raising of taxes in bad economic times. It is a policy whose validity was in dispute among economists. For example, Paul Krugman's opinion was: "'The boom, not the slump, is the right time for austerity at the Treasury.' So declared John Maynard Keynes in 1937, even as F.D.R. was about to prove him right by trying to balance the budget too soon, sending the United States economy (which had been steadily recovering up to that point) into a severe recession. Slashing government spending in a depressed economy depresses the economy further; austerity should wait until a strong recovery is well under way. Unfortunately, in late 2010 and early 2011, politicians and policy makers in much of the Western world believed that they knew better, that we should focus on deficits, not jobs, even though our economies had barely begun to recover from the slump that followed the financial crisis. And by acting on that anti-Keynesian belief, they ended up proving Keynes right all over again. In declaring Keynesian economics vindicated I am, of course, at odds with conventional wisdom." (Krugman 2011) The austerity imposed by the EU on the Greek government had not worked. The austerity imposed upon Ireland and Spain had worked. As we earlier analyzed, the difference in the crisis situation was that the financial crisis in Greece was in public-debt market; whereas in Ireland and Spain, crises were in private-debt markets. In a public-debt market, the government is spending too much and collecting too little taxes. Increasing taxes and decreasing spending by firing government workers and reducing government services plunges a country with a public-debt crisis into a steeply deep economic recession.

The explanatory relationship between the *Society and Performance* is *(10) performance*; and performance of societies in the Euro crisis did experience economic recessions/depressions triggered by their fiscal crises. This performance occurred concurrently with the EU 'austerity' policy imposed upon the nations seeking 'Troika' (EU, IMF, ECB) loans. The two explanatory relations of (6) *policy* and (10) *performance* occurred simultaneously; but they were not 'causally' related. Policy did not cause performance, nor performance cause policy; instead they were functionally related. Financial crisis triggered the functional need for EU loans (bail-out funds); austerity policy demanded increases in taxes and reduction in public employment and pensions. Reduction in employment and decreased pensions resulted in less market demand and commercial retrenchment. Thus there was a statistical 'correlation' between crisis, policy, and performance—due to the functional connections between government finances, taxes, employment, and market demand. Societal systems contain functional connections but not causal connections. For the Euro crisis, Martin Wolf examined the correlation between austerity policy and economic performance in the EU nations. He wrote: "Paul Krugman had an interesting blog on the New York Times website on austerity and growth in the eurozone ('Keynes Was Right', Krugman 2011). I thought it would be interesting to examine the question, using the latest data from the International Monetary Fund's World Economic Outlook database. I have defined the fiscal tightening as the percentage point change in the structural (or cyclically-adjusted) general government deficit from 2008, the year of the crisis, to the forecast for 2012. The assumption is that this change represents the results of policy, rather than cyclical effects. I have taken growth as being the proportional change in GDP from 2008 to 2012. The result is… the bigger the structural tightening, the larger the fall in GDP.…The 8 % points of structural fiscal tightening in Greece lowered its GDP by 12 %." (Wolf 2012) In Greece, the economic depression from 2010 to 2012 there was a 17 % decline in GDP. In the cases of Spain and Ireland, economic recessions were… 2 and 6 %. Clearly the experience of austerity policy upon economic decline was more severe in a nation under a public-debt crisis than under a private-debt crisis.

The explanatory relationship between the *Reason and Process* is *(15) System*; and the system in the event was the European Monetary Union, for which the European Central Bank (ECB) was established to administer the Euro financial system. And the explanatory relationship between the *Group and Action* is *(13) operations*; and the ECB administered currency operation and, in the Euro crisis, the ECB also added a second operation of 'lender-of-last-resort' to European banks (to save the European credit part of the monetary union).

The explanatory relationship between the *Society and Process* is *(9) Regulating;* and in the Euro crisis, an additional authority was added to the ECB for regulating the large banks of the European Union.

The explanatory relationship between the *Group and Society* is *(11) Infrastructure;* and the European Monetary Union system was established to facilitate the commercial infrastructure in Europe for expanding market and trade opportunities.

The ECB had been only attending stabilizing the euro as a low-inflation currency. But the Euro crisis erupted because financial bubbles had been building in private debt markets (e.g. Ireland and Spain) and in public debt markets (e.g. Greece); and without authority for this, the ECB had paid no attention to the financial bubbles in European credit. Also the Euro crisis erupted because international banks had been trading in derivatives markets with fraudulent risk ratings; and without authority for this, the ECB had paid no attention to high-risk trading by international banks in Europe. Accordingly, the additional authority which the European Union added to the ECB during the Euro crisis was authority to regulate private banking in the European Union (EU).

Initially the authority to regulate central banks in the nations of the EU had not been assigned to the ECB by the EU. In fact, the respective central banks in European nations in the crisis (e.g. Ireland, Spain, Portugal, Greece) had failed their own national functions to regulate banks in their nations. The Irish Central Bank had allowed Irish Banks to fund a property bubble, as did the Spanish Central Bank and the Portuguese Central Bank. Also the Greek Central Bank had not pressured its Greek governments to financial transparency and even purchased Greek sovereign bonds.

Also the Central Banks in France and Germany had not prevented their international banks from trading in fraudulent derivatives. James Kanter wrote: "Banks in the European Union should quarantine their risky trading activities from their everyday savings and lending operations, as a way to safeguard the financial system and avoid future bailouts at taxpayers' expense, a panel of financial experts recommended

Tuesday. The recommendation, from a group led by the Bank of Finland's governor, in some ways recalls the old Glass-Steagall Act in the United States, which for decades after the 1929 stock market crash kept stock trading and other investment banking activities separate from retail lending. The U.S. restrictions were repealed in 1999, and many critics have said that the change paved the way for the sort of risk taking that eventually required Washington to bail out the country's biggest banks in 2008. The European proposal would stop short of requiring full separation of investment banking and commercial banking into two different companies, as Glass-Steagall did. Instead, banks that engaged in risk-taking activities beyond a certain level would have to be put into a separate unit of the same company." (Kanter 2012a, b) Thus many of the national central banks in the European Monetary Union were not properly doing their financial job of regulating credit in their nations.

Model of an International Central Bank

We see from this empirical example of the case of the European Central Bank (ECB), that if an International Bank Central (ICB) were to operate in a global context, an ICB would need to have the authority to (1) stabilize international currency integrity, (2) ensure international credit integrity, and (3) regulate national central banks. To stabilize international currency (or international currency exchange rates), currency needs to maintain no or very low inflation rates. To stabilize international credit integrity, banks need to not fund financial bubbles in private or public debt markets. To stabilize international banking, a national central bank should properly regulate the operations of banks in its country for financial integrity and transparency—not doing in-house trading, nor issuing high-risk fraudulent financial products.

The first historical lesson from the Euro crisis is that the central banks in each nation require international regulation, particularly about their international obligations over and beyond their national responsibilities. It was the National Bank of Greece which both sanctioned the Greek governments' policies of fiscal profligacy and also bought excessive amounts of Greek sovereign bonds (to annually fund Greek government deficits)—ultimately contributing to the Greek bond bubble (which brought down the Greek economy in 2010 and continues to paralyze Greece through 2015). Moreover, as seen in the case of the Spanish fiscal crisis, it was the European Central Bank and the IMF which needed to bail-out the Bank of Spain, when that central bank had bailed out Spanish private banks from their real estate bubble. National central banks are under the influence (control) of their national governments and may not be properly regulating the private banks in their national regimes.

The second lesson from the liberal hegemonies of the Dutch and British is that: for each nation to be included in a stable system, its central bank should be obligated to both the public and private financial institutions in the nation.

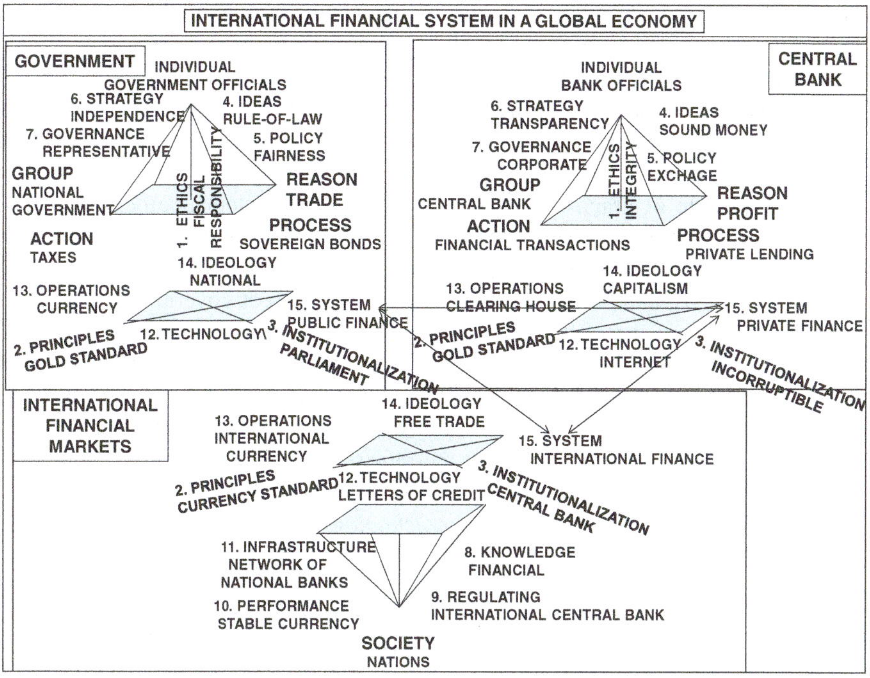

Fig. 8.3 Managed systems of government and central bank within self-organizing international financial markets

To design these two lessons into a model of an international central bank, one must graphically model two managed systems, one of the government and one of the central bank for each nation—and then, in addition, identify the international scene as a self-organizing system; and this is depicted in Fig. 8.3.

Each managed system of government and central bank has a pyramid of: *Individual* leadership over the *Group* (government or bank) and the *Actions*, *Reasoning*, and *Process* of each group's activities. And beneath each Leadership pyramid is the *Socio-Technical System* of the government or bank by which each operates. For the government, the system is the public finance of the nation. For the central bank, the system is the private finance of the nation.

The socio-technical systems of public and of private finance both interact with the financial markets, the self-organizing system of international finance. These are system interactions between the financial systems of nations and the capital flows around and between nations, as international finance.

The connections between these systems are based upon the *ideas, policies, strategy, governance, and ethics*—all of which empirically exist at a given time within the managed-systems of public and private finance.

For example, the two basic *Ideas* in a government and in its central bank are the *Rule-of-Law* and *Good Money*—which together must underlie the effective *Regulation* of the self-organizing financial markets. When governments do not act under the *rule-of-law* and banks do not operate with *trustworthy currency*, no financial system can be effective or stable. *Ideas* are basic to societies and social-technical systems. So too, the *Ethics* of *fiscal responsibility* and *banking integrity* are basic to the stability of financial systems. This is why an institutional analysis of economics and finance is essential for modeling the socio-technical systems of an economy.

The advantage of graphing all this is that one can systematically address the important *institutional issues* about the interaction of these systems. For the public and private financing in each nation, one can discuss issues of *leadership, strategy, governance, ideas, and policies*—in the managed-system of government and in the managed-system of the central bank. Also one can discuss issues in a nation of *operations, ideology, technology, principles, or institutionalization*—in the interacting systems of public and private finance. By depicting the institutionalization of the international-financial-system (in which capital flows between nations) as a self-organizing system, one can talk about the *infrastructure, performance, regulation, or knowledge* of the self-organizing world of international finance. Also one can discuss issues about *operation, ideology, technology, principles, or institutionalization* in the international system of finance.

The systems of public and private finance and international financial markets interact with one another, connecting the managed-systems of a government and its central bank to the self-organizing system of the international markets. This graphic model depicts how the financial systems of societies institutionally interact. A graphic approach may at first appear complicated, but the systems of national and international finance are complicated. Trying to simplify such systems (say down to algebraic equations of import-exports) just leaves out much of the important empirical information about how international capital really flows. A graphical approach is mathematically basic to any institutional analysis of financial and economic system. A topological approach does not preclude the use of algebraic equations in models, particularly when flows can be quantitatively measured in the institutional connections of a graph.

The first system requirement for a stable international system is that each nation which participates in the system must have sound financial policies in its government and also an effective central-bank regulatory policy over its private banks. Nations which do not meet these requirements should not be included in the international financial system.

Earlier we had noted that the Sobel-Kindleberger description of a 'liberal hegemon' provided five key aspects of public good, as Sobel summarized: "…maintaining a relatively open market for distress goods, providing countercyclical, or at least stable, long-term lending; policing a relatively stable system of exchange rates; ensuring the coordination of macroeconomic policies; and acting as a lender of last resort by discounting or otherwise providing liquidity in financial crisis." (Sobel 2012) These are central bank functions. To construct a stable but non-hegemonic international system, this suggests that there need be an international central

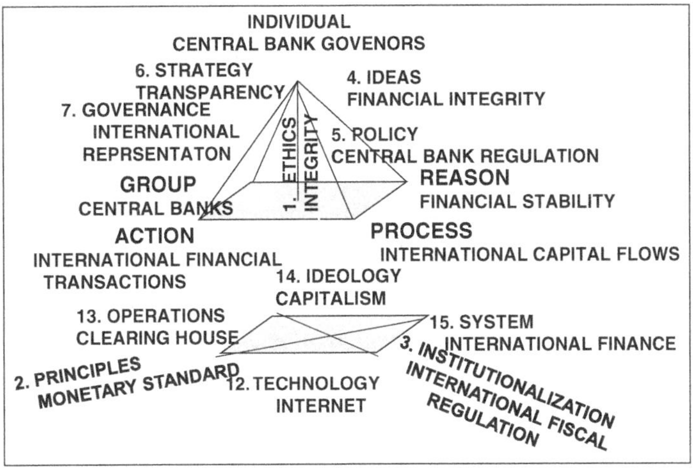

Fig. 8.4 Managed system of an international central bank

bank, which regulates the central banks of each nation participating in the international system.

> *The international grid should be organized with international central bank under which all national central banks are regulated. Central banks of each nation need to be under some international regulation.*

We graph an international central bank managed-system in Fig. 8.4.

The *Group* involved in an International Central Bank (ICB) would include the *central banks* of nations which agree to being regulated by the ICB. The *governance* of the ICB should be by *international representation*. (There is precedent for 'international representation' in the governances of the World Bank and the International Monetary Fund, which we will later discuss.) The *ideas* of the ICB should center on *financial integrity*. The *policy* of the ICB should be national *central bank regulation. Reasoning* in the managed system of the ICM should be toward international *financial stability*. The *strategy* of ICB should be to introduce *transparency* into international capital flows.

The condition of 'transparency' presently does not exist in international capital flows. Earlier, we noted that Nicholas Shaxson estimated a large percentage of the contemporary flows of international capital are for (or from) illegal activities. Shaxson wrote: "Most people are dimly aware of the murky world of offshore finance. But how big is the problem? The OECD reckons that about half of all the world's cross-border trade involves structures for concealing money … as corporations and rich individuals shuffle profits around to avoid taxes and for yet more nefarious reasons … There are basically three forms of dirty money. One is criminal money: from drug dealing, say, or slave trading or terrorism. The next is corrupt money, like the late former Nigerian dictator Sani Abacha's looted oil billions.

The third form, commercial money—what our finest companies and richest individuals hide from our tax collectors—is bigger. The point is that these three forms of dirty money use exactly the same mechanisms and subterfuges: tax havens, shell banks, shielded trusts, anonymous foundations, dummy corporations, mispricing schemes... all administered by... mainstream banks, lawyers, and accountants." (Shaxson 2011)

In the socio-technical system of the ICB, the *operations* provide a *clearing house* for transactions between national central bank. The *system* is *international finance;* and the *technology* is the *internet* of electronic financial transactions. The *principles* of ICB is to administer an international *monetary standard.* The institutionalization of the ICB is to administer *international fiscal regulation.* The *ideology* of the ICB is for a productive *capitalism.*

Using the model for an International Central Bank, we can now construct a model of a cooperative (hegemonic) international financial system, as in Fig. 8.5.

The small figures of the nations 1–3 indicate that an institutional model of each nation is necessary for every nation to participate in an international central bank arrangement. The lines indicate that the connections from each nation's central bank to the international central bank is one for the regulation of central banks. The line connecting the institutionalization procedures of the international central bank

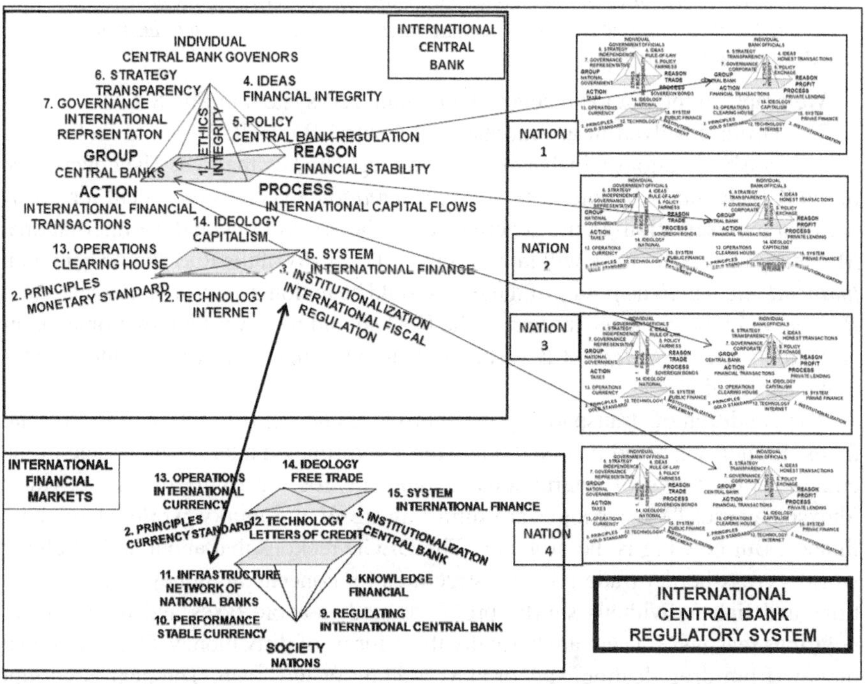

Fig. 8.5 Institutional infrastructure for an international central bank

to the self-organizing system of international financial markets indicates that the function of the international central bank is to stabilize the infrastructure of international banking.

This model consists of two managed systems in each participating nation of public and private financial systems. As the arrows indicate (drawn from each nation's central bank toward the International Central Bank), the central banks in the national financial systems network together through the ICB. The International Regulation of the Institutionalization in the managed-system of the ICB then provides the function of Regulation over all the national central banks participating in the self-organizing system of international finance.

In the models, the socio-technical-system of each component has the criterion of 'institutionalization' as a specification. In any societal system, how the functions of a society are established, institutionalized, is a critical feature of the society. As seen in the history of the Dutch hegemony, their financial system operated as a stable system, institutionalized with government-fiscal-soundness and banking-integrity. Regulation is the key societal feature for the regulation of institutionalized procedures, so that activities are functional and effective and not corrupted.

History: Bank for International Settlements

Historically, there is an International Bank for Settlements (BIS) for financial transactions between national central banks; but BIS is not itself an international central bank. BIS has no regulatory authority over banks, has no international currency to regulate, and does not act as a Bagehot lender-of-last-resort to banks. Hence it is not a central bank. Traditionally, central banks have contributed to the stability of national financial systems through: (1) national fiscal policy, (2) GDP growth, (3) currency integrity, and (4) lender-of-last-resort. But these have been the responsibilities only if national central banks, with the exception of the European Central Bank.

The challenge now is about global financial systems, in which the many national financial systems are embedded. BIS is a cooperative organization whose members are national central banks. BIS did not play a major role in stopping the Global Financial Crisis of 2007–2008; nor did it even participate in solving the Euro crisis of 2009–2015. It is interesting to ask, why not? A central bank traditionally plays an important role for financial stability—as the lender-of-last-resort to private banks in stopping runs on them. Why did not the BIS play such a role in 2007–2008 global crisis? And why did it play no role in the Euro crisis of 2009–2015? Instead as we have reviewed, it was the International Monetary Fund (IMF) and the European Central Bank (ECB), as two of the 'Troika' which included the European Union (EU), which played the important roles in 2010. The IMF and World Bank are banks which loan funds to member governments; but neither is an organization of central banks, as is BIS.

BIS operates as a kind of 'club' for heads of central banks to meet for a weekend once a month to communicate with each other. Financially it provides this organizational service by acting as a bank for central banks to exchange currency or credit with one another. "The Bank fulfils this mandate by acting as a forum for discussion and decision-making among central banks and within the international financial and supervisory community, a centre for economic and monetary research, a prime counterparty for central banks in their financial transactions; and agent or trustee in connection with international financial operations." (BIS 2007)

Thus the BIS is not involved with attempting to establish any form of an international currency, such as the European Central Bank which was established to operate the European currency of the Eurodollar. The BIS facilitates financial transactions between central banks (outside of any private financial market open to the public) but does not extend a credit line to any central bank (not a lender-of-last-resort to central banks). Finally, BIS is not charged with regulating any national central bank.

In 2006, members of the BIS included: "Central banks or monetary authorities of Algeria, Argentina, Australia, Austria, Belgium, Bosnia and Herzegovina, Brazil, Bulgaria, Canada, Chile, China, Croatia, the Czech Republic, Denmark, Estonia, Finland, France, Germany, Greece, Hong Kong SAR, Hungary, Iceland, India, Indonesia, Ireland, Israel, Italy, Japan, Korea, Latvia, Lithuania, the Republic of Macedonia, Malaysia, Mexico, the Netherlands, New Zealand, Norway, the Philippines, Poland, Portugal, Romania, Russia, Saudi Arabia, Singapore, Slovakia, Slovenia, South Africa, Spain, Sweden, Switzerland, Thailand, Turkey, the United Kingdom and the United States, plus the European Central Bank." (BIS 2007)

The history of BIS began after the First World War: "Before 1914, central banks of the western industrialized world had cooperated occasionally under the classical gold standard. The financial disruption and the strenuous efforts to restore the gold standard after the First World War further underlined the need for close cooperation. It was not until the Young Plan was elaborated in 1928–1929 that the idea took concrete shape. The Young Plan, adopted in January 1930 at the Hague Conference, primarily dealt with the reparation payments imposed on Germany by the Treaty of Versailles. In order to give the reparations issue a more commercial, and thus politically less sensitive, character, the Hague Agreement entailed the creation of the Bank for International Settlements to take over the functions previously performed by the Agent General for Reparations in Berlin and to act as a trustee for the Dawes and Young Loans, the proceeds of which were partly reinvested in the German economy. In addition, the BIS would promote central bank cooperation in general." (BIS 2007)

BIS was located in Basel, Switzerland, beginning in May 1930 with 24 European central banks as members. But the U.S. depression also began the same year and soon spread to Europe: "However, the high hopes were soon dashed by the 1931–1933 financial crises, in which the BIS failed to play the role of lender of last resort, notwithstanding noteworthy attempts at organizing support credits for both the Austrian and German central banks in 1931. Moreover, the financial crisis brought the reparations issue to an abrupt end (1932 Lausanne Conference), thus eliminating one of the Bank's original raisons d'être. After the devaluation of the pound sterling in September 1931 and of the US dollar in March 1933, the BIS participated in a number of—unsuccessful—attempts to end exchange rate instability by restoring the gold standard, culminating in the World Monetary and Economic Conference of June-July 1933 in London. After 1933, and definitely after the collapse of the Gold Bloc in 1935–1936, the BIS had little choice but to limit itself to undertaking banking transactions for the account of central banks and providing a forum for central bank governors to help them maintain contact in a world increasingly dominated by the pursuit of autarky and by international confrontation rather than cooperation." (BIS 2007)

During World War II, BIS assisted the German central bank transferring looted funds: "The precariousness of wartime financial neutrality was underlined when after the war it transpired that the gold used by the German Reichsbank during the war to honor its prewar obligations towards the BIS partly originated from the looted gold reserves of the Belgian and Dutch central banks. This gold was subsequently returned by the BIS to its rightful owners (Agreement with the Tripartite Commission for the Restitution of Monetary Gold, Washington, 1948). In July 1944, the United Nations Bretton Woods Conference adopted a resolution calling for the liquidation of the BIS, on the grounds of its supposed domination by the Axis Powers during the war and because its traditional field of activity would henceforth be largely covered by the soon to be created International Monetary Fund (IMF) and the International Bank for Reconstruction and Development (IBRD, or World Bank). However, in 1946 European central bank governors started to meet regularly in Basel once again. Soon it became clear that the BIS had an important role to play in making the Bretton Woods system work in the European context, and in 1948 the liquidation resolution was officially revoked." (BIS 2007)

Europe moved toward integration establishing the Organization for European Economic Cooperation (OEEC, later OECD): "In the 1950s, the BIS acted as agent for the European Payments Union (EPU) as a part of the OEEC….The EPU was designed to assist the European countries in restoring exchange rate convertibility, as intended by the Bretton Woods agreement. The EPU system operated by offsetting trade balances between countries through multilateral compensation, initially largely in credit but increasingly in gold or gold-convertible dollars." (BIS 2007)

However, the Bretton Woods system established after the Second World War to reintroduce an international gold standard, came apart in the 1960s, with the U.S. withdrew its dollar from a gold standard: "In fact, throughout the 1960s, the growing inherent instability in the Bretton Woods system called for close monetary cooperation to try to counter recurring problems such as the weakness of the pound sterling and, most importantly, the increasing pressure on the gold parity of the US dollar (fixed at $35 per ounce since 1934). Pressure on the dollar's gold parity resulted from an insufficient supply of gold and from the weakening of the US balance of payments. In the context of the BIS, an array of instruments was put into place to relieve these strains. These included the so-called Gold Pool, whereby central banks intervened directly on the London gold market, and a network of mutual support facilities (swaps) between the major central banks. Special support credits were arranged through the BIS as the need arose: for the pound sterling in 1961

(Basel Agreement) and in subsequent years, for the French franc in 1968, and two so-called Sterling Group Arrangements in 1966 and 1968 to help resolve the sterling balances problem. These joint initiatives proved in the end insufficient to prevent the breakdown of the Bretton Woods system in August 1971, when President Nixon closed the US 'gold window'." (BIS 2007).

After 1960, the financial world operated again without a gold standard: "With the collapse of the Bretton Woods system, central banks found themselves confronted with the very different reality of managed floating. Political factors compounded by the 1973 oil crisis prevented a market-induced return to stability and prompted continued central bank intervention. Within the BIS context, financial stability issues gained increasing prominence. The G10 central banks set up a Euro-currency Market Standing Committee to monitor the rapidly expanding euro-currency market. The globalization of financial markets and the highly publicized failure of a number of international banks in the wake of the 1973 crisis led to the establishment of what would later become the Basel Committee on Banking Supervision to study the prudential aspects of international banking in 1974. These efforts led to the 1975 Basel Concordat on the sharing of supervisory responsibilities of banks' foreign activities between host and home-country authorities; and the 1988 Basel Capital Accord, recommending a risk-weighted capital ratio for internationally active banks. A negotiation round to review and update the Basel Capital Accord was started in 1997, and led in 2004 to the endorsement by the G10 central bank governors and heads of supervision of a new capital measurement and capital standards framework (Basel II). Throughout this period, the BIS continued to provide emergency assistance where needed, increasingly on a global scale as witnessed by the credit facilities provided to the central bank of Mexico in 1982 and 1995 and to Brazil in 1998." (BIS 2007) Thus the BIS began to move some involvement toward regulation of international banking by establishing standards for measuring capital risks in banks (Basel II)—but still without the authority to enforce such standards.

In 1979, the European Monetary System (EMS) was established and a European currency unit (ECU), the euro-dollar, was set; and in 1991, the Massstrict Treaty established the European Monetary Institute (EMI), which was replaced by the European Central Bank (ECB) in 1994. This changed the focus of BIS: "The EMI's move from Basel to Frankfurt in November 1994 brought the BIS's direct involvement in European monetary unification to an end. The increased globalization, deregulation and sophistication of financial markets have focused the attention of the BIS firmly on issues related to the soundness of the international financial architecture and the threats posed by systemic risks. These issues, as discussed and studied in the various central bank expert meetings and groupings set up in the context of the BIS, are of interest to the central bank community worldwide." (BIS 2007)

Thus in the institutional history of the BIS was never intended to become a global central bank, regulating the functioning of national central banks. Consequently, in the current global financial system what is missing in system control are: (1) no stable international currency, (2) no stability of international credit, and (3) no international regulation of international banks in the world. Accordingly, there are no institutional mechanisms for ensuring a stable financial system in the world.

Consequently, financial instabilities, such as the Global Financial Crisis of 2007–2008 and the Euro Crisis of 2010–2015, can recur and recur. But what if BIS ever aspired to be an international central bank (to regulate the central banks in the international financial grid), how must it evolve? It would need to implement an institutional structure along the lines of the model for an International Central Bank, as previously described.

Summary

One of the societal functions of a central bank in a nation is to regulate the financial banking system of the nation. Without proper central bank regulation, banks can be operated improperly, leading to bank runs. The problem of the present international financial system is that there is no international central bank regulating the central banks of each nation. Thus the international banking system as a whole is unregulated. To create an international central bank would provide a way for the self-organizing system of international finance to be under some regulatory control—regulating the central bank operations of each member nation. System control would be over the fiscal integrity of each member nation's government and over the regulatory integrity of the central bank of the nation.

References

Alderman, L. (2015). *Deal or no deal, Greece faces a difficult aftermath.* Retrieved 2015, from http://www.nytimes.com/2015/07/10/business/international/deal-or-no-deal-greece-faces-a-difficult-aftermath.html?_r=0

BIS Archive Guide. (2007). Retrieved from www.bis.org

Eddy, M. (2013). *Europe inches closer to establishing a Banking Union.* Retrieved May 8, from http://www.nytimes.com/2013/05/09/business/global/09iht-germanbank09.html

Eichengreen, B. (2008). *Globalizing capital: A history of the international monetary system.* Princeton, NJ: Princeton University Press.

European Commission. (2012). *High-level expert group on reforming the structure of the EU banking sector presents its report.* Brussels: European Commission. Retrieved October 2, from http://europa.eu/rapid/press-release_IP-12-1048_en.htm?locale=en; http://ec.europa.eu/internal_market/bank/docs/high-level_expert_group/report_en.pdf

Ewing, J. (2015). European Central Bank expands mandate as it struggles to keep zone intact. *New York Times.* Retrieved May 24, from http://www.nytimes.com/2015/05/25/business/international/european-central-bank-expands-mandate-as-it-struggles-to-keep-zone-intact.html

Higgins, A., & Jolly, D. (2013). Deal on banking union will test goal of United Europe. *New York Times.* Retrieved December 19, from http://www.nytimes.com/2013/12/20/business/international/deal-on-banking-union-will-test-goal-of-united-europe.html

Kanter, J. (2012). Europe's Banks urged to keep trading and lending operations separate. *New York Times.* Retrieved October 2, from http://www.nytimes.com/2012/10/03/business/global/europes-banks-should-isolate-risky-businesses-expert-group-says.html

Kanter, J. (2012). European leaders hail accord on banking supervision. *New York Times*. Retrieved December, 2012, from http://www.nytimes.com/2012/12/14/business/global/eu-leaders-hail-accord-on-banking-supervision.html

Kirby, P. (2015). Greek debt crisis: Is Grexit inevitable? *BBC News*. Retrieved June 29, from http://www.bbc.com/news/world-europe-32332221

Krugman, P. (2011). Keynes was right. *New York Times*. Retrieved December 29, from http://www.nytimes.com/2011/12/30/opinion/keynes-was-right.html?_r=1

Sobel, A. C. (2012). *Birth of hegemony*. Chicago: University of Chicago Press.

Shaxson, N. (2011). *Treasure Islands: Uncovering the damage of offshore banking and tax havens*. New York: St. Martin's Press/Palgrave McMillan.

Thomas, L., & Eavis, P. (2015). As Greece deadline looms, European Central Bank plays key role. *New York Times*. Retrieved June 21, from http://www.nytimes.com/2015/06/22/business/european-central-bank-plays-dual-role-in-greek-crisis.html

Trichet, J-. C. (2013). The euro zone and the global crisis. *New York Times*. Retrieved March 15, from http://www.nytimes.com/2013/03/16/opinion/global/the-euro-zone-and-the-global-crisis.html

Wolf, M. (2012). The impact of fiscal austerity in the eurozone. *Financial Times*. Retrieved April 27, from http://blogs.ft.com/martin-wolf-exchange/2012/04/27/the-impact-of-fiscal-austerity-in-the-eurozone/

Chapter 9
Gaming-the-System

Introduction

Even good people get tempted. The basic truism about any financial system is that's its about money; and the truth about money is that there will always be people to cheat, to steal it. Money is the repository of wealth and what better to steal—than money? This is why financial systems must be regulated. Financial systems are temptations to theft and corruption, which do not contribute to the public good due to a lack of proper regulation. We saw in the model of the international financial grid that abuse of financial integrity is deep, widespread, and costly to the public good. We conclude this book with examining cases of theft—individual corruption and institutional corruption—the case of Libor in the twenty-first century and the case of the South Sea Bubble in the eighteenth century.

History: The Case of Libor

In the case of Libor, deliberate corruption among bank traders altered the Libor index during the first decade of the twenty-first century. The Libor index began as a convention among banks in London, to set a daily average interest rate for loans between banks.

Landon Thomas wrote: "Libor (short for the London Interbank Offered Rate) is the interest rate that affects trillions of dollars' worth of corporate and consumer loans each year. It is supposed to be a neutral figure that reflects how much it costs a bank to borrow money … In the early days of Libor, starting in the late 1960s and into the 1980s, the fact that the rate banks used to borrow money was set and governed by a small group of like-minded bankers based in London was not seen as a problem. In fact, according to Minos A. Zombanakis, a former banker at Manufacturers Hanover who says he made the very first loan based on Libor by

F. Betz, *Stability in International Finance*, SpringerBriefs in Economics,
DOI 10.1007/978-3-319-26760-9_9

inventing the product on the fly, it was a sense of responsibility and trust between banks that underpinned the rate's success. Mr. Zombanakis, who is 85 years old and retired in his home country of Greece, recalls that first Libor loan—$80 million extended by a group of banks to Iran, as if it were yesterday. 'We had to fix a rate, so I called up all the banks and asked them to send to me by 11 a.m. their cost of money,' he said. 'We got the rates, I made an average of them all, and I named it the London interbank offer rate.' For more than 15 years, the banks set the rate more or less as Mr. Zombanakis described—by throwing out the highest and lowest rates and compiling an average of the remaining ones. Then, in 1986, the British Bankers' Association was asked by its member banks to assist in the setting of the benchmark rate. It has overseen the process ever since, even as the club of gentlemen bankers making syndicated loans in the City of London evolved into the opaque and impersonal multitrillion-dollar interbank market." (Thomas 2012)

In the beginning, it was bankers' sense of responsibility and trust (integrity) which was essential to the accuracy of Libor—at first but not later. After 1986, the British Bankers' Association supposedly oversaw the procedures for setting the rate. But their oversight failed, and at some point, the rate became rigged. Peter Eavis wrote: "Eighteen banks currently supply data for setting dollar-denominated Libor. According to regulators, Barclays traders sought to skew Libor to benefit their bets. These trades were executed using financial contracts called 'derivatives' that were linked to Libor." (Eavis 2012)

It happened that the Libor rate was important not only to British banking but also to European and American financial systems. Gary Gensler wrote: "Americans who save for the future, use credit cards or borrow money for tuition, cars and homes deserve assurance that the interest rates on their savings and loans are set in a reliable and honest way. That's why the revelation that the British bank Barclays attempted to manipulate the London interbank offered rate, or Libor—one of the benchmark rates used to determine the cost of borrowing around the world—is so disturbing. But the Barclays case isn't only about misconduct by large financial institutions. It also raises questions about the reliability and accuracy of these key interest rates, which are largely determined by the private sector, without significant government oversight. When you save money in a money market fund or short-term bond fund, or take out a mortgage or a small-business loan, the rate you receive or pay is often based, directly or indirectly, on Libor. It's the reference rate for nearly half of adjustable-rate mortgages in the United States; for about 70 % of the American futures market; and for a majority of the American swaps market, where businesses hedge risks from changes in interest rates." (Gensler 2012)

At the time, Gary Gensler was head of a U.S. regulatory agency, Commodities Futures Trading, which was assigned (after 2009) a new responsibility to regulate financial derivative markets. As part of his responsibility, he looked into the Libor index. Gensler noted some odd things about the Libor rate. Gary Gensler wrote: "These changes in the markets raise questions about the integrity of this important benchmark. First, why is Libor so different from another benchmark interest rate for borrowing in United States dollars—Euribor, or euro interbank offered rate? Both rates are calculated on the basis of banks' answers to roughly the same question.

For Libor, a bank is asked at what rate it thinks it can borrow, while for Euribor, a bank is asked at what rate it thinks other banks are able to borrow. And yet the Euribor for dollar borrowings is about twice as high as the comparable Libor. Second, why have Libor and other benchmark rates typically not been aligned, since 2008, with the borrowing rates that would be implied by foreign exchange markets? A long-established financial theory known as interest rate parity says that the difference in interest rates between two countries should be roughly in line with the expected change in exchange rates between the countries' currencies. (If it isn't, that opens an opportunity for arbitrage, the practice of taking advantage of price differences.) Until 2007, as the theory predicted, the difference between the borrowing rate in one currency and the lending rate in another could typically be derived from foreign currency exchange rates. In the last few years, that hasn't been the case, and this divergence between theory and practice has yet to be adequately explained. Third, why is the volatility of the dollar-denominated Libor so much lower than the volatility of other short-term credit market rates? Just like stocks and bonds, short-term interest rates experience a certain volatility. But Libor has less severe swings than comparable rates. In addition, the variation in rates that some banks submit to the British Bankers' Association (the private group that oversees Libor) don't seem to match the variation in the rates for their credit default swaps (financial instruments that are similar to insurance and are one measure of a bank's credit risk). There have been times when the swap rates have widened for particular banks (suggesting a growing credit risk) even as their Libor submissions have remained stable (suggesting that the banks' borrowing costs haven't changed). Anyone saving or borrowing for the future has a real stake in the integrity of Libor and in the answers to these questions." (Gensler 2012)

Gensler was intrigued by these three puzzling aspects. Firstly, the Libor rate was not tracking with other rates based upon borrowing in the United States (such as the Euribor or euro interbank offered rate). Interest rates on different kinds of loans should track together, all based upon economic fundamentals of the current situation. Secondly, since 2008, the Libor rate did not track with changes in foreign exchange markets, again as all such changes should be based upon current economic fundamentals. Thirdly, the volatility (range of change) of the Libor rate was much less than the volatility of other rates in short-term credit markets, again something odd due to similar economic fundamentals in credit markets. Gensler thought that was something might be wrong; and why had previously no government regulator examined this accuracy of the Libor index? Perhaps the previous lack of interest in Libor was because many of the government regulators at the time had instead espoused a policy of 'deregulation', believing that financial markets always perform 'perfectly'. If individuals as regulators do not believe in the efficacy of government regulation, they can ignore all the empirical evidence of corruption, in a societal system they are supposed to be regulating. *Particular individuals' characters provide a historic 'context' to any sociological institutional process (e.g. bureaucratic rationality); just as conversely, institutional procedures provide a historic context to individual behaviors.*

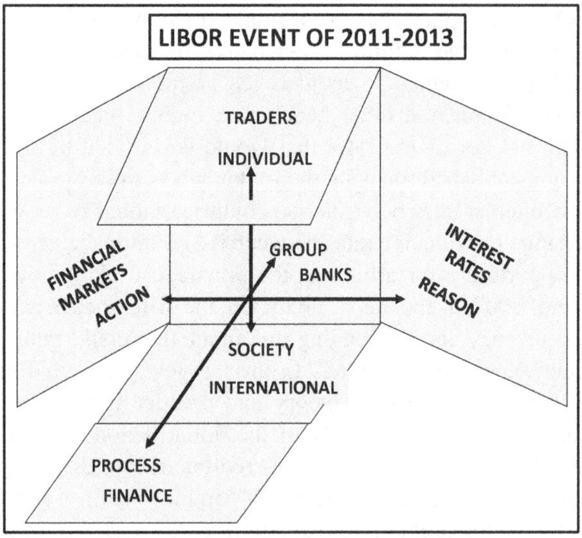

Fig. 9.1 Perceptual space of Libor event

Gensler began his investigation of Libor and discovered fraud—not by traditional crooks and thieves, but by white-collar employees (traders) 'gaming a system'. Floyd Norris wrote: "The Libor market, we now know, was a fraud. There were few, if any, real trades backing the indicator. This week the scandal claimed its second top European banker and treated us to more of those delightful emails and electronic chats in which traders discuss their deceptions. 'Don't worry mate—there's bigger crooks in the market than us guys!' wrote an official of Rabobank, the large Dutch lender, after he agreed to a request from one of the bank's traders in 2007 to submit a phony rate for Libor rates in yen. He was right about that. As more cases are disclosed, there will no doubt be more big fines and more assurances from senior executives that they had no idea what was going on.'" (Norris 2013)

We analyze the Libor event in the cross-disciplinary framework of societal dynamics Fig. 9.1.

INDIVIDUAL—In the Libor event, the *Individuals* involved were traders employed by integrated banks, such as Barclays.

SOCIETY—The *Society* was the international financial society, involving many nations.

GROUP—The *Group* consisted of many banks in different nations, British, European, and American.

PROCESS—The *Process* focused upon Finance, specifically the financial transactions of loans.

ACTIONS—The *Action* was the manipulation of Libor index for the Financial Markets around the world.

REASON—The *Reasoning* focused upon establishing appropriate interest rates for loans, based upon the rates of current short-term loans between banks—establishing interest rates that would be beneficial to a bank's profits from trading.

Libor was supposed to be a daily average rate-of-interest on inter-bank loans (interest rate on over-night loans between banks, in order to help balance their previous day's transactional accounts). The Libor index was used to set, on a daily basis, a whole range of interest rates on different kinds of loans (mortgages, etc.) However, traders in banks made daily bets on the direction of various kinds of interest rates; and they wanted the Libor rate to go up or down, in correspondence with their recent bets on interest rates. So they conspired to fix the Libor rate—a fraudulent bank practice by some but not all banking employees (mostly involving traders in the large integrated banks in Europe and America). These traders in banks were not really 'trading'—buying and selling things. They were gambling, making bets on the directions of interest rates.

Next we can analyze system control in Fig. 9.2. 'Libor' was an index used in the *Control* of the Managed Systems of Banks as a guide to setting interest rates on all kinds of loans. The *Group* involved were the banks in many the countries of the world. The *Reason* was thinking about how to establish a measure of interest rates in financial markets based upon one current activity of loans between banks. The *Society* involved in the Libor case was international, banks in many different countries using the index-rate.

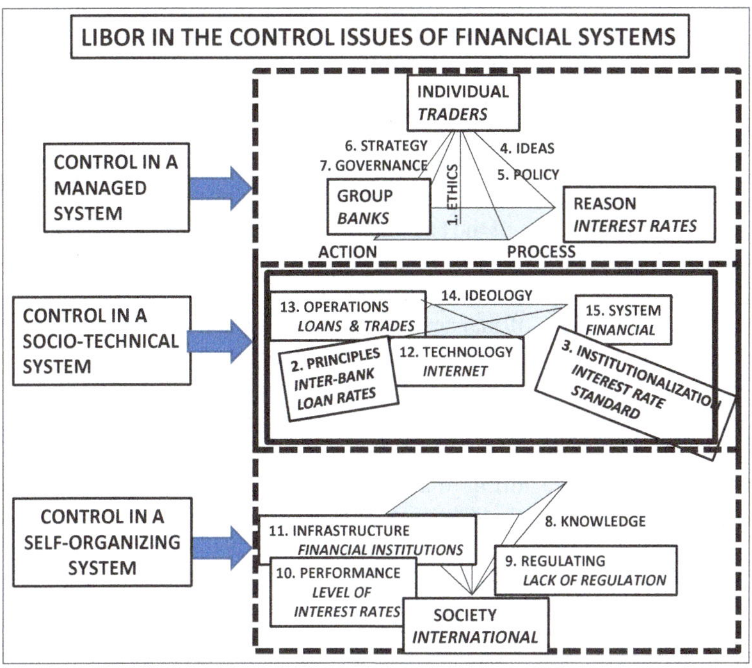

Fig. 9.2 Control issues of Libor event

The Libor rate was of particular interest to *Traders* in banks, trading on the differences between loans, exchange rates, etc. The *(15) System* involved was the financial systems in different nations. The *(13) Operations* are loans and trades, facilitated by financial transactions over the *(12) Technology* of the Internet. Interest rates on different types of loans were *(3) Institutionalized* under a general standard of the *(2) Principle* of the Libor rate. The *(11) Infrastructure* was the financial institutions, providing a societal level of *(10) Performance* for finance at current levels of interest rates. But the Libor rate lacked effective government *(9) Regulation*, depending only on a London private bank association which allowed abuse of the Libor rate-setting. One sees that the failure of societal control in the principle of Libor as a current interest rate standard was a failure in the *(9) Regulation* of the self-organizing system of the *(11) Financial Infrastructure.*

Traders were the *Individuals* employed in the trading divisions of banks, who wanted the manipulation of Libor rate as their *(6) Strategy* for fraudulent trading which generated large profits for the banks; and in the *(7) Governance* of the banks, top management ignored the fraud, as traders were generating large profits. Cheating was the *(1) Ethics* practiced by the participating traders and silently condoned by their top management overseers. *Traders made bets on the direction of interest rates; and by manipulating the base Libor rate, tilted interest rates, up or down, in the direction of their bets.*

The bankers' self-organized *(9) Regulating* board simply did not regulate the Libor rate setting procedure, even though rumors of fraud were rampant in the trading community. The rule for *(9) Regulation,* used by the self-organized British Bankers' Association, was to 'see-no-evil' and 'hear-no-evil'.

The self-organizing view of a societal system can be further analyzed by viewing the 'explanatory relations', connecting the different classes of Individuals to the Society. In Fig. 9.3, the graph analyzes these interactions in the forms of two kinds of managed-systems, government and business, above a socio-technical system (e.g. financial system) of a self-organizing society (nation). From this view, one sees that no single person is in charge of the basic societal systems of politics and of economy. No one is in charge of a self-organizing society; instead individuals are in charge of managed-systems of government organizations and managed-systems of business organizations. Both kinds of managed-systems, government agencies and business companies constitute the infrastructure, of the self-organizing aspects of society.

Looking to the <u>right side</u> of the explanatory topology at the Businesses, one sees that the *Individuals* were the traders employed in the *Group* of banks. The traders' *(6) Strategy* was to fix the Libor rate, using their *(4) Idea* of collusion with bank employees, resulting in a shared *(1) Ethics* of cheating. Their *Reason* was to gain bonuses from their *Actions* of fixed trades, in the *Process* of derivatives trading. The *(7) Governance* of the banks by their CEOs turned a 'blind eye' away from seeing such collusion. The banks' *(5) Policy* was not to enforce compliance about bank integrity.

In contrast, looking to the <u>left side</u> of the explanatory topology at the Government Agencies, a key *Individual* was Gary Gensler, head of the Commodities Futures Trading Commission in the *Group* of regulatory government agencies. Gensler's *(4)*

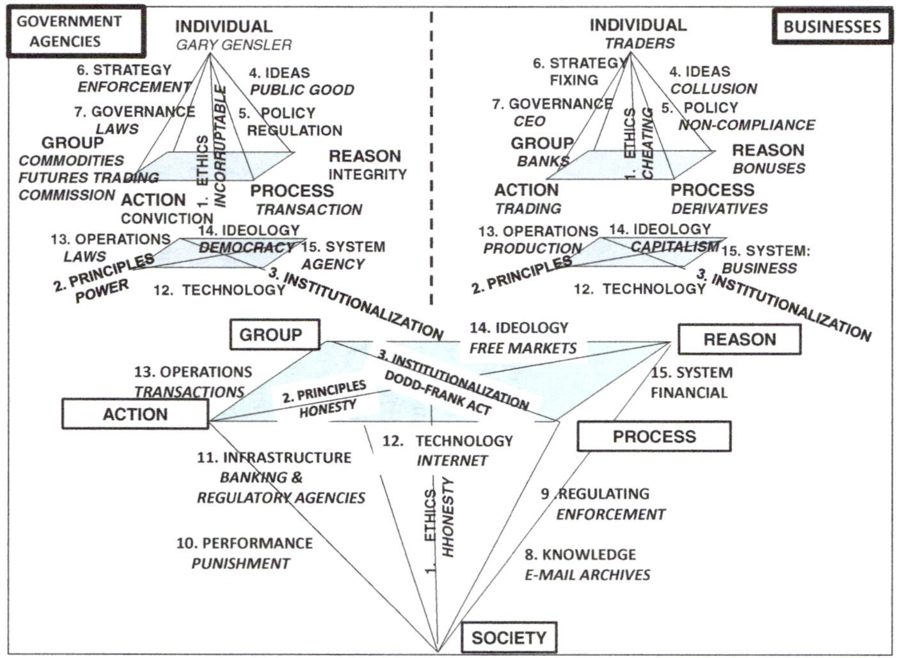

Fig. 9.3 Libor in self-organizing systems

Ideas were about the public good which can be attained through a *(5) Policy* of government regulation. His agency's *Action* was to convict individuals and banks which violated the *(7) Governance* laws on the *Process* of financial transactions. The *Reasoning* of the agency was to ensure the integrity of financial transaction. The *(1) Ethics* of the agency was incorruptibility—to serve without corruption and to find and convict corruption in the financial trading system.

Operating in the socio-technical financial system were two managed-systems of government agencies and private businesses. Together these provided the *(11) Infrastructure* of the nation's financial *(15) System*, with the *(13) Operations* of financial transactions, under the *(14) Ideology* of free markets, using the *(12) Technology* of the Internet for financial business. The *(3) Institutionalization* of the law of the Dodd-Frank Act provided the *(2) Principles* of honesty legally in the *(9) Regulation* of the financial system. The Commodities Futures Trading Commission enforced this *(9) Regulation* of the derivatives markets for the *(1) Ethics* of honesty—enabling an honest *(1) Performance* through punishment of corruptions in the *(15) Financial System.*

Individual Corruption

Some individuals in authority can corrupt a system, acting alone, or in groups, or in conspiracy. Some of the explanatory relationships are particularly critical to understanding 'corruption'. Corruption of a *Society's* societal systems is always by an *Individual.* Corruption occurs when the ethics of an individual violates the principles institutionalized for proper performance of the system (and regulators do not catch the individual's ethical violations). *This is highlighted in Fig.* 9.4. In analyzing the case of Libor, one can see that some of the explanatory relations are particularly important to limit individuals' abuses of the system: *(15) System, (2) Principles, (3) Institutionalization, (9) Regulating, (1) Ethics.* These are highlighted in Fig. 9.4.

The *Individuals* involved in the Libor case were traders employed in banks, CEOs of the banks, and Gary Gensler, head of the U.S. Commodities Futures Trading Commission (CFTC). A *(15) System* is the kind of socio-technical system important to the functioning of a society. In the case of Libor, the system was the financial system of the world, using standardized interest rates for loans. The *(1) Ethics* of the socio-technical system expresses the 'virtue' of the operations of the system. In the case of Libor, the ethics of bankers and traders should have been in the 'integrity' of their honest reporting of interbank-loans interest rates. Instead the ethics of some traders were to cheat (while their CEOs saw no evil). In contrast Mr. Gensler's ethics was to enforce honest ethical behavior in the banks and its employers.

The *(9) Regulating* of a socio-technical system should consist of overseeing and enforcing rules of the operations of an economic system—for honest, safety, and stability. In the case of Libor, the trading operations involving financial derivative contracts had been unregulated. In 2009 with U.S. government's passage of the Dodd-Frank Act, a new regulation of the U.S. derivatives market was assigned to

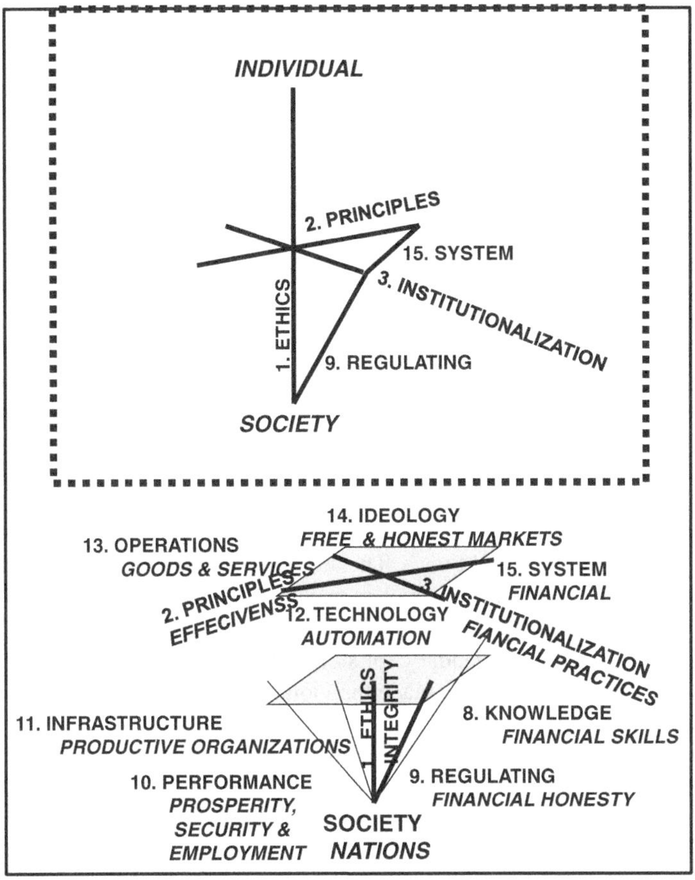

Fig. 9.4 Self-organizing relationships which limit individual corruption

the Commodities Futures Trading Commission (CFTC); and its head, Gary Gensler, began investigating the honesty of the Libor interest rate index.

The *(2) Principles* for the socio-technical system expresses the rules for proper functioning of the system. In the case of Libor, the principles should have consisted of good banking principles, providing capital loans for effective production in an economy. Instead, banks were engaging mainly in trading to generate profits. Then unethical bank traders cheated daily on the setting of the standard rate—in order to profit upon derivative trades influenced by the rate.

The *(3) Institutionalization* of the social-technical system should provide the practices for effective operations in the function. In the case of Libor, the practices were intended to be overseen by the private British Bankers' Association, but instead the Association failed to do any proper oversight of Libor.

In a self-regulating society, the ethics of individuals acting in directly-managed organization are constrained (or not constrained) by proper *Ethics, Principles, Institutionalization, and Regulating*. Without such proper constraint, greedy individuals (through irresponsibility or fraud or corruption) abuse the socio-technical systems of a self-organizing society.

Financial markets are not necessarily empirically perfect; but require proper regulation for integrity, in order to actually operate toward the 'ideal' of a perfect market. Even bankers/traders in integrated banks (the banks-too-big-fail) will cheat, motivated by enormous bonus rewards. Bankers/traders too are merely human.

Epilogue

After the fraud was revealed, then some regulatory punishments began. Floyd Norris wrote: "This week's penitent financial institution, Rabobank, showed just how international a fraud this was. The bank settled with authorities in the Netherlands, Britain, Japan and the United States. The authorities said the fraud was carried out by more than two dozen traders and managers at the bank's offices in London, New York, Utrecht, Tokyo, Singapore and Hong Kong. The bank's chairman resigned. When the Libor scandal exploded last year, with Barclays as the initial villain, there was a narrative that made the violations seem understandable and perhaps provoked at least a little sympathy for the banks. They had lied about their borrowing costs during the financial crisis, concealing how difficult a time they were having. Perhaps they should not have done so, but who was really harmed? It turns out that the financial crisis did not cause the fraud; it merely made it so obvious that regulators finally noticed. It had been going on for years, aided by an international culture that treated market manipulation as a matter of course. If a bank did not have its own good reason for manipulating the market, then a trader would agree to do so as a favor for a trader at another institution. Why not? Maybe he would need a favor on another day. 'You know, scratch my back, yeah, and all,' a Rabobank trader said." (Floyd Norris 2013)

On March 14, 2014, further steps in the Libor event were continuing to unfold: "The Federal Deposit Insurance Corporation has sued 16 big banks that set a crucial global interest rate, accusing them of fraud and conspiring to keep the rate low to enrich themselves. The banks, which include Bank of America, Citigroup and JPMorgan Chase in the United States, are among the world's largest. The F.D.I.C. said it sought to recover losses that the rate manipulation caused to 10 United States banks that failed during the financial crisis and were taken over by the agency. The lawsuit was filed on Friday (March 14, 2014) in Federal District Court in Manhattan. The banks are accused of rigging the London interbank offered rate, known as Libor, from August 2007 to at least mid-2011. The F.D.I.C. also sued a trade group, the British Bankers' Association, that helped set Libor." (Associated Press 2014)

It was not European but U.S. government regulators who uncovered the Libor scandal. Joe Nocera wrote: "One of the big criticisms of the original team of financial regulators brought in by President Obama is that too many of them had worked in Bill Clinton's Treasury Department. That, of course, was the Treasury Department run by Robert Rubin and then by Lawrence Summers—an agency with a bias toward deregulation. Those regulators had supported the elimination of Glass-Steagall, the 1930s law that separated investment banks from commercial banks, and were disinclined to regulate derivatives, 'those financial weapons of mass destruction,' as Warren Buffett liked to call them. One of those old Rubin hands was Gary Gensler. An 18-year veteran of Goldman Sachs, Gensler had been the assistant secretary of financial markets under Rubin, and then later undersecretary for domestic finance, and he shared his boss's deregulatory bias. When President Obama was picking his regulatory team, he chose Gensler to be the chairman of the Commodities Futures Trading Commission. Now, Gensler is about to leave that post. And if people once doubted how tough he would be as a regulator, there is no doubt now: he may well be the single best appointment Obama made." (Nocera 2013)

The change in the American regulatory environment was a new law passed in 2009, which finally gave government authority to regulate financial derivatives. Joe Nocera wrote: "When Gensler came into office, the CFTC's job was to regulate the futures market. It was a small agency, with fewer than 700 employees. Then came the Dodd-Frank reform law, which gave the commission enormous new responsibilities. It was charged with writing dozens of rules to regulate derivatives, and to oversee a $400 trillion market. 'I hadn't realized how much authority was delegated to regulators,' he said. But he embraced the challenge. Derivative trades had always been conducted in the shadows. Gensler brought them into the light… Thanks to the trading commission's new rules, the government now has a good feel for the derivatives market. And the added transparency has also had the effect of lowering prices, which is what inevitably happens when all the market participants can see what is being bought and sold… If regulating the derivatives market were all Gensler had done, it would have been plenty. But the CFTC was also the agency that cracked the Libor scandal. A few months after being sworn in, in May of 2009, he saw an article about Libor—the interest rate banks charge to each other for interbank lending—that piqued his curiosity. 'I asked our head of enforcement—should we look into this?' The result, 3 years later, was the unveiling of an enormous scandal involving traders at more than a dozen financial institutions. Gensler said: 'I remember thinking that if it's true—that the Libor rate was being manipulated by traders—that is a really bad thing… It took 20 months before we had actionable evidence… which finally happened last year.' Barclays then agreed to pay a fine of $450 million for manipulating the Libor rate. Subsequently, the CFTC settled with five other financial institutions. A handful of traders had been indicted." (Nocera 2013)

This example emphasizes the particular roles which different individuals play in institutions of a society. Although in official positions for government regulation of financial systems, some individuals, such as Robert Rubin and Lawrence Summers, did not believe in regulation and so did little or no regulation when they occupied their institutional positions. In fact, both were active in getting U.S. laws passed in 1999, which 'deregulated' U.S. banks from their restrictions of the Glass-Steagall act (passed 60 years earlier). This allowed the 'too-big-to-fail' banks to integrate, which set the context for the global financial collapse in 2007–2008. See for example (Morgenson and Rosner 2011) and (Betz 2014). In contrast, when Gensler (also a former banker like Rubin) took up a regulatory position, he acted to regulate the societal system of finance by investigating the Libor fraud. Individual character matters in the social science of institutional behavior. This provides additional evidence for the proposition that all 'grand' social theories (such as macro-economics) can never be 'context-free'—but instead are always context-dependent upon the time place and individuals in the history of societal events. Here no macro-economic theory (e.g., problems or benefits of economic regulation) can never be context-independent (as Rubin and Summers supposed). *Methodologically, macro social science theory (grand theory) should always be expressed empirically in a context of a micro theory of societal history (middle-range theory).*

The total costs of the Libor fraud are difficult to estimate. Keri Geiger wrote: "Paula Ramada, who earned a doctorate in economics at the Massachusetts Institute of Technology, says she knows how to calculate how much an investor lost when banks allegedly rigged benchmark interest rates. Now she just needs a team of analysts—and a client to fund the work. Ramada is among a growing number of mathematicians and analysts trying to tackle a key question to emerge from the Libor scandal: If banks manipulated rates tied to $300 trillion in instruments ranging from mortgages to student loans, how much do the firms owe investors? With lawsuits wending through courts, the damage payments could climb into the billions of dollars…. Ramada and her team of researchers at London Economics, a U.K. consulting firm, propose a two-step approach. They look for divergences between Libor and other benchmark interest rates that track the cost of unsecured funding to banks, such as the Federal Reserve's Eurodollar deposit rate, as well as instruments linked to the banks' credit risks, such as credit-default swaps. The second step is to recalculate payments on specific contracts. For that, investors will need documents from their trades. "The problem comes when a company doesn't have accurate records on each and every interest rate product," Ramada says. Libor rates were probably 25 basis points to 35 basis points (a basis point is one hundredth of a percentage point) lower than they should have been from late 2007 through early 2009, according to a preliminary estimate from Marc Vellrath, chief executive officer of economic consulting firm Finance Scholars Group. His company, like Ramada's, is conferring with plaintiffs' lawyers who want to quantify their damages. The methodologies for determining damages may become a battleground, with opponents arguing over computer modeling, a decade of market prices, and the fine print on derivatives-trading agreements—if they still exist." (Geiger 2013)

What next happened institutionally to the regulation of Libor, government regulation? Nothing. There was merely a transfer from British to American shores, and it remained under private non-regulation. Nathaniel Popper wrote: "The administration of a distinctly British institution is being handed over to an American company. The parent company of the New York Stock Exchange won a contract on Tuesday to administer and improve the benchmark interest rate known as Libor, long run by the British Bankers' Association. The move could help provide a fresh start for Libor, or the London interbank offered rate, which is used to determine the cost of short-term loans around the world. The banks that help set the rate each day have been accused of conspiring to rig the rate for their own benefit before and during the financial crisis, leading to billions of dollars in fines and a few arrests. The move is a symbolic blow to a British financial industry that has been rocked by scandals and forced to look to the outside for leadership. Last week, a Canadian, Mark Carney, took over leadership of the Bank of England. The London Stock Exchange was among the four companies that also bid for the Libor contract, said a person briefed on the process, who spoke on the condition of anonymity ahead of a public announcement." (Popper 2013)

Not everyone was pleased with the decision to continue the international financial index, under private operation. Floyd Norris wrote: "Mr. Gensler said in his speech: 'In the U.S., Libor is the reference rate for 70 % of the futures market and more than half of the swaps market. It is the reference rate for more than $10 trillion in loans. Such a huge market created ample incentives to cheat … The frauds being prosecuted now involved interest rate manipulations of only a few hundredths of a percentage point … Unfortunately, nothing fundamental is being changed. Libor lives on.' Regulators who wanted to change that, most notably Mr. Gensler, have been outmaneuvered by those who did not want to risk damaging one of the biggest and most lucrative markets around." (Norris 2013)

However, some assignments of irresponsibility did occur. Ben Protess and Mark Scott wrote: "Regulators delivered the first blow in a major investigation into whether big banks had improperly set key interest rates that affected how consumers and companies borrowed money around the world. On Wednesday, Barclays agreed to pay $450 million to resolve accusations that it had tried to manipulate rates to benefit the bank's own bottom line … The settlement is the first in a series of potential cases against other financial firms, including HSBC, Citigroup and JPMorgan Chase … The Barclays settlement, which offers clues about the scope of the inquiry, may provide a template for future actions." (Protess and Scott 2012)

British indignation about banking (despite previous failure of British regulatory effort) assigned responsibility to an 'American', as head of the British bank of Barclays. Ben Protess and Mark Scott wrote: "Robert Diamond, the bank's chief executive, expressed contrition and underscored the recent changes at Barclays. Mr. Diamond said that he and three other top executives had voluntarily agreed to give up their bonuses this year. Most of the traders involved in the case have left the bank, according to people briefed on the matter. Mr. Diamond said in a statement: 'The events which gave rise to today's resolutions relate to past actions which fell well short of the standards to which Barclays aspires in the conduct of its business. When we identified those issues, we took prompt action to fix them and cooperated extensively and proactively with the authorities.'" (Protess and Scott 2012) *The cultural context of individuals, of course, contribute to their ethical orientation in societal institutional procedures.*

First, the chairman of Barclays resigned. Mark Scott and Michael J. De La Merced wrote: "Marcus Agius, the chairman of Barclays, resigned on Monday, less than a week after the big British bank agreed to pay $450 million to settle accusations that it had tried to manipulate key interest rates to benefit its own bottom line … ' A former banker at Lazard, Mr. Agius joined the Barclays board in 2006 and became its chairman in 2007. He was also the honorary chairman of the British Bankers' Association, the organization that oversees one of the key rates in question, the London interbank offered rate, or Libor. Mr. Agius tendered his resignation as chairman of the trade association on Monday." (Scott and De La Merced 2012)

Also Mr. Diamond's regrets were not sufficient for British regulators. Andrew Ross Sorkin wrote: "The conventional explanation is that Diamond, 61, was ousted last July after regulators in Washington and London uncovered a 'pervasive' scheme by several banks, including Barclays, to manipulate a key interest-rate benchmark known as the Libor, or London interbank offered rate … Despite all the headlines—and there were hundreds of them—Bob Diamond's role in the scandal was minimal, and perhaps wildly overblown. It may have been the nominal cause for his dismissal, but what really drove his departure was that he had become, as one member of Parliament described him, the 'unacceptable face of banking' … On July 2, less than a week after the Libor scandal broke, King summoned Barclays' chairman, Marcus Agius, to his office, in the imposing Bank of England Building in the heart of London's financial district. According to Agius, King told him, 'Bob Diamond no longer enjoyed the support of his regulators.' The next morning, Diamond resigned … Martin Wolf of The Financial Times said: 'After the financial crisis, the British establishment became very divided over what's the model for the big banks that we want to see. Bob represented investment banking big time. He represented the success of it—but also the sense that investment banking is dicey and not a completely sound business. He represented a way of doing business that we've become very uncomfortable with'." (Sorkin 2013a, b)

A few other bank officers resigned, particularly those who were supposedly in charge of ensuring banking honesty, the compliance officers. Julia Werdigier wrote: "Barclays said on Wednesday that Hector W. Sants would not return to his post as compliance chief after taking a leave of absence because of exhaustion and stress last month. Mr. Sants, a former head of Britain's financial regulator, resigned after concluding that he would not be able to return to work in the near term, Barclays said in a statement … Mr. Sants is not the only senior financial executive in London to take a leave in recent years because of stress. But his resignation stands in contrast to the actions of António Horta-Osório, chief executive of the Lloyds Banking Group, who returned to the bank after a 2-month leave at the beginning of 2012." (Werdigier 2013)

Traders with explicit emails about the fraud were placed on leave. Chad Bray wrote: "Nearly a dozen traders have been placed on leave at five large banks in recent days, amid a wide-ranging investigation into potential manipulation of the foreign-exchange market. Authorities in Britain, the United States, Switzerland and Hong Kong are investigating whether traders colluded to rig some areas of currency trading, a market that overall generates more than $5 trillion of trades daily. In particular, they are looking at discussion logs in chat rooms between currency traders at various firms and whether those discussions corresponded with improper trading activity, according to people briefed on the investigation. On Friday, two British banks, Barclays and Royal Bank of Scotland, both placed traders on leave amid heightened scrutiny by regulators … Six traders were placed on leave at Barclays and two traders were placed on leave at Royal Bank of Scotland, these people said. They join currency traders who were placed on leave at Citigroup, Standard Chartered and JPMorgan Chase in recent weeks. In many cases, the traders have been placed on paid leave pending the outcome of the investigation … " (Bray 2013)

With the explicit emails, some traders were then indicted. Mark Scott wrote: "Two former brokers at RP Martin Holdings made their first court appearance in London on Friday in connection to charges tied to the manipulation of global benchmark interest rates … Both sets of charges contend that the men conspired with employees of UBS, the Dutch bank Rabobank, HSBC and other financial institutions to manipulate the benchmark rates for personal financial gain, according to the charge sheet." (Scott 2013)

Some traders were convicted and sentenced. Peter J. Henning wrote: "At the sentencing hearing for Kareem Serageldin, a former senior executive at Credit Suisse, Judge Alvin K. Hellerstein of the Federal District Court in Manhattan pointedly asked why someone in such a position would engage in misconduct. The judge asked, 'Why do so many good people do bad things?' That is the conundrum of many white-collar crime cases: successful business people act in ways that put careers and personal fortunes at risk for seemingly modest gains, and sometimes the misconduct benefits their company but themselves only indirectly. Mr. Serageldin was the global head of the structured credit group at Credit Suisse, responsible for overseeing its subprime mortgage securities portfolio. He was indicted in February 2012 for inflating the value of bonds held by the bank to cover up losses as the collapse in the housing market hit in late 2007. As seen in other recent cases, there were recorded telephone conversations in which Mr. Serageldin and other defendants discussed keeping the prices high to protect their positions in the hope that the housing market would turn around. When internal inquiries into the valuations were made, the defendants did their best to cover up what they had done, a losing battle that led the bank to disclose the mismarking in February 2008. Judge Hellerstein imposed a 30-month prison term, a punishment below the recommended sentence for the violation. In explaining the reason for the reduction, the judge noted that Mr. Serageldin's conduct 'was a small piece of an overall evil climate inside that bank and many other banks.'" (Henning 2013)

Observers were puzzled about the ethics. Peter Henning also wrote: "Perhaps misconduct by some groups can be ascribed to the belief that so long as everyone else seems to be doing something, it cannot actually be wrong. Continuing investigations into global banks' manipulation of the London interbank offered rate, or Libor, as well as foreign currency exchange rates are replete with examples of traders exchanging information and boasting of their ability to artificially raise or lower a benchmark rate. These are not isolated instances, but part of a pattern of conduct over months and even years. So it cannot be chalked up to the heat of the moment. What is so puzzling about people who have led otherwise good lives is that they are unlikely to have engaged in the misconduct if it is presented to them in stark terms. Ask a Wall Street trader, for example, whether he or she would trade on material nonpublic information received from a corporate insider, and the answer from most would be 'no'—at least if there was a reasonable chance of being caught. But under pressure to produce profits for a hedge fund or a bank, traders are often on the look-out for an 'edge' on the market that can slowly take them closer to crossing the line into illegality." (Henning 2013)

Summary

The idea of 'self-organizing societal systems' is a fundamental concept to both to economic theory (e.g. price-equilibrium markets) and political science theory (e.g. democracy). Both industry and government operate as self-organizing systems. A self-organizing societal system is one in which control lies in local organization and not in a central authority. In a self-organizing economic system, control is local, as competition between businesses for shares of a market. In a capitalistic democracy, while a government provides a central authority, it does not provide direct control over either political association or economic activity. Self-organization in a political system means that control ultimately is local, in the form of honest elections between contending political parties

However, local control can also be corrupted both in an economy and in a government. Corruption by fraudulent business practices (such as Pareto schemes) can cost an economy. Corruption by fraudulent electoral practices can cost a democracy. Corruptions can trigger system distortions or even system failure.

Within the single social science discipline of economics, traditional macro-economic theorists might have labeled 'corruption' as merely a 'market failure'. But any significant manipulation of a financial system goes beyond 'failure' to the very 'essence' of a market, which is fairness—the societal fairness in a proper economic trade. Particularly, a financial system basically depends upon financial 'integrity'. Hyman Minsky wrote: "Banking is not money lending… The fundamental banking activity is 'accepting', that is, 'guaranteeing' that some party is credit worthy. A bank, by accepting a debt instrument, agrees to make specified payments if the debtor will not or cannot. Such an accepted or endorsed note can be then sold in the open market." (Minsky 1982)

Bank finance needs to be conducted in an honorable way, as financial integrity in the guaranteeing of the credit of a borrower. This guarantee is based upon a banking procedure called 'due diligence' in the processing of the loan. Due diligence creates the 'public good' in banking as well as the private good of credit. The 'public good' of banking lies in the bank's guaranteeing of the credit-worthiness of the borrower. Since 'accepting and guaranteeing' a debt is the fundamental act of banking, a particular bank's integrity is its competitive advantage, in the market place of finance. A financial system can break down because of bad behavior of bankers, acting without integrity and committing financial fraud. Financial systems without integrity are crooked and can distort, even destroy, an economic system—plunging a society into depression.

References

Associated Press. (2014, March 14). F.D.I.C. Sues 16 big banks over rate rigging. *The New York Times*.

Betz, F (2014). Disequilibrium Pricing—Greek Euro Crisis. *Theoretical Economics Letters, 4*, 897–909. http://dx.doi.org/10.4236/tel.2014.49113.

Bray, C. (2013). Currency Traders Put on Leave Amid Investigation. *The New York Times*, November 1.

Eavis, P. (2012, June 27). A rate-setting mechanism of far-reaching effects. *The New York Times*.

Geiger, K. (2013). *Calculating the cost of the Libor scandal to investors*. New York: Bloomberg. Retrieved June 27, from http://www.bloomberg.com/bw/articles/2013-06-27/calculating-the-cost-of-the-libor-scandal-to-investors

Gensler, G. (2012). Libor_ Naked and exposed. *New York Times*. Retrieved August 6, from http://www.nytimes.com/2012/08/07/opinion/libor-naked-and-exposed.html?_r=0

Henning, P. J. (2013, November 25). When good people do bad things. *The New York Times*.

Minsky, H. P. (1982). *Can 'it' happen again? Essays on instability and finance*. Armonk, NY: M. E. Sharpe.

Morgenson, G., & Rosner, J. (2011). *Reckless endangerment: How outsized ambition, greed, and corruption led to economic Armageddon*. New York: Henry Holt and Company.

Nocera, J. (2013, November 15). The little agency that could. *The New York Times*.

Norris, F. (2013, October 31). After fraud, the fog around Libor hasn't lifted. *The New York Times*.

Popper, N. (2013, July 9). NYSE Euronext to take over administration of Libor. *The New York Times*.

Protess, B., & Scott, M. (2012, June 27). Barclays settles regulators' claims over manipulation of key rates. *New York Times*.

Scott, M. (2013, July 19). Ex-brokers appear in court in Libor case. *The New York Times*. July 1, 2012, 8:48 pm

Scott, M., & de la Merced, M. (2012, July 1). Chairman of Barclays resigns. *New York Times*.

Sorkin, A. R. (2013a, May 2). Robert diamond's next life. *The New York Times*.

Sorkin, A. R. (2013b, October 29). The things traders say, Dutch Bank Edition. *The New York Times*.

Thomas, L. (2012, July 5). Trade group for bankers regulates a key rate. *The New York Times*.

Werdigier, J. (2013). Hector Sants resigns from Barclays. *The New York Times*.

Chapter 10
Riding the Bubble

Banking System Abuse

What we have reviewed are several ways a banking system can be abused in financial transactions with some private good but no public good. Private good is when some economic agents earn wealth; and public good is when private gain benefits the whole society as well. Abuses of the public good occur in two kinds of banking corruption, individual corruption and institutional corruption. The case of Libor was deliberate corruption of the index by a group of individual traders, lying about the index. The case of mortgage securitization in the 2007–2008 Wall Street collapse was deliberate corruption by investment banking institutions, selling off rents from capital assets and thus destroying their future liquidity (toxic assets).

However, due to the long-term tendency of financial markets toward price disequilibrium, there is another kind of institutional bias which can create instability—an institutional practice of knowingly encouraging and taking advantage of a growing financial bubble—the profits from 'riding the bubble'. To see a historical case of this, we briefly review one of the earliest bubble in modern financial history, the English South Sea Bubble.

History: South Sea Bubble

Modern banking began in England in the 1600s from practices of placing valuables with shops fashioning gold jewelry, called 'goldsmiths'. The goldsmiths fashioned jewelry from gold and had vaults and security for keeping the shops safe. Next goldsmiths began to temporarily loan gold coins to owners of the stored valuables (based upon the collateral value of the stored valuables). Thus goldsmiths had begun the commercial banking activities in England, lending money based upon collateral. Peter Temin and Hans-Joachim Voth wrote: "Modern commercial banking grew out

F. Betz, *Stability in International Finance*, SpringerBriefs in Economics,
DOI 10.1007/978-3-319-26760-9_10

of the activities of London goldsmiths at the beginning of the eighteenth century.... Banking is not at all like the production and sale of jewelry. What we call 'goldsmith banking' was a new economic activity in the seventeenth and eighteenth centuries; it flourished before the term banking was used to describe the taking of deposits and the making of loans." (Temin and Voth 2012)

In the European Middle Ages, Catholic countries' governments prohibited interest on loans as 'usury', a sin. In the 1500s in England, King Henry III embraced Protestantism, and he formally allowed interest on loans at 10 %. His daughter, Queen Elizabeth, lowered the legal limit on interest to 8 %. Later in King Charles' reign the rate was lowered to about 6–8 %, the range in which interest remained throughout the seventh and eighteenth centuries in Britain (Andreades 2014).

Earlier, we reviewed the history of England's Glorious Revolution and the beginning of the modernization of English finance. Peter Temin and Hans-Joachim Voth summarized: "In the late 1710s, English politicians could look back at a political revolution that had succeeded in spectacular fashion. Parliament had changed the rules of succession to the English throne. A new political alignment had become nearly permanent. On the Continent, England had successfully led an anti-French coalition in a sequence of wars between 1689 and 1713. The monarch of France had to recognize the exclusion of the Stuarts; pro-Stuart risings in 1715 and 1719 had been crushed successfully.... At the same time, the public debt situation was clearly not ideal. An explosion of debt had followed the Glorious Revolution, most of it used to fight wars. By 1719, total public debt had expanded to £41.6 million, up from £14.2 in 1700—a rise by a factor of three.... In 1700, the national debt amounted to 3.33 times the annual revenue; by 1719, it stood at a factor of 6.9, more than twice as high. By the 1780s, it would rise to a factor of 19. Servicing the national debt required more than a quarter of revenue. In 1719, fully half of all tax, customs, and other revenues was spent on interest and capital repayments." (Temin and Voth 2012)

Thus public debt grew, but taxation was insufficient to fund the wars. In the 1700s, the British Parliament began financial inventions to service the national debt. The first of these innovations resulted in the 'South Sea Bubble'. Peter Temin and Hans-Joachim Voth wrote: "The United East India Company was chartered in 1708 and also lent substantial sums to the government in exchange for its charter. It was an active trading company, incorporating a potential rival into the venerable East India Company. It was widely traded, but its innovations were in managing its great empire of agents rather than in reforming government finance. The South Sea Company was founded in 1711 and given trading rights with the 'South Seas'—Spanish America. The trading rights derived from the Treaty of Utrecht, which concluded the War of the Spanish Succession in 1713. The privileges as finally agreed were more limited than initially hoped. The company received the right to send one ship per year to South America, as well as the privilege of supplying slaves." (Temin and Voth 2012)

The South Sea Company was a British government creation, with some trading rights in South America. Stock in the company could be bought and sold by the public. The connection of the South Sea Company to the 'South Sea Bubble' was in its role in financing the British government. The government had previously sold 'annuities' to the public to raise money. The idea of stock in a South Sea Company was that (1) operations could increase, (2) the stock price rise, and (3) the Company would acquire the government annuities. The government gave the right of the South Sea Company to issue stock to purchase annuities, and the government would pay the Company on the interest of the annuities it held. Some annuities lasted a long time (some expiring only in 1807), and the government did not have the right to force their redemption. The South Sea Company's idea was to let the Company buy up annuities with their stock and receive the interest payments of the annuities. The government might then more easily deal with the debt through the company, than through annuities held by individuals. Peter Temin and Hans-Joachim Voth wrote: "The South Sea scheme of 1720 was an attempt to convert annuities into equity in a way that enticed debt-holders to participate voluntarily. In this respect, the scheme largely succeeded—about two out of every three annuitants eventually participated in the conversion scheme." (Temin and Voth 2012)

Robert Wenick traces the origin of the company to John Patterson: "The original idea for what became known as the South Sea Bubble has been ascribed to Defoe, But it appears, in fact, to have come from the fertile mind of John Paterson, a talented Scot who had migrated to London like so many of his impoverished countrymen. Paterson was by no means an impractical fool; one of his brain children was the Bank of England.... In 1710, Paterson was still inventing, still persuading. This time he came up with a scheme for a company that would dominate trade with the South Seas—that is to say the coasts of the Spanish possessions in South America. That England was currently at war with Spain didn't matter. The long War of the Spanish Succession, which had been drenching Europe in blood for more than two decades, was finally winding down, and Earl Robert Harley, who was secretly beginning peace negotiations, thought this was a tremendous opportunity to extract some trade concession from the Spaniards." (Wernick 2014)

Although it was Paterson's idea, the entrepreneur who ran the system was a scrivener. Robert Wenick wrote: "Enter John Blunt, by profession a scrivener, a man who copied in elegant writing the contracts and the legal documents that had to accompany all business transactions. He also acquired knowledge of the details, the fine print in the documents, and he learned how to put this knowledge to good use, as subscribers to South Sea stock... John Blunt had begun his career by leaping into the shifting world of the new joint-stock companies, where the supply of fools seemed to be unlimited. People had money that needed investing, and there were so many projects for them to put their cash in that it didn't seem to make any difference what was offered." (Wernick 2014)

It was Blunt who was inventive about the financial operations. Robert Wenick wrote: "Financial skullduggery as we know it now was then in relative infancy, so Blunt had to improvise as he went along. Realizing that to keep the scheme going required a constant flow of money, he worked out an efficient pumping system. Because he had government approval, he would periodically float a new loan at favorable interest rates, then promptly put out a new issue of stock under attractive terms that would entice the money right back in.... In a fast-moving market, the profits could be enormous. One British government official collected in a single transaction 249,530 £, representing the difference between market value and the 50,000 £ registered as his purchase price a few months before." (Wernick 2014)

The South Sea Company was conceived as a government financial instrument. Peter Temin and Hans-Joachim Voth wrote: "In contrast to the East India Company and the Bank of England, the South Sea Company did not run a flourishing commercial operation. Only one ship with a consignment of textiles ever sailed under the company's flag to South America before its overseas assets were seized by Spain in 1718. The slave trade, which had the potential to yield great profits, also failed to flourish. From its very beginning, the company was more involved in handling government debt than foreign trade. In 1713, shortly after its inception, the company had exchanged £10 million of government debt for shares. The South Sea Company received interest of 6 % in perpetuity on this loan." (Temin and Voth 2012)

But if the commercial activities were not to grow, how could the value of the stock in the South Sea Company increase? It could increase (and did) by issuing more stock—and then more stock. Peter Temin and Hans-Joachim Voth wrote: "The South Sea Company's next major venture was the debt conversion of 1719. So-called lottery bonds, issued in 1710, combined a loan to the government with a lottery ticket. These securities were relatively illiquid and often traded at a steep discount. Investors therefore had an incentive to exchange them for company stock that traded liquidly at close to par. The value of the stock seemed secure, as it was principally backed by government debt. The South Sea Company exchanged £1,048,111 of lottery bonds for newly issued stock and received annual interest payments (at a slightly lower rate than the original bondholders) from the government. As a result, the government saved money, former debt-holders saw the value of their securities rise, and the company netted a considerable profit. This was a basic form of "financial engineering." (Temin and Voth 2012)

The Company shares were tradeable whereas the government lottery bonds were illiquid; and thereby investors readily traded their lottery bonds of a new issue of Company stock. *This was indeed 'financial engineering' and the beginning of a financial bubble.*

The South Sea Company business was turning out to be issuing new stock offerings. Peter Temin and Hans-Joachim Voth wrote: "The Company proceeded to issue fresh shares in four subscriptions, at higher and higher prices. Subscriptions were offered on generous terms. Shares in the second subscription, for example, went on sale on April 29. They cost £400 and could be purchased with a down payment of £40, or 10 %, with the rest becoming due in quarterly installments (with the final payment due in August 1721). Prices of the subscriptions quickly rose, in line with the share price. Within a week subscribers turned a profit of 10–150 %. The newly issued shares were taken up with alacrity by the political class, nobility, gentry, merchants, bankers, and anyone who could get onto subscription lists. Most members of the government were involved. Fully 578 Members of Parliament and the House of Lords subscribed to the stock (or borrowed against it). They bought stock for £1.7 million and borrowed another £1.8 million. In contrast to the 1719 operation, the exchange ratio between shares and bonds was not set in advance, which meant that bondholders could theoretically be bought out with ever fewer shares as the share price of the South Sea Company increased.... as the company issued shares at higher and higher prices, it was redistributing cash flow rights from new subscribers to the old owners of stock." (Temin and Voth 2012)

The new shares were not used to buy out older shares but increased the total of shares. As each new issue was at a higher price, the value of older shares increased, but the total shares also increased. The increase in share price could only happen with a new offering, one new offering after another—a Ponzi scheme. Peter Temin and Hans-Joachim Voth wrote: "The purchase of South Sea stock gave new subscribers a chance to benefit from additional stock issuance in the future. In such an operation, the value of their shares would also benefit from the rising price of new subscriptions. Note that for this mechanism to work, no actual purchase of bonds is necessary—it is enough that it is planned. New investors are willing to buy because they hoped that they will gain if prices continue upward. The prospect of future issuance can turn the negative value of the current transaction into a purchase that, at least in expectations, makes sense at some point in the future.... The structure we just described is, of course, that of a classic Ponzi scheme. The secret to success is to join early (and to get out before things fall apart). As long as there is a good chance that another wave of investors will enter, it is a good idea to participate." (Temin and Voth 2012)

A Ponzi scheme works because investors do not recognize the scheme—until too late! Peter Temin and Hans-Joachim Voth wrote: "Did contemporary investors understand this basic incentive structure? Or were they struggling to make sense of the intricate changes to cash flows as a result of financial engineering? The details of the South Sea operations were certainly complex, and there is some evidence that investors and the general public did not find it easy to see through it all. The *Flying Post*, a newspaper at the time, argued on April 9, 1720, that the intrinsic value of South Sea Company stock would be £448 if the share price went to £300. At £600, it would be £880. We do not know how these numbers were calculated; it is clear that they cannot be correct. The basic structure is right, with higher share prices justifying a higher fundamental, but the relative prices are wrong—the intrinsic value can never catch up to the price at which the last issue was undertaken." (Temin and Voth 2012)

Yet in any Ponzi scheme or any financial bubble, a few often recognize the scheme. In case of the South Sea Bubble, Peter Temin and Hans-Joachim Voth wrote: "Other contemporaries had a clearer understanding of what was going on, and they explained their insights publicly. The *Theatre*, another newspaper, argued in late March 1720 that South Sea stock—then trading at 200—was only worth 140. Archibald Hutcheson, the MP for Hastings in 1720, was highly skeptical of the South Sea Company. He published several treatises on the conversion scheme. He set out in detail who was gaining and who was losing from the various subscriptions." (Temin and Voth 2012)

In a bubble, some do see through the film of the bubble, but most don't—which is why bubbles grow until they blow up.

Peter Temin and Hans-Joachim Voth wrote: "Demand for the new shares was brisk, and the books were filled quickly. Many aristocrats were turned down, as were applications to buy from the court (residing in Hanover for the summer) and from Walpole. The latter was told by his bankers that they had not subscribed themselves, 'not thinking it worth the bustle'. Observers noted a shift in the composition of subscribers; merchants and bankers were largely absent. MPs and members of the House of Lords, who had taken up stock for between £350,000 and £795,000 in the earlier subscriptions, now only subscribed to £77,000." (Temin and Voth 2012)

Finally, all financial bubbles burst. Peter Temin and Hans-Joachim Voth wrote: "Ponzi schemes end when no more new investors join the fray. The day the transfer books were opened, after the summer closure, selling was massive. The company immediately closed the transfer books again, trying to keep the share price artificially high by 'locking in' potential sellers. By late August, the scheme was starting to unravel at another end as well. The company found itself short of cash to pay debt-holders. Desperate to prop up the sagging stock price, the directors promised dividends of 50 % of the stock's face value, approximately 6 % relative to the market price. It did not help. Thereafter, the price started to slide quickly. By mid-September, it fell below 400. Then the price moved even lower: The Sword Blade Company, founded to produce sword blades, was used as the financial arm of the South Sea Company. It became insolvent in late September. Thereafter, the price of South Sea stock fell precipitously. It ended the year below 200, up on the year, but down over 80 % from the midsummer peak." (Temin and Voth 2012)

Not only did naïve investors participate in the bubble, but so did sophisticated investors, such as the goldsmith banks participating in the bubble; and one of the most successful of these banks was Hoare's Bank. Hoares' Bank profited quite well from riding the bubble—entering early and leaving before the bubble's collapse.

Peter Temin and Hans-Joachim Voth wrote: "We analyze how one sophisticated investor with high-powered incentives—Hoare's Bank—behaved during the South Sea Bubble. Like all goldsmith banks, its partners were liable for losses without limit—their own personal fortune was at stake. Hoare's also made large bets while receiving customers' deposits.... The bank executed securities transactions for its clients, and it also traded actively on its own account. Hoare's had done so since the earliest entries in the account ledgers, dating from 1702. Since the inception of the South Sea Company, it had invested in its shares, as well as those of the Royal African Company, the East India Company, and the Bank of England, in addition to various forms of government debt. The bank traded actively in South Sea stock, executed trades for customers, and dealt extensively in other securities in 1720. Yet it was most active in trading South Sea stock." (Temin and Voth 2012)

In the first sale of the Company stock in 1720, Hoare's purchased stock. Then Hoare's continued to trade in the stock while the bubble grew. Peter Temin and Hans-Joachim Voth wrote: "Hoare's participated in two subscriptions in 1720, making only one payment in each case.... When Hoare's bought, the market on average rose substantially. From the day of the purchase to the next, South Sea stock on average rose by 3.3 % more than on days when the bank did not buy. Over 5 days, the outperformance amounted to 12.9 %, and over 10 days, to 14.7 %.

These numbers are quite large—the 10-day performance, for example, implies an annual gain of 1686 %. The same is true when we examine returns after Hoare's sold. The price of South Sea stock always declined, and in a major way over 5- and 10-day horizons, falling by 6.7 and 10.7 % more than on days when Hoare's was not selling." (Temin and Voth 2012) Hoare's Bank was a sophisticated banking firm and understood the financial implications of the bubble. It participated early in the bubble, making huge profits.

Then Hoare's Bank exited from the market. Peter Temin and Hans-Joachim Voth wrote: "Hoare's Bank was a successful investor. It was not a perfect investor; the bank sold off its holdings too early in the bubble. The lesson is that it is better to sell too early in a bubble than get caught by selling too late.... Hoare's trading record was impressive by almost any standard, and it was not due to chance.... Hoare's skillfully 'rode the bubble'." (Temin and Voth).

Sophisticated financial investors can recognize bubbles but also ride the bubble early enough to make fortunes. Peter Temin and Hans-Joachim Voth wrote: "After the collapse in share prices, in October, the bank returned to its earlier practice of lending at the current market value... On November 27, 1721, it was time for the partners at Hoare's Bank to take profits. Henry Hoare, the senior partner, had £21,000 transferred to his private account; Benjamin, the junior partner, £7000. These were not the normal distributions to the owners of the bank at the end of the annual accounting period; the partners were reducing their involvement in trading stock and distributing profits. Proprietary trading during the South Sea Bubble had been phenomenally successful—the partners probably earned as much in 1720–1721 by buying and selling stock as they had during the 20 years previous." (Temin and Voth 2012) Financial bubbles can make fortunes for successful riders of the bubble, as is depicted in Fig. 10.1.

ACTION—A financial bubble called the 'South Sea Bubble' occurred in England in 1720.

GROUP—A private company, the South Sea Company, was chartered by the British Parliament to trade in government annuities. Banks such as Hoare's Bank participated in purchases of the company's stock.

REASON—The reasoning was to replace tradeable company stock for untradeable government annuities.

PROCESS—The financial process was the issuing of company stock in exchange for government annuities, whose interest would then be paid to the South Sea Company.

INDIVIDUAL—John Paterson thought up the scheme and convinced Parliament to pass an enabling act; John Blunt was the scrivener who ran the company; and Robert Walpole was the member of Parliament to clean up the debris left by the bursting of the South Sea Bubble.

SOCIETY—The British Nation was the society in which the financial bubble occurred.

Who pays for bubbles? The foolish investors pay. Peter Temin and Hans-Joachim Voth wrote: "After the collapse of the South Sea Company's share price, investors who had bought at inflated prices were faced with substantial losses.

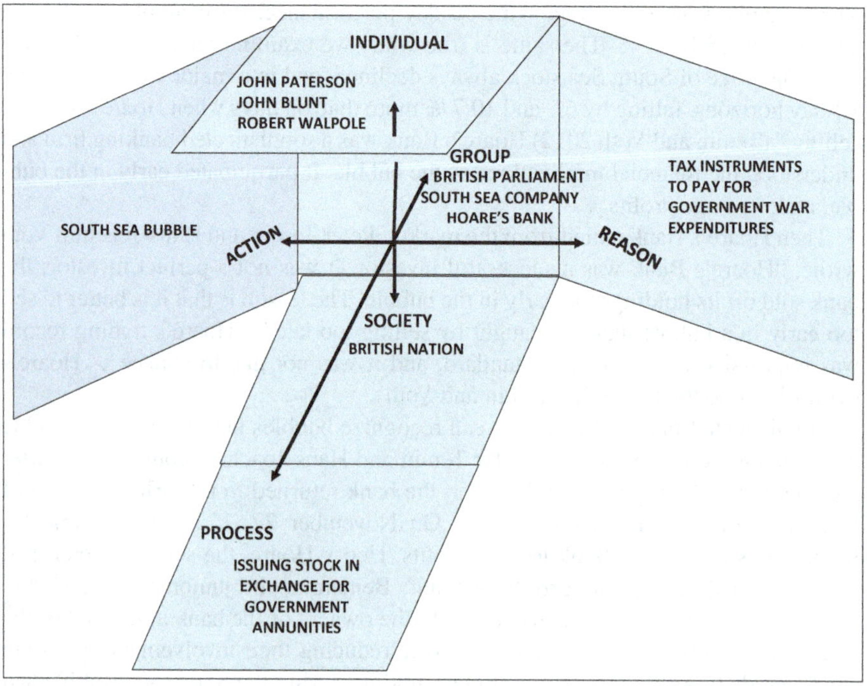

Fig. 10.1 South sea bubble event

Amid recriminations from those who had paid £1000 per £100 in stock in the third and fourth subscriptions, the South Sea Company hatched plans to be taken over by its old rival, the Bank of England. The year ended in scandal, with a House of Commons committee investigating, and the company's cashier fleeing the country. Eventually, the estates of the company's directors were confiscated. The investigating committee of the House of Commons found evidence of widespread corruption in the government. Chancellor of the Exchequer John Aislabee, who had been a great promoter of the conversion scheme, was imprisoned. Several other ministers were impeached as a result of what became a major scandal. The Whig party's standing, and even the position of King George I, was seriously undermined by the conversion scheme gone wrong." (Temin and Voth 2012)

The British government made some attempts to modify the consequences, but people lost money. Peter Temin and Hans-Joachim Voth wrote: "Sir Robert Walpole became First Lord of the Treasury.... The deal brokered by Walpole and approved by Parliament in August 1721 involved the Treasury waiving its claim of seven million pounds against the company from the conversion scheme. Subscribers were given the right to stop paying further installments. Subscription prices were adjusted ex post. The price of the first two was kept as initially agreed. For the last two, when subscribers had agreed to pay 1000, the price was lowered to 400. This, in effect, reversed the vast redistribution from late to early subscribers to a much lower order of magnitude. The terms of the two conversions of government debt were also adjusted. This ensured equal treatment of those who had converted in August with those who had swapped bonds for shares in April. Finally, investors who had borrowed against South Sea stock only had to repay 10 % of the loan received. Shares held by the company were distributed among shareholders, increasing their right to cash dividends. The company still possessed £8 million, which was divided among the shareholders. Holders of long annuities lost one-quarter of what they would have had without conversion. Holders of redeemable debt lost one-half, and holders of short annuities lost about two-thirds. Although these losses were significant, it was far better than a total loss." (Temin and Voth 2012) Still, loses are loses.

Some of the government debt obligations from the South Sea Bubble lasted into the twenty-first century. Stephen Castle reported: "Share prices went through the roof, speculation ran wild and money poured into ill-fated ventures before the boom turned, inevitably and catastrophically, to bust. After that financial crash in 1720, called the South Sea Bubble, the British government was forced to undertake a bail-out that eventually left several million pounds of debt on its books. Almost three centuries later, Britons are still paying interest on a small part of that obligation. Now, prompted by record low interest rates, the British government is planning to pay off some of the debts it racked up over hundreds of years, dating as far back as the South Sea Bubble. George Osborne, the chancellor of the Exchequer, said that in 2015 Britain would repay part of the country's debt from World War I, and that he wanted to pay off other bonds for debt incurred in the eighteenth and nineteenth centuries." (Castle 2014)

Riding a Bubble: Short-Term Private Good versus Long-Term Public Good

What we have seen in the example of the South Sea Bubble is that bubbles provide an opportunity for instant fortunes and instant bankruptcy. Therefore, for sophisticated financial institutions, bubbles are not all bad—a short-term private good of instant fortune.

For this reason, some economists have identified an institutional bias toward the occasional bubble. Hans-Werner Sinn has noted as a tendency of financial institutions to focus upon short-term profitability without regard to long-term risk, and he argued this tendency is the basis of the modern 'casino capitalism'. Hans-Werner Sinn wrote: "The losses piled up in the financial crisis (of 2008) and the speculative business models that have been revealed are beyond anything conceivable and suggest a comparison between the world of finance and a gambling casino… But what was it precisely that pushed the financial world near the abyss? The answer is multifaceted: it was a gambling instinct, but not a blind one like that seen in gambling casinos… Wall Street banks took part in a gamble that in itself had a positive probability of winning… The basic principle that is responsible for the huge profits of investment banks is the legal institution of limited liability, as limited liability permits earning profits from mere risk-taking by privatizing profits and socializing losses." (Sinn 2010)

Sinn emphasized that after U.S. investment banks transformed from partnerships (with unlimited liability) into corporations with 'limited liability', there was an institutional incentives toward gambling—to profit in the short-term even at risk in the long-term. By going public and issuing stock, investment banks in the U.S. became financial corporations and officers were protected from losses by limiting their liability only to the equity they owned in the bank corporation. This encouraged investment banks to reduce bank capital and lend 'leverage', lend multiples of their capital. In this way and in good years, banks could earn large profits. For example in 2006, Goldman Sachs earned a return-on-capital of 40 % and Bear-Sterns earned 26 % (Sinn 2010). But then Bear-Sterns went bankrupt in 2008; while Goldman Sachs didn't. What was the difference? Bear-Sterns was not 'bailed out' by the U.S. government in 2008; while Goldman Sachs and other banks received bail-out funding. This was what Sinn meant by 'socializing losses'—getting the government to bail-out bank failures.

Sinn argued that the 'limited-liability' of bank corporations encourages executives to focus upon short-term profit making by taking long-term risks. In the short-term, if a financial product earns large commissions, even if very risky in the long-term, the executives can make millions in short-term bonuses. For example, the CEO of Goldman Sachs's bonuses added up to 54 million dollars in 2007 and 2008, even as the financial system collapsed in 2008. The U.S. government bailed out the Wall Street banks in 2008; and the CEO of Goldman Sachs bonus was $24 million in 2009. So even if Goldman Sachs had collapsed in 2008, the CEO still had multiple millions of wealth. In the case of Bear-Sterns bankruptcy in 2008, the CEO at that time had already cashed over one hundred million dollars in stocks in the previous years. Thus for executives of banks with limited liability and large executive bonuses, there is a probability of success for the executive, if large bonuses can be earned in the short-term before banking bankruptcy in the long-term.

Sinn argument about the 'casino' banking of investment banks in the financial grid is that there is a built in institutional bias (limited liability) for banking executives to gamble large in the short-term, irrespective of dire consequences for the bank in the long-term. One can call this: 'short-term private good and long-term public bad'.

> *Thus abuse and instability of the international financial grid can be traced to two institutional features of modern banking: leverage in speculative trading and leverage in short-term risk-taking.*
>
> *And since 'financial leverage' and 'limited liability' are both essential features for effective modern banking, they cannot be eliminated but only controlled.*
>
> *This is the basic argument for proper regulation of the international banking grid—regulation (1) to control excessive use of leverage in market speculation (prevent financial bubbles) and (2) to control excessive risk-taking (prevent fraud and corruption).*

Instead of financial bubbles and high risk-taking and tax-avoidance and corruption in the present casino-banking form of the financial grid—what kind of international central bank might bring integrity and stability into the financial grid of international banking?

Regulation and Public-Private Good

Economists use the phrase 'public good' to indicate a product/service produced in a society which is shared by all members of society. This is in contrast to the term 'private good' in which the product/service is consumed only by a particular member of society. A private good is an easier term to understand within the economics discipline, since private goods are produced and sold by businesses. Public goods are the domain of government; and government is studied outside of economics in political science.

Yet some economists do emphasize the importance of the concept, as Martin Wolf wrote: "Public goods are the building blocks of civilization. Economic stability is itself a public good. So are security, science, a clean environment, trust, honest administration, and free speech. The list could be far longer. This matters, because it is hard to secure adequate supply. The more global the public goods, the more difficult it is. Ironically, the better we have become at supplying private goods and so the richer we are, the more complex the public goods we need. Humanity's efforts to meet that challenge could prove to be the defining story of the century….(now) a central element of debate is how to avoid extreme financial instability. Such instability is a public bad. Avoiding it is a public good." (Wolf 2014)

Wolf defined the term: "What, for those unfamiliar with this terminology, is a public good? In the (economics) jargon, a public good is 'non-excludable' and 'non-rivalries'. Non-excludable means that one cannot prevent non-payers from enjoying benefits. Non-rivalries means that one person's enjoyment is not at another person's expense. National defense is a classic public good. If a country is made safe from attack everybody benefits, including residents who make no contribution. Again, enjoyment of the benefits does not reduce that of others. Similarly, if an economy is stable, everybody has the benefit and nobody can be deprived of it." (Wolf 2014)

This is a positive view of a public-good, but not all economists have regarded the term as positive. Wolf wrote: "Public goods are an example of what economists call 'market failure'. The point is generalized in the language of "externalities"—consequences, either good or bad, not taken into account by decision-makers. In such cases, Adam Smith's invisible hand does not work as one might like. Some way needs to be found to shift behavior. Public goods usually involve some state provision. Externalities usually involve a tax, a subsidy or some change in property rights. Free-market economists, such as Tyler Cowen of George Mason University, prefer the latter. But even that requires effective public action, if only via the apparatus of the law." (Wolf 2014)

In financial regulation, one public good is to prevent collapses. Wolf concluded: "Economists have tended to assume that the market economy is inherently stable. If so, stability is supplied automatically. Unfortunately, this is not so. A free-market economy can expand credit without limit, at zero cost. Since money supply is simply the liability counterpart of private credit decisions, instability is baked in the economic cake. For this reason, economic stability is a public good we find quite hard to supply. The consequences of the repeated failure to do so can also be dire. Even the late Milton Friedman believed that government intervention, via the central bank, was needed to prevent long chains of banking collapses." (Wolf 2014)

Public good is a concept used not only in economics but also in political science. One can turn to political science as a cross-disciplinary way to enrich the economic idea of 'public good'. In the twentieth century, political theory turned upon two different ideas about the nature of society. Was society basically divisive and not civil? Or was society basically cooperative and civil? Was society empirically and normatively divisive (implacably divided)? Or was society empirically divided but integrative? The 'divisive view' on society was held by communists; and the 'civil view' on society was held by those advocating democracy.

Those who viewed society as basically cooperative and not one of internal war advocated democracy, a society governed in a representative form with elected officials from contending parties. Democratic ideology viewed all society as an integrative society, a civil society. For example the political scientist, Bent Flyvbjerg, wrote: "A strong civil society is a crucial condition of strong democracy. Empowering civil society is a central concern for the project of democracy… But what is 'civil society'?… Most writers on civil society agree… that civil society has an institutional core constituted by voluntary associations outside the sphere of the state and the economy. The fundamental act of citizenship in a pluralist democracy is in forming (voluntary) associations…. The task of maintaining and redefining the boundaries between civil society and state are the two interdependent and simultaneous processes: the expansion of social equality and liberty, and the restructuring and democratizing of state institutions." (Flyvbjerg 1998)

The idea of a civil society allows the voluntary association of citizens in a state to act freely and independently of state institutions. Freedom of the citizen to voluntarily associate enables the democratic goals in the pursuit of social equality and liberty and limitation to the arbitrary exercise of state power. In an authoritarian government, all voluntary associations are controlled by the state, as well as controlling state institutions. There is no freedom for citizens in an authoritarian (e.g. communist) state, only the obedience to dictates of the state.

But the idea of a 'civil society' introduces methodological complications in political science research. This idea of a 'civil compromise' (civil cooperation) raises the problem about (1) the existence of power and (2) the distribution of power within society. The idea of a 'civil compromise' can have a normative implication: what ought to be a 'civil compromise'? This is the methodological problem of normative judgments versus empirical judgments—idealism or realism. Within contemporary political science in the last half of the twentieth century, this problem between the ideal or real (normative or empirical) was the central methodological issue. And this was so, not only in political science, but in all social sciences. What is real about the nature of society, and what is ideal? The distinction between a societal reality and a societal ideal is the methodological fulcrum of societal theory.

To illustrate this, Bent Flyvbjerg focused upon the writings of two influential political scientists of the late twentieth century: Jurgen Habermas and Michael Foucault. Flyvbjerg saw their differences as that of methodology: (1) Habermas approached research in political systems as a study of idealism in political theory—normative theory; (2) Foucault approached research in political systems as a study of realism in political theory—empirical theory.

Jurgen Habermas described political activities by focusing upon and identifying the political ideals around which people gather, associate, and identify. Habermas called this 'discourse-ethics' of the politics. By the term 'discourse', Habermas indicated that social ideals are discussed openly in the politics as a justification of political action. By the term 'ethics', Habermas was indicating that the ideal of the discourse provided an ethical agreement around which a group associates.

But also there is a reality about power in all political situations—the reality of how power is actually used, as opposed to how the power is justified. This is what Michel Foucault emphasized as an essential feature of social science methodology. Foucault argued that in any political situation (even focused around a 'discourse-ethics') there was also another view about power—which is a 'realism' about politics, an analysis of power, 'power analytics' of a situation.

For example, one of the ideals of American democracy is for equal opportunity and equal treatment under law—Habermas's discourse ethics But in reality not every American has the same access to legal systems, education, safety, health etc. People of means have better opportunities in life, and wealthy folk can hire more expert lawyers than can poor folk—Foucault's' power analytics.

Flyvbjerg argued that these two approaches capture the modern political science methodological duality of idealism or realism: "The works of Habermas and Foucault highlight an essential tension in modernity. This is the tension between consensus and conflict.... Habermas is the philosopher of Moralitat (morality) based on consensus. Foucault... is the philosopher of wirkliche Historie (real history) told in terms of conflict and power." (Flyvbjerg 1998)

A 'consensus about power' in a group is constructed around an ideal expressed in the discourse-ethics of the group (idealism). The 'reality of how power is really exercised' in a group is expressed in the power-analytics of the group (realism). Public good is a discourse-ethics theory of an economy (idealism). Private good is a power-analytics theory of an economy (realism).

In regulatory actions, one can clarify the complexities of ethics and power by using a taxonomy of the two dichotomies (public good & private good and discourse-ethics & power-analytics), Fig. 10.2.

ETHICS AND POWER IN REGULATION

	PUBLIC GOOD	*PRIVATE GOOD*
DISCOURSE ETHICS	REGULATORY LAW	REGULATORY INFLUENCE
POWER ANALYTICS	REGULATORY PRACTICE	REGULATORY COMPLIANCE

Fig. 10.2 Idealism and realism in the exercise of public good and private good

Financial regulation in economic systems is complicated by the two kinds of goods, public and private and by the two aspects of ethics and power. Regulatory law is the expression of the discourse ethics in the public good of a financial institution. Regulatory practice is how law is actually administered within the context of political power. To optimize the private good in the exercise of regulatory practice, private financial institutions attempt to influence the political process for legislating and implementing regulation. Private firms can also exert their own private good to the extent they comply with the spirit of regulatory law (discourse ethics) in addition to the practice of regulatory law (power analytics). *Regulation exists in a context of both discourse-ethics (public good) and power-analytics (private good). Regulation should balance public and private good—in the idealism of ethics and in the realism of politics.*

Hyman Minsky emphasized the regulation in the form of bank examination had increased in importance as banks became larger: "With the attenuation of customer and collegiate surveillance as a result of the risk absorption by broadly defined central banking, bank examination becomes increasingly important as an instrument for constraining the exposure to risk of banks. Bank examination is largely perfunctory—the domain of accountants who look for proper procedures, documentation, and obvious fraud—rather than an inquiry into the economic viability and the exposures to risk of banking organizations." (Minsky 2008)

Regulation of the banking industry should attend to the 'economic viability and risk-taking' of the financial structure. Economic theory which is intended to underpin regulatory principles for financial systems should provide an empirical and normative grounding for financial regulation—both the 'power analytics' and 'discourse ethics' of economic systems. Issues which should be addressed include:

- The appropriateness of a *financial transaction* and the conditions under which it creates both private and public good (e.g. trading or gambling);
- The appropriateness of a *financial institution*, and the conditions under which it creates both private and public good (e.g. bank or shadow bank);
- The appropriateness of *relationships between financial institutions*, and the conditions under which they create both private and public good (e.g. internal shadow banking in integrated banks);
- The appropriateness of *financial market operations*, and the conditions under which they facilitate both private and public good (e.g. unregulated derivatives markets);
- The appropriateness of the *relationships between the financial institutions and a central bank*, and the conditions under which both private and public financial good are protected (e.g. financial institution access to Federal central bank 'discount window' loans).

References

Andreades, A. (2014 April 4). *History of the Bank of England*. Kindle Edition.
Castle, S. (2014). That debt from 1720? Britain's payment is coming. *New York Times*. Retrieved December 27, from http://www.nytimes.com/2014/12/28/world/that-debt-from-1720-britains--payment-is-coming.html?_r=0
Flyvbjerg, B. (1998). Habermas and Foucault: Thinkers for civil society? *British Journal of Sociology, 49*(2), 210–233.
Minsky, H. (2008). *Stabilizing an unstable economy*. New York: McGraw Hill.
Sinn, H.-W. (2010). *Casino capitalism*. Oxford: Oxford University Press.
Temin, P., & Voth, H.-J. (2012). *Prometheus shackled: Goldsmith Banks and England's financial revolution after 1700*. Oxford: Oxford University Press.
Wernick, R. 2014. *The South Sea Bubble*. New Word City, Inc. Kindle Edition.
Wolf, M. (2014). *The Shifts and the Shocks: What we've learned—and have still to learn—from the financial crisis*. London: Penguin Books.

CPSIA information can be obtained
at www.ICGtesting.com
Printed in the USA
FSOW03n2152250316
18485FS

9 783319 267586